ECONOMICS IN PERSPECTIVE

BOOKS BY
JOHN KENNETH GALBRAITH

American Capitalism:
The Concept of Countervailing Power

A Theory of Price Control

Economics and the Art of Controversy

The Great Crash, 1929

The Affluent Society

The Liberal Hour

Economic Development

The Scotch

The New Industrial State

The Triumph

Indian Painting
(with Mohinder Singh Randhawa)

Ambassador's Journal

Economics, Peace and Laughter

A China Passage

Economics and the Public Purpose

Money: Whence It Came, Where It Went

The Age of Uncertainty

Almost Everyone's Guide to Economics

The Nature of Mass Poverty

Annals of an Abiding Liberal

A Life in Our Times

The Voice of the Poor

The Anatomy of Power

A View from the Stands

Economics in Perspective:
A Critical History

ECONOMICS IN PERSPECTIVE

A CRITICAL HISTORY

John Kenneth Galbraith

HOUGHTON MIFFLIN COMPANY
BOSTON
1987

Library of Congress Cataloging-in-Publication Data

Galbraith, John Kenneth, date.
Economics in perspective.
Includes bibliographical references and index.
1. Economics — History. 2. Economic history.
I. Title.
HB75.G274   1987   330'.09   87-3644
ISBN 0-395-35572-9

For Eric Roll,
friend of fifty years,
whose guidance on these matters
will be evident to all.
And,
out of enduring affection,
for Freda Roll.

TO ACKNOWLEDGE

ALL WRITERS are more in debt to friends than they usually know. My obligation is especially great, and without doubt even greater than I realize. Two of my Harvard colleagues, Robert Dorfman and Henry Rosovsky, gave me help on particular points, and Professor Dorfman read the entire manuscript through in an earlier form. Therese Horsey managed my office affairs while I was writing it and absorbed a myriad of distractions that would otherwise have engaged my time or aroused my temper. Eric Roll, Lord Roll of Ipsden, my friend for many, many years, to whom this book is dedicated, has been an enduring source of ideas on all these matters.

But special in all respects is my debt to two beloved allies. Edith Tucker typed and then retyped these pages and did the infinity of research and checking that was required. I once asked her if she was not tired of the task; with great skill she evaded the question.

Andrea Williams, my partner in all writing enterprises for nearly thirty years, read and reread the manuscript and, as ever, persuaded me to the clarity of expression and rules of grammar from which I too often lapse. To her, my exceptional word of thanks.

And, finally, my love and thanks go to Catherine Galbraith, who over the three years of this writing gave me the encouragement, affection and, above all, the tolerance for which all writers yearn and which only the fortunate are accorded.

CONTENTS

ECONOMICS IN PERSPECTIVE

I

A Look at the Landscape

THERE CAN BE no understanding of economics without an awareness of its history; in the academic world this is acknowledged. Yet the history of economic ideas has not been a popular or always rewarding field of study, and the reasons are not hard to find. There are many books on the subject of no slight scholarly accomplishment; all economists owe their authors a major debt. But in searching for academic excellence or in protecting against professional criticism, even the best scholars have spread themselves widely over the important and also the expendable. They cannot have it said that this point or that made by Adam Smith or David Ricardo or Karl Marx was missed. In consequence, the really controlling ideas, right or wrong, have frequently been lost in the mass; what continues to be of interest or relevance in our time has been obscured.

And there is a yet more serious problem: much and perhaps most of this writing has assumed that economic ideas have a life and development of their own. Progress in the subject matter is made in the abstract; one scholar shows a compelling talent for innovation, and others amend and improve on his work, all without close reference to the economic context.

In fact, economic ideas are always and intimately a product of their own time and place; they cannot be seen apart from the world they interpret. And that world changes — is, indeed, in a constant process of transformation — so economic ideas, if they are to retain relevance, must also change. In the last one hundred years the great corporate enterprise, the trade union, depression and war, increasing and increasingly dispersed affluence, the changing nature of money and the new and enhanced role of the central bank, the declining role of agriculture with the counterpart urbanization and growth of urban poverty, the rise of the welfare state, the newly assumed responsibility of the government for overall economic performance, the emergence of socialist states, have all dramatically altered, even revolutionized, economic life. As the subject matter of economics has changed, so necessarily has the subject.

But, at best, change in economics has been reluctant and reluctantly accepted. Those who benefit from the *status quo* resist change, as do economists who have a vested interest in what has always been taught and believed. These are matters to which I will return.

Further, it must be said, much past writing on the history of economic ideas has been aggressively dull. There are a significant number of learned men and women who hold that any successful effort to make ideas lively, intelligible and interesting is a manifestation of deficient scholarship. This is the fortress behind which the minimally coherent regularly find refuge.

The foregoing paragraphs will suggest my purpose in this history. I seek to see economics as a reflection of the world in which specific economic ideas have developed — the ideas of Adam Smith in the context of the early trauma of the Industrial Revolution, those of David Ricardo in its later, more mature stages, those of Karl Marx in the era of unbridled capitalist power, those of John Maynard Keynes as a response to the unrelenting disaster of the Great Depression. Where, as before the rise of capitalism or in the subsistence economies of our own time, there was — or is — little that is interesting and even less to be discovered in economic life, I accommodate to this fact. Economic ideas are not very important when and where there is no economy.

I am not averse, on occasion, to peripheral detail in the development of economic thought if it adds in an interesting way to the story. But I am principally concerned to isolate and emphasize the central idea or ideas of the specific author, school or time and to focus, above all, on those which have a continuing and modern resonance. That which was transitory I try scrupulously to ignore, as also any scholarship in the mainstream that did not greatly alter or deflect that stream.[1]

Because this is a history of economics and not merely of economists and their thought, I go beyond the scholars and scholarship to the events that shaped the subject. And as necessary to the events that shaped the history of economics when there were no economists. The last century in the United States, as I will tell, was a time of intense economic discussion — of banking and banking policy, money and monetary policy, international trade and tariff policy. But until well into its last decades there were almost no economists to lead or even to participate in that discussion. To confine myself in this history to formal economic expression would be to ignore a great and sweeping current in the flood of economic ideas.

I have said that in the past the writing on this subject, or much of it, has been dull, sometimes ostentatiously obscure. I cannot think this necessary. The central ideas and their context are alive with interest; they have retained mine for over half a century, since I first encountered them in 1931 at the University of California at Berkeley under the guidance of two persuasive scholars, Leo Rogin and the stately Carl C. Plehn.[2] I would like to think that they can

1. I do not, as one example, deal at any length with John Stuart Mill, a truly major figure but one wholly in the mainstream. And I pass over the great German writers on economic history in the last century who had little effect on its course, although here I should confess that I also suffer from a lack of motivating interest.

2. Instruction by or association with four older Harvard teachers — C. J. Bullock, a man of powerfully pre-Cambrian convictions, A. E. Monroe, Overton Taylor and, needless perhaps to add, Joseph A. Schumpeter — continued and heightened my enthusiasm.

Perhaps I might be permitted another point. The systematic life of economics extends over two hundred years since Adam Smith. Slightly to my surprise, I realize that I have been professionally present and have known most of the participants for a full one quarter of that time.

3

be as absorbing to others. Nor do these matters challenge understanding. As I have urged on earlier occasions, there are no useful
propositions in economics that cannot be stated accurately in clear,
unembellished and generally agreeable English.

I must now say a word on the practical uses of history — history
such as this. The claim that I make is one that should be made
with care.

As economics is practiced, all will agree, it is obsessively concerned with the future. Every month in the United States men and
women of assumed wisdom fan out over the Republic to give their
views on the economic prospect, as also on the social and political
outlook. Thousands turn out to hear them. Business executives or
their companies pay heavily for the privilege of listening and, if
wise, treat the knowledge so gained with intelligent disbelief. The
most common qualification of the economic forecaster is not in
knowing but in not knowing that he does not know. His greatest
advantage is that all predictions, right or wrong, are soon forgotten.
There are too many of them, and if the elapse of time is considerable, not only the memory of what was said will be gone but so
will an appreciable number of those making or hearing the predictions. As Keynes observed, "In the long run we are all dead."

If indeed economic knowledge were impeccable, the economic
system as it now exists in the nonsocialist world would not survive. Were it possible for anyone to know with precision and certainty what was going to happen to wages, interest rates, commodity
prices, the performance of different firms and industries and the
prices of stocks and bonds, the one so blessed would not give or
sell his information to others; instead, he would use it himself, and
in a world of uncertainty his monopoly of the certain would be
supremely profitable. Soon he would be in possession of all fungi-
ble assets, while all contending with such knowledge would suc-
cumb. Perish the thought that anyone thus favored should be a
socialist. The modern economic system does, in fact, survive not
because of the excellence of the work of those who forecast its

future but because of their supremely reliable commitment to error.

Yet there is a redeeming possibility: we can attempt to understand the present, for the future will inevitably retain compelling aspects of what now exists. And the present, in turn, is profoundly a product of the past. As the ensuing pages will tell, what we now believe in economics has deep roots in history. Only as these are perceived — only as we view the past as regards prices and production, employment and unemployment, the distribution of income and wealth, saving, banking and investment, the nature and promise of capitalism and socialism — can the present, and therewith, in some slight measure, the prospect, be understood in any appreciable way. To that understanding these pages are addressed.

But not exclusively. Not everything is to be measured by a stern, utilitarian yardstick. There is, or should be, in these matters room for enjoyment for the sake of enjoyment. The history with which I here deal is, I like to think, interesting for its own sake. There is much about it, in both its facts and its absurdity, that may challenge and delight the curious mind. I would be sorry, indeed, were there no such response to these pages.

A word must now be said on the nature and content of economics itself.

"Political Economy or Economics," said Alfred Marshall, the great University of Cambridge teacher whose textbook was the light and sometimes the despair of many students of the college generations early in this century, "is a study of mankind in the ordinary business of life."[3] This allows of a wide field; not much in human behavior can be excluded as irrelevant. For practical purposes, however, the scope of inquiry and concern must be narrowed to the questions most commonly asked. And we must keep in mind that these questions change greatly in urgency with the changing context and over the passing years.

Central to all economic analysis and instruction is the question

3. Alfred Marshall, *Principles of Economics*, 8th edition (London: Macmillan, 1920), Vol. I, p. I.

of what determines the prices that are paid for goods and for services rendered. And how the proceeds from this economic activity are distributed. And what determines the share going to wages, interest, profits and, although less distinctly, the rent of land and other fixed and immutable objects used in production.

Over most of the modern life of economics these two subjects, the theory of value and the theory of distribution, have been the ultimate concern. It is still thought that economics came of age when these two matters were tackled systematically in the latter part of the eighteenth century, most notably by Adam Smith. But here, at the very center of the subject, there has been formidable change with the changing context. In earliest times, as we shall presently see, neither the factors determining prices nor those setting the levels of wages, interest and other distributive shares were of much relevance. With production and consumption centered on the household, there was no necessity for a theory of prices; with slaves there was no compelling need for a theory of wages.

In very recent times, although the change has not been conceded by the more scrupulously conventional economists, the importance of price determination and of the factors setting the distributive shares has once again declined. Prices in a poor or meager society are the prices of grim essentials; the price of bread does much to determine how much people will eat. In a generally affluent world, by contrast, if the price of bread is high, then something else of no great significance is forgone in order to pay for it. Or something else is consumed. Many purchases and much ensuing consumption are now inconsequential; so, accordingly, as compared with past times, are the prices charged and paid. Again the importance of seeing matters in their context.

Along with what determines prices and the distributive shares go the other central questions. The first is how income distributed as wages, interest, profits and rent is diffused or concentrated — how equitable or inequitable is the income distribution. The explanations and rationalizations of the resulting inequality over the centuries have commanded some of the greatest, or in any case some of the most ingenious, talent of the economics profession. In nearly all of economic history most people have been poor and a comparative few have been very rich. Accordingly, there has been a compelling need to explain why this is so — and, alas, on frequent occasion, to tell why it *should be* so. In modern times, with rising and increasingly general affluence, the terms of this subject have greatly changed. The distribution of income remains, however, the most sensitive business with which economists deal.

Next, economics is concerned with what leads to better or worse economic performance in the aggregate. The earlier question was what damaged or improved the state of trade, as it was then called. The current reference is to what depresses or stimulates economic growth. And what causes fluctuations, rhythmic or otherwise, in the production of goods and services. Emerging here also is the now urgent, though relatively new, problem of why it is impossible in the modern economy to find useful employment for so many people who are willing to work. In the 1800s, unemployment was scarcely discussed; only in this century has the difficulty of achieving an adequate supply of goods given way to the far greater, far more discussed difficulty of finding adequate employment for as many people as possible in the production of goods.

Along with all these questions goes consideration of the institutions that are involved in economic activity — in the production and pricing of goods and services and the distribution of the proceeds. Here enters the role of the business enterprise, great and small. And of banks and central banks and of money in its diverse forms and functions and the special problems of international commerce. And of government and the policies it pursues, as these bear in greater or lesser measure on all of the aforementioned processes and institutions.

Finally, and less specifically, there is the larger political and social framework in which economic life proceeds. What of the nature and efficacy of capitalism, free enterprise, the welfare state, socialism and communism? With these matters, it may be noted, the mood of economics undergoes a rather major change. It ceases to

7

be a dispassionate, putatively scientific subject and becomes a theater for strongly expressed argument. The most detached scholar, the most avowedly practical business executive, the politician least subject to any confining intellectual process, all react with visible, even violent, emotion. Such reaction this history will, nonetheless, seek to avoid.[4]

All these questions, the solutions to them that are avowed and the courses of action, public and private, that are urged are the subject matter of the history of economics. The obligatory starting point for any study of this history is, needless to say, in the classical world.

4. Yielding, not unwillingly, to my publisher and editor, I have subtitled this book *A Critical History.* Any competent history, as all will agree, involves criticism or, in any case, critical judgment. But I am here more than marginally concerned to identify error and, I might add, to have the enjoyment that comes from doing so.

II

After Adam

THERE CAN at any given time be an absence of answers to
the questions suggested in the last chapter because economic thought has not developed to the requisite level of
sophistication. Or there can be an absence of answers because the
questions themselves have not yet arisen. With distinguished
exceptions, most historians of economic thought have attributed
the failure to provide answers to the first default. More is to be
attributed to the second.

In the time of the Greek city-states and the Athenian Empire and
later in the age of Rome, many, if not most, of the problems mentioned did not, in fact, exist. The basic industry of both Greece and
Rome was agriculture; the producing unit was the household; the
labor force was the slaves. The intellectual, political, cultural and
a substantial measure of the residential life centered on the cities,
and it is of these — Sparta, Corinth, Athens and most notably
Rome — that the history is written. But the ancient cities, large or,
as was the common case, very small (Rome and a few Italian cities
excepted), were not economic centers as that term is now understood. There *were* markets and craftsmen, most of the latter slaves;
there was, however, little industrial activity of a kind that would
now be recognized as such.[1]

1. David Hume could "not remember a passage in any ancient author, where the
growth of a city is ascribed to the establishment of a manufacture." Quoted in M. I.
Finley, *The Ancient Economy* (Berkeley and Los Angeles: University of California
Press, 1973), p. 22.

The use or consumption of goods — primitive shelter, elementary nutrients, perhaps some drink, some cloth, little else — was infinitesimal for all but a minute governing minority. For this minority the greatest consumption was in services — again the slaves. Ancient Greece and Rome were not, a far from controversial point, consumer goods economies.

It is somewhat unclear how the inhabitants of the Greek and Italian cities, including Rome, paid for the foodstuffs and wine they drew from the countryside. Most of the material goods were probably bought with the rents and other revenues or exactions that accrued to absentee landowners who lived in the cities and that were now recycled to pay for the product of the farms and vineyards. Perhaps also in some cases the city dwellers were simply paid in kind. Or their revenue may have come in the form of taxes, which could be used in turn to pay for the produce. And the silver mines provided revenue to Athens, as military tribute did to Rome. It is certain that grain and other products came in volume to the ports of the Piraeus and Ostia, but it has never been quite so clear what those ports sent out in return.[2]

Discussion of the economic questions of this era is principally to be found in the writings of Aristotle (384–322 B.C.), and there is not a rich yield. No one can read his works without secretly suspecting a certain measure of eloquent incoherence on economics — "secretly" because, the author being Aristotle, no one can wisely suggest such a thing. But more to the point, very few of the questions with which economics later became concerned applied to the society of which Aristotle spoke. Those problems with which he was occupied — to which, indeed, he was impelled — had a notably ethical intonation. In the words of Alexander Gray, a distinguished student of the history of economic ideas, "Economics

2. On this see Finley, *The Ancient Economy*, pp. 123–149. A careful and persuasive authority on these matters, Finley was a professor of ancient history at the University of Cambridge from 1970 to 1979.

[in ancient Greece] was not merely the attendant and the hand-maiden of Ethics (as perhaps she should always be); she was crushed and blotted out by her more prosperous and pampered sister, and later excavators, in search of the origins of economic theory, can only dig out disconnected fragments and mangled remains."[3]

The elementary character of economic life apart, the most important reason that ethical questions were addressed to the exclusion of economic ones in the ancient world was the existence of slavery. "At all times and in all places the Greek world relied on some form (or forms) of dependent labour to meet its needs, both public and private. . . . By dependent labour I mean work performed under compulsions other than those of kinship or communal obligations."[4] Since wages were not paid for labor, it followed in a reasonably evident way that there could be no view of how wages were determined. And, as was true in Athens and in the Greek cities generally, because slaves did the work, labor had a derogatory aspect that helped to exclude it from scholarly consideration. The ethical justification of slavery and the terms of the treatment of the slaves became, instead, the interesting questions, as in this defense of the institution by Aristotle: "The lower sort are by nature slaves, and it is better for them as for all inferiors that they should be under the rule of a master. . . . Indeed the use made of slaves and of tame animals is not very different."[5]

*

3. Alexander Gray, *The Development of Economic Doctrine* (London: Longmans, Green, 1948), p. 14. Gray was for many years a professor of political economy at the University of Edinburgh.

Aristotle's thoughts on economics are most conveniently available (if the volume can still be found) in *Early Economic Thought*, edited by A. E. Monroe (Cambridge: Harvard University Press, 1924).

4. M. I. Finley, *Economy and Society in Ancient Greece*, edited by Brent D. Shaw and Richard P. Saller (New York: Viking Press, 1982), p. 97.

5. Aristotle, *Politics*, Book 1, in *Early Economic Thought*, p. 10. Aristotle adds, "It is clear, then, that some men are by nature free, and others slaves, and that for these latter slavery is both expedient and right." He was, it may be observed, equally certain as regards women. "Again, the male is by nature superior, and the female inferior; and the one rules, and the other is ruled; this principle, of necessity, extends to all mankind." *Ibid.* Returning to lecture in a modern university or to receive an honorary degree, Aristotle would be accorded a somewhat qualified welcome.

There was a similar problem as regards interest in the absence of capital. People borrow money and pay interest for two reasons. They want to have capital goods or working capital with which to make income — to have machinery and equipment that will contribute to earnings or to have goods in process of manufacture and sale from which income will be made. Or, alternatively, interest is paid because someone with less money borrows it from someone with more to satisfy variously urgent personal needs, to permit present extravagance or to repair extravagance in the past. If capital goods and working capital are of little visible importance in the economy, as was true in the household economy of Aristotelian Greece, then the greatest part of the lending and borrowing is of the second sort, that is, for personal needs.[6] In such circumstances interest is not viewed as a production cost but rather as something the more favored charge the less fortunate or the less wise. So again, like slavery, it raises a problem in ethics — what is right, just and decent in relations between those who are amply supplied with money and the feckless or needy.

Not surprisingly, Aristotle strongly condemned the taking of interest: "The most hated sort [of moneymaking], and with the greatest reason, is usury. . . . For money was intended to be used in exchange, but not to increase at interest."[7] For the same reason — that interest was an unworthy exaction from the less fortunate arising from the possession of the money by the more fortunate — interest continued to be strongly condemned throughout the Middle Ages. And here there is a point for later emphasis: only when interest was redefined as a payment for productive capital — when it became compellingly evident that the one who borrowed money made money out of doing so and should, in all justice, share some of the return with the original lender — did it become reputable. Religious precept and the accepted ethic were then, not

6. "The pattern of Greek moneylending for non-productive purposes is indubitable." Finley, *The Ancient Economy*, p. 141.

7. Aristotle, *Politics*, Book 1, in *Early Economic Thought*, p. 20.

01104 אא32

exceptionally, adjusted to this circumstance. But the taking of interest on loans for personal need or use continued to have a slightly unwholesome, even suspect, reputation. Here the very distant past has echoes in the present: interest for personal loans remains even today subject to a certain measure of opprobrium and is thought to require regulation. The loan shark is excoriated and is widely assumed, not without reason, to be unduly prone to criminal association.

Without wages and interest in the ancient world there could not be a theory of prices in any modern sense. Prices derive in one way or another from production costs, and production costs were not a visible function in the slave-owning household. So it remained for Aristotle to ask only whether prices were just or fair, a concern that would be central to economic thought for most of the next two thousand years and the basis for the question posed to this day: Is that really a *fair* price? Nothing has so engaged economic attention over the centuries as the need to persuade people that the price given by the market has a justification superior to all ethical concern; to this also I will return.

Aristotle gave attention to another problem with ethical overtones that was to be a continuing one for economists: Why are some of the most useful things the least valued in the market while some of the least useful command the highest price? Well into the nineteenth century, economic writers would still be struggling with the reason for the difference between value in use and value in exchange — with the fact that bread and clean drinking water are useful and relatively cheap while silks and diamonds are much less useful and decidedly more expensive. Surely there is, or was, something ethically perverse here. It would be considered a major advance in economics when this problem was finally solved.

On improvement in trade, the distant predecessor of the concern for economic growth, Aristotle, like the Romans who followed him, confined himself to suggestions for better agricultural organization and practice. And, as did the Romans, he ascribed great moral superiority to farming, a view that would be echoed strongly by French economic writers in the eighteenth century and that has powerful resonance among farmers today.

On money in its more elementary forms and uses there cannot be a great deal said. It is merely a commodity that, because of its divisibility, durability, adequate but not unlimited availability and consequent acceptability, occupies an intermediate role in exchange. Silver, gold, copper, iron, seashells, tobacco,[8] cattle and whiskey have, along with paper and bank deposits, all so served. It is only as its use as money gives a commodity a certain personality, mystique and scarcity that its price — what one has to surrender in other commodities for its possession — becomes a special problem. And it is only as the commodity gives way to purely representational forms — paper or bank deposits — that any very grave mystery develops as to what determines the value of the money or, in common language, the general level of prices as established by the value of the money. By Aristotle's time, in the fourth century B.C., coinage of metal in Greece had been long established; already in the fifth century B.C., Herodotus (c. 484–c. 425 B.C.) had rendered his superb *non sequitur* on the subject: "The manners and customs of the Lydians do not essentially vary from those of Greece, except in . . . [the routine] prostitution of the young women. They are the first people on record who coined gold and silver into money."[9] Aristotle describes the origins of money with admirable clarity and succinctness, observing that

8. In the American experience tobacco has, of all these items, had the best run so far. It was used as money in the southern colonies for around a century and a half, which exceeds by a substantial margin the eras of eminence of gold, silver or the paper notes and bank deposits of modern times. See my *Money: Whence It Came, Where It Went* (Boston: Houghton Mifflin, 1975), pp. 48–50. Where money is concerned, there has been a strong archaic instinct that has always argued for a return to earlier use, notably in the past to silver and in recent times to gold. Perhaps one day, led by some vigorously regressive senator from North Carolina, there will be a demand that we get back to a tobacco standard.

9. Herodotus, *Clio*, Book 1, translated by the Reverend William Beloe (Philadelphia: M'Carty and Davis, 1844), p. 31. It is more than probable that coined money was earlier in use on the Indus Plain, and on all matters having to do with money, including paper currency, there is an even greater presumption of priority in favor of the Chinese.

the various necessaries of life are not easily carried about, and hence men agreed to employ in their dealings with each other something which was intrinsically useful and easily applicable to the purposes of life, for example, iron, silver, and the like. Of this the value was at first measured by size and weight, but in process of time they put a stamp upon it, to save the trouble of weighing and to mark the value.[10]

Having identified the nature of money and coinage, Aristotle goes on to a consideration of moneymaking, which, in its pure form, he finds abhorrent. "Some men turn every quality or art into a means of making money; this they conceive to be the end, and to the promotion of the end all things must contribute."[11] As with his position on usury, this observation of Aristotle's has remained accurate over the centuries. A superior modern example of his case is, no doubt, the young financial deal maker who surrenders all personal effort and conscience to pecuniary return and measures all personal achievement by its result. Perhaps Aristotle should still be read on Wall Street.

However, when he goes on, one senses not without effort, to distinguish between legitimate and illegitimate forms of moneymaking, it need not detain us. One must here risk the unpardonable truth, which is that he does not make a great deal of sense.

Scholars who have not found Aristotle wholly rewarding on the Athenian economy have turned to Xenophon (c. 440–c. 355 B.C.), a student of Socrates and a man of practical turn of mind, who, long after his campaign with the younger Cyrus and the writing of his immortal account of it in the *Anabasis*, concerned himself briefly

---

10. Aristotle, *Politics*, Book 1, in *Early Economic Thought*, p. 17. Aristotle mentions silver but not gold. Over the long range of monetary history silver has been by far the more important of the two metals. It was for silver that Jesus was turned in to the local authorities; silver, not gold, was the great treasure of the New World; gold was adopted by the European trading community as an international medium of exchange only in the 1870s. Silver was dropped from free coinage in the United States in 1873 with a resulting controversy that dominated American politics (and the oratory of William Jennings Bryan) for the next quarter century.

11. Aristotle, *Politics*, Book 1, in *Early Economic Thought*, p. 19.

with economics. In his *Cyropaedia*, and in anticipation of Adam Smith, he tells of the advantage accruing to a large, as opposed to a small, city in the opportunity for specialization by trade — for the division of labor. And in *On the Means of Improving the Revenues of the State of Athens*[12] he considers the sources of the relative prosperity of the city and the means for enhancing it. The prosperity he attributes to the excellence of the surrounding agriculture — not something that is entirely obvious to the modern visitor — and he holds that it would be enhanced by extending hospitality and privileges to foreign merchants and seamen, not excluding the Spartans with whom he had notoriously consorted; by giving proper attention to public works; by sending all possible labor to mine silver, which he sees as a major component in the Athenian balance of payments, as it would now be called; and, above all, by keeping the peace. The difference between prosperity and catastrophe Xenophon attributes in the flattest possible language to war: "For those states, assuredly, are most prosperous, which have remained at peace for the longest period; and of all states Athens is the best adapted by nature for flourishing during peace."[13] It is a seriously troubling matter that only rarely in the next twenty-four hundred years have economists addressed the economic costs of war and the economic rewards of peace and taken a strong professional stand on the choice. It is not too late.

A final question raised by the Greeks that is of impressive modern relevance concerned the larger organizing and motivating force in the economy: Should it be, to put the matter rather too bluntly, self-interest or communism?

This arose because of the presumed or suspected commitment to communism of Plato (c. 428–c. 348 B.C.), a man not easily dismissed. His imagined state has its origin essentially as an economic entity — as an assemblage of the various occupations and professions necessary for civilized life. But presiding over, guiding

12. In *Early Economic Thought*, pp. 33–49.
13. Xenophon, *On the Means of Improving the Revenues of the State of Athens*, in *Early Economic Thought*, pp. 46–47.

and protecting the state are the guardians, who live a life of ascetic renunciation; they are denied property beyond the bare essentials; their income is rigorously limited to need. "Should they ever acquire homes or lands or moneys of their own, they will become housekeepers and husbandmen instead of guardians, enemies and tyrants instead of allies of the other citizens."[14] There can be free enterprise at the bottom; power must be with those at the top who avow a pure communist ethic.

Plato's inclination to communism, however partial, has been a source of no slight concern for the more sensitive historians of the subject. Alas that so universal a figure might have rendered himself subject, had he endured, to surveillance by the Federal Bureau of Investigation and denunciation by the late Senator Joseph R. McCarthy. Professor Alexander Gray, a stalwart conservative,[15] is at pains to point out that Plato's state is the communism of a limited group, the communism of the military encampment; it is not at all committed — like later manifestations — to revolt or to concepts of social, economic and political equality. On the contrary, it divides firmly as between the rulers and the ruled, the beautiful and the damned; there is no true communist tendency here. But reassurance had come even earlier from the position taken by Plato's most renowned pupil, Aristotle, who is solidly on the side of property and self-interest: "How immeasurably greater is the pleasure, when a man feels a thing to be his own; for the love of self is a feeling implanted by nature and not given in vain. . . . No one, when men have all things in common, will any longer set an example of liberality or do any liberal action; for liberality consists in the use which is made of property."[16]

As sufficiently observed, it was ethical judgment, not the dry expository concerns of economics, that motivated Aristotle and the other great mentors of the Greeks. But already we see a tendency

14. Plato, *The Republic*, cited in Gray, p. 19.
15. See footnote 3 in this chapter.
16. Aristotle, *Politics*, Book 2, in *Early Economic Thought*, p. 25.

that recurs throughout the history of the subject and is central to its understanding: on slavery, the position of women and public interest *vis-à-vis* self-interest, ethical judgments have a strong tendency to conform to what citizens of influence find it agreeable to believe; they reflect what I have elsewhere called the Convenient Social Virtue.[17] Over the intervening two and a half thousand years between Grecian times and our own, we shall find economists articulating the Convenient Social Virtue to the consequent applause. But we will also find some who, out of the great dialectic of mind, voice and adverse interest, challenge what the privileged, contented and influential find it comfortable to believe. It is only thus that economic discussion is to be understood fully.

Those who have written on the history of economic ideas are overwhelmingly in agreement on the small, even negligible, contribution of the Romans. They extended the praise of agriculture so that it became a paean. To this were added many suggestions on agricultural methods and management — that of the self-sufficient estate, perhaps needless to say, not that of the commercial enterprise. There were doubts about the efficiency of slavery; Pliny (c. A.D. 23–79) observed that "it is the very worst plan of all to have land tilled by slaves let loose from the house of correction, as indeed is the case with all work entrusted to men who live without hope."[18] In the later Empire, when the estates had grown very large, there was much regret over the passage of the smaller cultivator and much concern over the great scale of the *latifundia*. This, also, is a worry that has endured: "We must, whatever happens, safeguard the family farm."

There was, however, one major Roman contribution that, being outside the conventional boundaries of economics, has escaped the more conventional economic discussion. That was Roman law and the role therein of private property.

The institution of private property far predates recorded history;

17. In *Economics and the Public Purpose* (Boston: Houghton Mifflin, 1973).
18. Pliny, *Natural History*, cited in Gray, p. 37.

in the most primitive of tribal communities, men laid claim to weapons, tools and, alas, to women of their own. Personal property is accepted in all societies, including the socialist world; possessions are everywhere an aspect of personality itself. But it was Roman law that gave to property its formal identity and to its possessor the *dominium*, or rights, that are now assumed. These rights were comprehensive; they included the right not only of enjoyment and use but also of misuse and abuse. Intrusion on them by others or the state would henceforth carry the burden of justification.

No institution in the nonsocialist world has rivaled in its importance private property and its use and pursuit; no institution has been so productive of social, economic or political discord. The conservative in the nonsocialist economy stands with unthinking eloquence for "the rights of private property," while those on the social left — liberals, in American parlance — contentiously but cautiously assert the higher claims of the state or the public interest. And on the question of public or private ownership of productive property turns the great difference between the capitalist and the socialist worlds. If Roman economic comment was slight, it was, nonetheless, the Roman genius to identify and give form to the institution that, more than any other, would be central to personal gratification, economic development and political conflict in the centuries to come.

III

The Enduring Interim

ALTHOUGH NOT RECOGNIZED as a part of the historical tradition of economic thought, the Roman commitment to the sanctity of private property, as it would now be called, was a tremendous legacy to economic and political life. It was to be the source of innumerable peasant uprisings against the power of landlords and aristocrats and eventually of the greatest social revolution of modern times — the socialist revolt against the power and the ability to win submission that accompany or once accompanied the possession of industrial (and also landed) property.

There was another, perhaps yet greater, legacy from the Roman era, if not specifically from Rome, and that was Christianity. This, building on and vastly extending the earlier Judean tradition, law and teaching, had three enduring effects. One was achieved through the example it established, one through the social beliefs and attitudes it inculcated and one through the specific economic laws it supported or required.

The example was that of Jesus, the son of an artisan, who showed that there was no divine right of the privileged; power could be with people who worked with their hands. Accompanied by disciples who were mostly of similar humble background, Jesus challenged the Herodian establishment and therewith the greatly more majestic power of Rome.[1] That one person or one small group from

1. On this last point I am guided by my friend and colleague Krister Stendahl, the former dean of the Harvard Divinity School. (He is now Bishop of Stockholm.) See his *Meanings: The Bible as Document and as Guide* (Philadelphia: Fortress Press,

such origins could gain such influence, distinction and authority was an example to be cited, an influence to be felt, for the next two thousand years. Those who in later times entered a protest against the established economic order would be called rabble-rousers, and it would be part of their defense that in His assault on the Jerusalem establishment — in denigrative terms, the moneychangers and usurers of the Temple — Jesus was their ultimate role model. To a far greater extent than many conservative Christians have liked to think, He legitimized revolt against evil or oppressive economic power. That priests in Central America who join the people in opposing rapacious or corrupt authority today believe themselves to be acting according to His example is a cause even now of much reputable distress.

The principal social attitude perpetuated by Christianity supported the equality of all mankind. All being children of God, all were, in consequence, equals in the brotherhood of man. In keeping with this instruction was an inevitable suspicion of wealth as a differentiation between brothers, a source for some of unequal power, prestige and enjoyment. By slight extension, there was also a sense of the superior virtue of the poor. Obviously and persistently troubling questions followed as to the institution of slavery and further questions as to wealth and the pursuit of wealth — so much so that some special distinction would henceforth accrue to the Christian who took a vow of poverty.

For the next two millennia, down to modern times, the great Christian slave owner and the devout man of wealth would have need to find special theological support for their good fortune, support that would frequently be available at some modest cost. Indeed, by the time of the Renaissance Popes, the Church itself would have become reconciled to the accumulation of wealth by its priests.

1984), p. 205 *et seq.* On p. 210, he notes the "increasing evidence that the role of Pilate was considerably greater in the execution of Jesus than the tradition and even the gospels lead us to think. . . . The crucifixion — a Roman execution — speaks its clear language, indicating that Jesus must have appeared sufficiently messianic, not only in a purely spiritual sense, to constitute a threat to political order according to Roman standards."

Indulgences would be marketed in an orderly manner; churchly offices would have their going price; the rich, once held to have a difficult access to heaven, would now enter in an expeditious way as their solvent survivors purchased a prompt passage for them through purgatory — a design that must have caused a serious congestion of the righteous poor in that inhospitable station.

Nonetheless, Christian attitudes toward both wealth and the equal standing of all men before God have survived such aberrations. With the Reformation they were affirmed by the theses of Martin Luther, as also in the later and improved standards of the Church of Rome. Along with a notably convenient accommodation to earthly needs, preferences and pleasures, there would be an accompanying persistence of original Christian doctrines calling for the rejection of worldly, meaning pecuniary, concerns.

The more specific relation of Christianity to economics centered on the laws pertaining to the taking of interest. Labor as a factor of production was considered to be good; Jesus and the Apostles spoke proudly of toil; the laborer was believed worthy of his hire. And the returns to the landowner were not severely criticized. But early Christian doctrine strongly condemned the exaction of interest; as with the Greeks, it was seen as extortion by the fortunately affluent from the unfortunate, unwise or impoverished who were pressed by needs and obligations beyond their means. That money might be borrowed so that the borrower could make more money from it still had no effective standing in Roman times and did not sanction the taking of interest. The need to find a justification for interest would, in fact, preoccupy some of the more innovative minds for the next eighteen hundred (and more) years; the moneylender for all this time would be a dubious, even reprehensible, figure, and if a Jew, and thus more ambiguously subject to the ban on the taking of interest, he would be a ripe object for anti-Semitism. One far from impeccable view[2] used the Christian restriction on the taking

2. Its principal exponent was Werner Sombart (1863–1941), the German historian-economist, a diligent but not completely reliable scholar. Intuitively and perhaps even openly anti-Semitic, Sombart sought in his later years to give a measure of

of interest to accord to the Jews a central role in the early development of capitalism, a thesis that sadly minimizes the ability of Christian doctrine to adjust to economic need and the signal importance of Christians — the Fuggers, Imhofs and Welsers — among the great early moneylenders of Europe.

The Christian doubts as to the righteousness of moneylending have never been wholly expunged. As noted in the last chapter, the loan shark is, to this day, outside the boundaries of conventional respectability, and only in relatively recent times have bankers been safely within. In the last century and on into the present one, John Pierpont Morgan, the most prominent of American bankers, established himself as a highly visible pillar of the Protestant Episcopal Church by, among other things, according the hospitality of his private railroad car to bishops and divines as they moved back and forth to church meetings. Some thought this a design for countering an otherwise predatory image as the greatest moneylender of his age.

Historians have looked earnestly and with little success for any formal expression of economic ideas in the scholarly and priestly thought of the one thousand years that followed the dissolution of the Roman Empire; the yield has again, as with the Greeks and Romans, been slight. And again the reason is not hard to find. The basic economic life of the Middle Ages bore little resemblance to modern economic society; accordingly, there was little that, as economics is now regarded, needed describing.

Specifically, the market, though growing in importance with the passing centuries, was a minor aspect of life. The great rural masses of men and women grew, made or killed what they ate or wore and surrendered a part of it to a hierarchy of lords or masters for their right to do so and their protection while thus engaged. As workers in the fields and cottages, "peasants could be slaves, serfs, freehold-

---

theoretical sanction to National Socialism. On this see Ben B. Seligman, *Main Currents in Modern Economics* (New York: The Free Press of Glencoe, 1962), pp. 18–21.

ers, share-croppers or tenants; they might have as their overlords the Church, the king, great noblemen, gentry of higher and lesser degree, or rich tenant-farmers,"[3] but whatever the relationship between master and worker, whether one of traditional status, obligation or compulsion, products and services were surrendered, not sold. This being so, this being the social situation of the overwhelming proportion of all people, it would be astonishing had there been any developed set of economic ideas as they are now understood. What was important once again was the intrusion of ethics on economics — the fairness or justice of the relationship between master and slave, lord and serf, landlord and sharecropper. A determining factor as regards income was the feudal conflicts or alliances by which one feudal lord enlarged his landed territory, and thus his revenues, at the expense of another. It is, appropriately, of these conflicts and not of the economic nexus that the established history deals. It might be added that this relation of landed territory to income has had an enduring effect on political and military thought. To this day the intellectually more retarded military strategist looks at a frontier on a map with the assumption that some landed feudatory has designs for bursting out to appropriate the acres and revenues across the border. That to seize and operate successfully a modern industrial economy is a more difficult task than simply to annex one's neighbor's land is a matter that has yet fully to penetrate the established military mind.

As a ruling circumstance, however, the absence of trade or a market in the Middle Ages must not be carried too far. There were now towns, if minuscule by later standards, and the higher feudatories had diverse needs or desires that were served by traders from near

3. Fernand Braudel, *Civilization and Capitalism, 15th–18th Century:* Vol. 2, *The Wheels of Commerce,* translated by Sian Reynolds (New York: Harper & Row, 1982), p. 256.
   Increasingly, as slaves became scarcer in the late Roman era and thereafter, one or another form of sharecropping took the place of slavery, as was the case after the Civil War in the United States.

and far or satisfied by purchase from the craftsmen of the local guilds. Here, indeed, was a market, but not being the norm of everyday relationships, it did not attract major attention or thought. Economics in all modern manifestations centers on the market; in a world in which the market was a subsidiary, even esoteric, aspect of life, economics as now known still did not exist.

Once again, however, there were exceptions. Such purchases and sales as did occur attracted the mind and pen of the greatest of the religious philosophers of his millennium, the wonderfully prolific Saint Thomas Aquinas, or Thomas of Aquina (1225–1274), an Italian-born citizen of France and, indeed, of all Europe. He was the first of the group of religious philosophers and scholars known to history as the Schoolmen. And money, the most magically alluring subject of economics, drew the attention of another unusually articulate divine, Nicole Oresme (c. 1320–1382), the Bishop of Lisieux.

As markets in the Middle Ages were only a small part of the structure of everyday life, so also they had their special characteristics: many sales, as of a horse or of cattle, were from one man to another; or they were by one or a handful of merchants to others; or they were under the regulation of the sellers of the product — of the guilds. The latter, the craft guilds, were a strongly characteristic feature of medieval economic life. They existed for many purposes: assurance as to quality of workmanship, highly agreeable social observances, political influence and notably, if not always successfully, regulation of prices and journeymen's wages. Exceptional rather than normal in all these medieval contexts was the impersonally determined or competitive market price. In all but the rarest cases there was evidence of superior and inferior bargaining power, a greater or lesser measure of monopoly power. This being so, the question of the fairness or justice of the price arose, just as it had with Aristotle and as it does in modern times when monopoly is involved. And it was to the fairness of the prices that Saint Thomas Aquinas addressed himself: "I answer that it is wholly

25

sinful to practise fraud for the express purpose of selling a thing for more than its just price. . . . To sell dearer or to buy cheaper than a thing is worth is in itself unjust and unlawful."[4] A fair price was thus enjoined as a religious obligation; default therefrom made the perpetrator subject not only to the moral condemnation of the community but to appropriate religious sanction, if not in this world, then in the next.

The concept of the just price survives, as I have indicated earlier, in the everyday reference to what is fair, reasonable or decent in a price as established in individual negotiation and by implication in the condemnation of the profiteer, predator, exploiter or unduly grasping seller or buyer. What was never decided by Saint Thomas, at least in any usefully secular way, is how a just price is determined. This too remains a matter on which the views of even righteous buyers and sellers have a wholly uncontrollable tendency to diverge. It cannot be supposed that it was a problem particularly welcomed by God, to whom Saint Thomas (and the other Schoolmen) ultimately referred it.

Here, then, is the greatest dialectic of economic life, that between morality and the market. The latter has been invoked over the centuries since Saint Thomas with even greater theological emphasis than the former:

"Leave it to the market."

"I only charge what the market will bear."

And with such reiteration the market has triumphed; Saint Thomas Aquinas's just price has become a theological curiosity, not something that even a devout theologian takes seriously. And the market has acquired a powerful morality of its own:

"You don't interfere with the market."

"One is entitled to a fair *market* price."

Yet, if exiguously, the notion of a higher order of justice than that of the market has also survived. A legislated minimum wage

---

4. Saint Thomas Aquinas, *Summa Theologica*, Question 77, "On Fraud Committed in Buying and Selling," in *Early Economic Thought*, edited by A. E. Monroe (Cambridge: Harvard University Press, 1924), pp. 54–55.

is seen as a necessary manifestation of such justice. As are minimum farm prices — "a fair price to the producer." And controlled rents in New York and other large cities. All these, in one established modern view, are greatly at odds with the efficiency of the market. They remain, nonetheless, as a distant — perhaps very distant — echo of the teachings of the Schoolmen.

Saint Thomas's just price, as noted, was highly subjective. On some other matters, however, he was wholly objective. Thus, in considering the question of whether a seller can or should sell a defective product, he affirmed that he must not knowingly do so, and if some defective item is innocently passed along, the seller must compensate the buyer when the fault is discovered. As to whether a seller is bound to admit to an imperfection in an otherwise acceptable product, he must, of course, do so unless "the defect is obvious, as in the case of a horse with only one eye."[5] Saint Thomas is a relevant guide to the recent agitation in the United States as to whether a used-car dealer should be required to post a list of the known defects in the vehicles he displays for sale. A bent fender would not need to be listed; a defective carburetor or transmission, according to Saint Thomas's rules, would have to be made known.

Saint Thomas also accepted and, indeed, strongly affirmed the ban on the taking of interest and combined this with consideration of the righteousness of trade in general. His condemnation of trade was not total:

> There are two kinds of exchange. One may be called natural and necessary, by means of which one thing is exchanged for another, or things for money to meet the needs of life. . . . The other kind of exchange is that of money for money or of things for money, not to meet the needs of life, but to acquire gain. . . . The first kind of exchange is praiseworthy, because it serves natural needs, but the second is justly condemned.[6]

5. Saint Thomas Aquinas, *Summa Theologica*, Article 3, in *Early Economic Thought*, p. 61.

6. Saint Thomas Aquinas, *Summa Theologica*, Article 4, in *Early Economic Thought*, p. 63.

With these words, professional traders — brokers, scalpers, speculators, middlemen — joined moneylenders in moral obloquy. Here, too, a long process of rehabilitation would be required. In France in the eighteenth century the Physiocrats, of whom the chapter after next will tell, would find trade essentially barren, unproductive of any real wealth. And to this day, when we think of wealth creation, there is a tendency to associate it with the production of hard saleable goods; buying and selling and the rendering of services have no similar standing. Also the trader was, until recent times, subject to some social stigma, this being the fate of anyone "in trade" in Britain until well into this century. Somerset Maugham, who was reared as an orphan in a clerical family, wrote eloquently of his uncle's sense of generosity when, as a country minister, he admitted to the graces of the Church a retailer or other tradesman.

One cannot but assume a sea change in attitudes in the one hundred years that separated the world of Saint Thomas from that of Nicole Oresme. Marginal and suspect in the thought of Saint Thomas, trade — merchant capitalism — is central to that of Oresme. The policy of the prince should now be to encourage trade and arrange the conditions that do so.

For Oresme this meant, principally, the proper management of money. It is not wholly an act of imagination to call him the first of the monetarists. Tracing briefly the history of money,[7] he showed how the coinage of gold, silver and copper — coins of fixed weight and reliable purity — replaced the awkward tedium of scales and the weighing of the metal. The responsibility for coinage he then placed squarely on the prince — the government. And having imposed this responsibility, he devoted many pages and the most urgent of language to telling the prince of his further duties. Above all, he must not debase — Oresme's word is *alter* — the pure metal content of the coin, and this injunction was frequently repeated:

7. In *Traictie de la Première Invention des Monnoies*. This, too, is available in the collection of the invaluable Monroe, pp. 81–102.

"Who, then, would trust a prince who should diminish the weight or fineness of money bearing his own stamp?"[8] Again, "There are three ways, in my opinion, in which one may make profit from money, aside from its natural use. The first of these is the art of exchange, the custody of or trafficking in money; the second is usury, and the third is the altering of money. The first is base, the second is bad, and the third is even worse."[9] And, "It is the sovereign's function to condemn and punish counterfeiters and those who practise any fraud upon money. How ashamed he should be, therefore, to be found guilty of a crime which he should punish in another by a disgraceful death!"[10] Oresme was particularly severe with the prince of an adjacent realm who slipped debased coins into the monetary circulation of his neighbor, and he was convinced that merchants would avoid doing business in a land where the coinage was unreliable. Good, reliable money is good for business.

Copper having become too plentiful in Oresme's day, he was for a coinage based on gold and silver — bimetalism. For the purposes of everyday transactions there should be a fixed ratio between the two; he mentioned, by way of illustration, ratios of 20 in weight of silver to 1 of gold, or 25 of silver to 3 of gold, the latter a considerably more favorable ratio for silver than the cry of 16 to 1 that rallied the American West at the end of the last century.[11] He recognized that changes in the supply of silver or gold would require changes in the ratio, but he pleaded that it be altered only in response to significant increases or decreases in that supply.

In economics there are some, even if not many, immutable laws — laws of an order of certainty of Calvin Coolidge's possibly apocry-

8. Oresme, *Traictie de la Première Invention des Monnoies,* in *Early Economic Thought,* p. 92.

9. Oresme, *Traictie de la Première Invention des Monnoies,* in *Early Economic Thought,* p. 95.

10. Oresme, *Traictie de la Première Invention des Monnoies,* in *Early Economic Thought,* p. 97.

11. See Chapter XII.

phal dictum that when many people are out of work, unemployment results. Of comparable stature is Gresham's Law, that bad money drives out good — that people and enterprises of all stations, if they are possessed of money, some of which is of solid substance and reputation and some that is debased or otherwise suspect, will pass on the bad and keep the good. Thus does the bad drive the good from circulation. This law is attributed to Sir Thomas Gresham, the great Elizabethan merchant, financier, diplomat and one of the founders of the Royal Exchange. It is one of the major misattributions of history. Oresme observed the tendency a full two centuries earlier, and it is unlikely that even he was the first, for it is the kind of economic discovery that anyone can make for himself or herself. Should one have, as of this writing, a stock of Mexican pesos and a stock of American dollars or Swiss francs, there is little doubt as to which a mentally viable person would dispose of for current needs and which he or she would hold for the future. And noticing that everyone did the same thing, someone would surely assert it as a law. The great truisms of economics have no clear discoverers; they are evident for all to see.

It remains that, were a choice possible, the law attributed to Sir Thomas Gresham should better be attributed to the Bishop of Lisieux.

There was more in this great span of time than the words of Saint Thomas and Oresme. But not much. And the reason will be evident. Economics, to repeat, does not exist apart from the relevant economic life. The rigid hierarchial structure of feudal society commanded and distributed goods and services not in response to price but in response to law, custom and the fear of condign and markedly painful punishments. The market was an esoteric exception; on it scholars, not surprisingly, did not dwell. Oresme, who did, was responding to a new and expanding world in which markets — and money — were strongly emergent. To that world and the economic ideas it nurtured, we now turn.

IV

The Merchants and the State

W E COME NOW to one of the most ardently debated periods in this history. It is the era of the merchants, the time of what is variously called merchant capitalism or mercantilism. It is thought of as extending for three hundred years, from very roughly the middle of the fifteenth century to the middle of the eighteenth, with the end vividly marked by the beginning of the Industrial Revolution, the American Revolution and the publication of *Wealth of Nations* by Adam Smith. Smith's great work appeared in 1776, the year of the American Declaration of Independence. The two events were not unrelated; both were in stern reaction to the economic policies and practices of the mercantilist era.

In these three centuries economics did not have an acknowledged spokesman, none such as Aristotle in Greece, Saint Thomas Aquinas for the Middle Ages and the Church-regulated feudal ethic, or Smith, Marx and Keynes in later years. "Mercantilism was anything but a 'system'; it was primarily the product of the minds of statesmen, civil servants, and of the financial and business leaders of the day."[1] As in the United States in the last century, economics and economic theories were expressed in a broad current of policy, not by individual economists or philosophers. There will be a later brief word on those who articulated the ideas of mercantilism; pri-

1. Alexander Gray, *The Development of Economic Doctrine* (London: Longmans, Green, 1948), p. 74.

marily we will understand economics in this era only as we see the controlling economic conditions of the time and their practical reflection in public and private action.

From far back in the Middle Ages, there had been an irregular but continuing expansion of trade within the European lands, between them and between Europe and the eastern Mediterranean. Now in the age of the merchants came a greatly increasing commerce carried on both locally and over long distances. There were markets of diverse aspect that sold cloth, yarn, wine, leather, shoes, corn (that is, wheat) and much else at fairs, in private houses, in great halls and in surrounding spaces.[2] Ships brought products from ever more remote lands. Banks appeared, first in Italy and then in Northern Europe. Money exchanges, where the coins of different countries could be weighed and exchanged, became a regular feature of commercial life. The merchant emerged from the feudal shadows to become a distinctive figure and if affluent and operating on an adequate scale, an acceptable and socially prestigious one. Over Europe as a whole the greatest social eminence continued to belong to the landed classes, the descendants of the feudal barons, many of whom still retained their special instinct for armed conflict and associated self-destruction. But already by the fifteenth century the merchant towns — Venice, Florence, Bruges giving way to Antwerp, Amsterdam, London, the Hansa cities — had merchant communities of distinction. Where everyone was in trade, the trader escaped stigma. These were, it might be added, communities of generally higher artistic and cultural achievement than that of the older landowning classes. To this day the most admired urban commercial and residential architecture remains that of the merchants.

In the merchant towns the great merchants were not merely influential in the government; they *were* the government. And

2. A full and lucid account of the development of markets in these years is in the previously cited *Civilization and Capitalism, 15th–18th Century:* Vol. 2, *The Wheels of Commerce,* by Fernand Braudel, translated by Sian Reynolds (New York: Harper & Row, 1982).

throughout all of Europe from the fifteenth to the eighteenth centuries they were increasingly influential in the new national states. Public policy and, in turn, public action reflected their views. Much of their influence, it may also be added, came from the fact that, to survive, the merchants had to be more intelligent than the inheriting members of the old landowning classes, and this intelligence extended to a very clear view of how the state could serve their interests.

Along with the proliferation of markets and the rise of the merchant class there were three other developments that were reflected in the economic attitudes and policies of the time. The first was the voyages of discovery to America and the Far East — in 1492, the Portuguese-trained Columbus to America; five years later, the Portuguese navigator Vasco da Gama to India; and in ensuing decades, others from Spain and Portugal and then from England, France and Holland. The result was a flow of new and exotic products into Europe from the East and, more important, a flood of silver and gold from the mines of the New World. One of the more persistent of historical myths holds that this flood comprised the accumulated treasure in gold of the Incas and the other peoples of the Americas; it was there to be picked up. In fact, as earlier indicated, the metal that was imported was mostly silver, and the silver was not found in ingots and ornaments but was wrested from the ground by the toil of tens and hundreds of thousands of Indians working for brief and bitter lives in the mines at San Luis Potosí and Guanajuato in Mexico and their counterparts elsewhere in New Spain. From 1531 to 1570, near the peak of the flood, silver represented from 85 to 97 percent in weight of the total treasure coming into Europe.[3]

The mines of the New World and the galleons that, subject to

3. These figures can be found in Earl J. Hamilton, *American Treasure and the Price Revolution in Spain, 1501–1650* (Cambridge: Harvard University Press, 1934), p. 40. Professor Hamilton, of Duke and Chicago Universities, is the acknowledged authority on the flow of precious metals into Europe and the resulting price revolution, as he chose to call it.

the exigencies of winds and weather and the occasional intrusion of pirates,[4] carried the precious metals to the Spanish peninsula were the precipitating factors in the second great development of these years, the great upward movement in prices. The treasure poured into Spain, where, according to law, it had to be coined; it then went on to the rest of Europe to pay for Spain's compulsive military operations and for Spanish imports. War in this period, it should be noted, was a highly important occupation with a major claim on public monies. Max Weber (1864–1920), the great German social scientist, estimated that some 70 percent of Spanish public revenues and around two thirds of the revenues of other European countries were so employed at the time.[5]

The effect of the great inflow of metal was a general rise in prices, an early manifestation of the Quantity Theory of Money. This is the historic theorem which holds that prices, the volume of trade being given, will vary in direct proportion to the supply of money. The price increase occurred first in Spain and then moved on to the rest of Europe, following the path of the silver and gold. Between 1500 and 1600, prices in Andalusia rose perhaps fivefold. In England, if prices during the last half of the fifteenth century, that is to say just before Columbus, are taken as 100, they were 250 by the end of the sixteenth century and around 350 in the decade of 1673 to 1682.[6] In modern Mexico, Brazil or Israel such price movements would be equated with currency stability. They showed at the time that a firm metallic currency — a gold and silver standard — was consistent with price inflation. The relationship between the supply of money and prices, a matter for later (and at times nearly

4. The role of the pirates, as Hamilton has observed, has also been greatly exaggerated. Most of the ships of the treasure fleets arrived safely in the Spanish harbors; it was the relatively few losses that were regretted and celebrated.

5. Quoted by Earl J. Hamilton in "American Treasure and the Rise of Capitalism (1500–1700)," in *Economica*, Vol. 9, No. 27 (November 1929), p. 340.

6. See Abbott Payson Usher after Georg Wiebe, "Prices of Wheat and Commodity Price Indexes for England, 1259–1930," in *The Review of Economic Statistics*, Vol. 13, No. 3 (August 1931), p. 103 *et seq.* Professor Usher is at pains to note that the price increase began somewhat before the great inflow of metal from the New World.

preclusive) economic attention, entered the economic comment of the day. Writing in 1576, when the metals were at full flow, Jean Bodin (1530–1596), the great political theorist and scholar, said, "I find that the high prices we see today are due to some four or five causes. The principal & almost the only one (which no one has referred to until now) is the abundance of gold & silver."[7] He went on to mention monopoly as the second cause.

The further effect of the great silver and gold inflow was on the volume of trade — the volume of merchant activity itself. There was a view, then as later, that the role of money is essentially neutral: money is a convenience in the buying and selling of goods, a bridge over the gap in time between the sale and purchase of goods, a convenient way of holding wealth. The state of trade — the volume of goods and services produced and made available for sale and purchase — is governed, it was held, by more fundamental, more sophisticated factors. There is, in fact, little doubt that the price revolution, the inflation, of the sixteenth and seventeenth centuries was a strongly stimulative force. It meant that, in contrast with a time of declining prices or deflation, there was written into the worth of any durable asset, any purchase for future sale, a strong chance for profit as denoted in current monetary terms in the expectation of an increase in prices. It is hard to believe that this, persisting over a long period of time as the metal continued to flow in from the Americas, had other than an impressive and encouraging influence on trade. It meant also, one may assume, that more and more people, having the possibility of possessing money, were more and more motivated to seek it for its own sake. This desire was perhaps most effectively articulated by Christopher Columbus himself. "Gold," he said, "is a wonderful thing! Whoever possesses it is master of everything he desires. With gold, one can even get souls into paradise."[8]

7. Jean Bodin, *Supplement* to *Les Six Livres de la République*, in *Early Economic Thought*, edited by A. E. Monroe (Cambridge: Harvard University Press, 1924), p. 127.
8. Quoted in Eric Roll, *A History of Economic Thought* (New York: Prentice-Hall,

What also is certain is that the great flow of silver and gold helped fasten the attention of merchants and governments on those metals and on policies that would enhance the amounts in their possession or under their control. This last was central to mercantilist thought and policy.

The third and most important development of these long years was the appearance and consolidation of the authority of the modern state, a process that was not wholly complete until the unification of Italy in 1861 and of Germany at Versailles a decade later. The earlier centuries had seen the decline of the feudal and compulsively feuding baronage and the emergence of princely and city authority. The national state was but the final step in a long chain of events.

With the rise of the national state came the close, even intimate, association between the state authority and the merchant interest. There has long been argument as to which came first: Did the state cultivate the merchants in service to its higher authority? Or was a strong state the necessary instrument of merchant power? Economics, like much else, is plagued by the problem of the precedence of the chicken or the egg. Gustav Schmoller (1838–1917), the German historian-economist, and Eli Filip Heckscher (1879–1952), the great Swedish economic historian and one of the masters of his trade,[9] held that service and subservience to the merchant interest was the natural tendency of the national state; the merchants provided the state with the economic resources that sustained its internal and external power. Sometimes in conflict with each other, sometimes in cooperation, the merchants helped create the power of the state and also to strengthen it. "The waverings of state policy during the long period in which mercantilism held sway cannot be understood without realizing the extent

---

1942), p. 61. The quotation is from a letter written from Jamaica in 1503, a letter that is also quoted by Marx in his *Zur Kritik der politischen Okonomie*. A slightly different version is in R. H. Tawney, *Religion and the Rise of Capitalism* (New York: Harcourt, Brace, 1926), p. 89.

9. Who dealt at length with these matters in the two volumes of *Mercantilism*, translated by Mendel Shapiro (London: George Allen & Unwin, 1935).

to which the state was a creature of warring commercial interests whose only common aim was to have a strong state, provided they could manipulate it to their exclusive advantage."[10]

In the contrasting view, nation building had a separate dynamic of power, and to this the influence and wealth of the merchants were merely contributing factors.

The difference of opinion cannot be resolved, but no one seriously questions the influence of the merchants in the new national states. Their interest was strongly served by both internal order and external protection, these as opposed to the old feudal rivalries and conflicts. And it was served by more specific policies on behalf of merchant well-being. From these needs and desires came the ideas and associated actions of mercantilism, and to them we now turn.

Mercantilism involved, needless to say, a marked break with the ethical attitudes and instructions of Aristotle and of Saint Thomas Aquinas and the Middle Ages in general. Since the merchants were patently in pursuit of wealth in a society where they were influential, perhaps dominant, such pursuit lost its evil or dubious connotation. The merchants were easy in their conscience. Protestantism and Puritanism[11] may have helped, but, as ever, religious faith was accommodated to economic circumstance and need.

As wealth and the pursuit of wealth became respectable, so, if it was not immoderate, did the taking of interest. This also was an adaptation to current reality. In the later Middle Ages, as we have sufficiently seen, the distinction between kinds of interest had already arisen. Interest could be indignantly condemned when it was an exaction by the fortunate from the needful. Or from some profligate baron or prince who, being important and articulate, was

10. Roll, p. 59.

11. " 'The capitalist spirit' is as old as history," R. H. Tawney observed, "and was not, as has sometimes been said, the offspring of Puritanism. But it found in certain aspects of later Puritanism a tonic which braced its energies and fortified its already vigorous temper." Tawney, p. 226.

an influential voice protesting the oppressive payments to which he was subject. But things were different when the borrower made money from his loan. Then, as a matter of simple equity, it could be held, he surely should share the gain with the lender who made it possible and compensate him also for the risk of loss. Both Catholic and Protestant church doctrine made the necessary concessions to economic circumstance, however reluctantly and gradually. The financing of merchant operations with borrowed money became legitimate. Merchants were not denied access to heaven.

The concept of the just price also receded in the face of mercantilism, for the overwhelming concern of the merchants was not that prices be too high but that, by competition, they not be brought too low. Of this more in a moment.

Wages had little or no part in mercantilist thought and practice. Here the role of foreign trade, as it would now be called, was a factor. The distant workers, be they slave, indentured or free, who produced cloth, spices, sugar or tobacco in remote lands, east and west, did not call for consideration. But neither did those nearer home. Domestic manufacturing was extensively in the household; there husband, wife and children worked into cloth the raw materials supplied them by the merchant. Again no wage as such was paid; the merchant entrepreneur simply paid for the work whatever was necessary to command the product. There was nothing here on which to erect a theory of wages, so none was prominent in mercantilist thought.

This household industry calls for a special word. In later centuries the factory system, with its myriad of organized and regimented workers, would evoke a powerful image of exploitation. Over household or cottage industry down to our own time would hover, by contrast, an impression of family independence and benign parental responsibility and command — a socially tranquil scene. Men and women of vulnerable tendency think even now of homely arts and crafts when they yearn for an escape from the more rigorous disciplines of the economic world. In India all governments and nearly all politicians are required, in the Gandhian tradition, to seek the revival of the cottage industries, including the spinning and weaving that brought the traders and the great trading companies to Madras, Calcutta and Bengal in the era of merchant capitalism. Forgotten, at least by many, is the terrible exploitation forced on men and women by the threat of starvation and thus on children by their parents. Nor is management by the head of a family always at a high level of efficiency or intelligence. More of those who have described or endorsed the homely romance of household industry over the centuries should have personally experienced its rigors when it was the sole source of income.

Coming to the avowed beliefs of mercantilism — or errors, as they would later be called [12] — there was, first, the merchants' negative attitude toward competition. Because they didn't relish it, monopoly or monopolistic control of prices and product was approved. Next, the merchants being influential in the state, there was a strong belief in the benignity of the state and in state intervention in the economy. Third and finally, this being much on the merchants' minds, there was agreement that the accumulation of gold and silver — pecuniary wealth — should be a primary goal of personal and public policy, to which end personal effort and public regulation should always be directed: "It is always better to sell goods to others than to buy goods from others, for the former brings a certain advantage and the latter inevitable damage." [13]

As the years passed and the merchant era receded, the competitive market would become a religious totem, with monopoly the one grievous flaw in an otherwise optimal system. The notion of national wealth coordinate not with the supply of money but with the whole production of goods and services would come to seem

12. "Mercantilism, as the reader may have observed, is even now not wholly dead, but its errors were exposed long ago." Allyn Young, a greatly influential professor of economics at Harvard before his death at an early age, wrote thus in a much remarked contribution to the 1932 and later editions of the *Encyclopaedia Britannica*, Vol. 7, p. 926.

13. Johann Joachim Becher, a German exponent of mercantilist thought, quoted in Roll, p. 62.

self-evident. Accordingly, it is easy to understand why mercantilist policy would be regarded with disdain and why nothing would come to condemn an economist or an economic policymaker so much as to say that he was showing a mercantilist taint. A better view should prevail. However, it must be recognized that mercantilism was a relevant and predictable expression of the merchant and princely interest of its time.

As just noted, the merchants in the mercantilist era did not like price competition; indeed, not many do today. The obverse, such as agreements or understandings between sellers as to price, grants or patents of monopoly from the crown for a particular product, a monopoly of trade with a particular part of the world, the prohibition of competitive production and sale of goods in the colonies of the New World, served the merchant interest. And so serving, they were then seen as the national interest. The tendency to identify a group interest with the national interest is not something to which any modern observer should react with surprise.

Likewise, a merchant's stock of precious metals was in that time the relevant index of his personal wealth, the simple, forthright measure of his financial competence. There is no tendency more commonplace than to assume that what is right for the individual is right for the state — the fallacy of composition, as it has come to be called. In its everyday modern form it holds that what is right as regards receipts, expenditures and debt for the household is right, *pari passu*, for the government. The mercantilist insistence on the accumulation of gold and silver as a matter of state policy has long been thought a fallacy of composition. It is not at all clear that it was. These, as noted, were years of persistent warfare. The precious metals bought ships and ordnance and were essential for sustaining soldiers on military campaigns. References to gold and silver as the "sinews of war" appear frequently in statements of mercantilist policy. It follows that rulers were right to associate military and national strength with policies that brought or seemed to bring these metals within their borders. Mercantilism had firm roots in national defense and aggression.

Its practical manifestation, the mercantilist decrees and legislation, involved the levy of customs duties and various other prohibitions on imports. Also the grants of patents of monopoly, which in Elizabethan England were given with great freedom, even down to such lesser essentials as playing cards. These grants were a public largesse that continued until curbed by Parliament during the reign of James I with the Statute of Monopolies, in 1623–1624. There was also the chartering of the great trading companies, of which a word later. Finally, there were persisting public efforts to limit the export of gold and silver. These, we may assume, were largely ineffective. Like modern exchange control, of which it was an early antecedent, the prohibition was easily evaded, and the evasion, unlike burglary or murder, did not greatly trouble the moral sense of the community or that of the perpetrator involved.

A legion of scholars has observed that the struggle of the mercantilist states to have a favorable balance of trade — to export more in value than they imported — was not a game in which all could succeed. Few economic truths are more evident. But this did not prevent any one country from making the effort. Nor does it now. Down to our own time every nation has looked at its balance of payments and wondered if it might not be improved.[14]

The years of merchant capitalism here being discussed were rich in the antecedents of policies of later account and controversy. Here was state intervention on behalf of industry, tariff protection, a policy on the balance of payments. But more important than any of these was the arrival of what was to become the dominant economic institution today, the great modern corporation.

In the beginning this was merely a temporary association of individuals joining their efforts and capital for a common task or voyage and to ensure a noncompetitive price for the resulting products as they were purchased and sold. The roots of such or similar associations extended back to the guilds of the Middle Ages. In the

14. With the notable exception, as this is written, of Japan in the mid-1980s.

fifteenth century the Merchant Adventurers, merchants selling cloth from England to the Continent, came together in a loose federation that, in time, took on a more cohesive form. Then in the Muscovy Company of 1555 and the Dutch East India Company of 1602, capital was no longer committed for a voyage or particular activity; it was, instead, a permanent support to operations. In the same period the highly durable British East India Company (1600–1874)[15] came into being, and in 1670 the elegantly entitled Gentlemen Adventurers, Trading into Hudson's Bay, which, its headquarters removed in recent times from Britain to Canada, still exists. The French East India Company was chartered in 1664. Each of these companies was accorded a monopoly of the trade in its assigned or preferred area. Each had also the need to resist, by armed action or its threat, the inroads of the other national monopolies that were similarly endowed. The corporation began as an instrument of trade but also, no less, of war.

In the late seventeenth and early eighteenth centuries the chartering of joint-stock companies, as they came to be called, continued, and for an increasing variety of purposes. Thus both trade with the American colonies and also their government were by chartered companies.

In the early 1700s, there was a further and more spectacular antecedent of modern corporate tendency: exuberant and mindless stock market booms in Paris and London. In Paris, under the auspices (and from some points of view because of the genius) of John Law, there was a wonderful inflation in the stock of the Mississippi Company (Compagnie d'Occident), which had been created to work the allegedly rich but, alas, wholly imaginary gold mines of Louisiana. In London there were the South Sea Company and a variety of other companies, including one to exploit a hitherto underutilized energy source, namely, the wheel of perpetual motion, and another, much celebrated in the history of speculation for its

15. Effectively, it came to an end after the Indian Mutiny of 1857.

reticence. It was "for carrying on an undertaking of great advantage, but nobody to know what it is."[16]

Although mercantilist doctrine can be understood primarily through the policies of the time and their less than formal advocacy, there were in all the new national states men who, in a somewhat coherent way, articulated its general principles — Antoine de Montchrétien (1576–1621) in France, Antonio Serra (precise dates unknown) in Italy, Philipp W. von Hornick (1638–1712) in Austria, Johann Joachim Becher (1635–1682) in Germany and Thomas Mun (1571–1641) in England being the most prominent. Scholars have found their work, on the whole, a limited resource, for all say at greater or lesser length much the same thing, and all are given more to assertion than to argument. One senses that the views are, without exception, not theirs but those of the merchants for whom they speak.

Thomas Mun was, in many respects, the most distinguished of these men and certainly the best known in the English-speaking world; his most noteworthy work, *England's Treasure by Forraign Trade or The Ballance of our Forraign Trade is the Rule of our Treasure,* was published in 1664, after his death. Like James and John Stuart Mill at a later time, he was employed by the great East India Company. While he was in its service, the company had permission to export for its purposes £30,000 in gold or silver for any voyage, provided it imported the same value within six months. This was a precise and practical mercantilist design for conserving

16. Charles Mackay, *Memoirs of Extraordinary Popular Delusions and the Madness of Crowds* (London: Richard Bentley, 1841; Boston: L. C. Page, 1932), p. 55. See Mackay for further details. In both France and England these episodes would leave an enduring residue of suspicion — of banks in France because the Banque Royale of John Law was at the center of the action; of corporations in general in England, which led to closer regulation by what were known as the Bubble Acts. In *Wealth of Nations,* turning sternly on the policies of the mercantilist period, Adam Smith would not exempt joint-stock companies from his criticism. Corporate executives and their spokesmen who cite Smith today as the source of all sanction and truth without the inconvenience of having read him would be astonished and depressed to know that he would not have allowed their companies to exist.

money, which Mun strongly favored in his early writing. Later, no longer compelled to this kind of special pleading, he relented and spoke earnestly against the profligacy of such a policy.

What relieves the tedium of mercantilist expression is its patent, sometimes emotional, even tearful, appeal to or for self-interest. Montchrétien, in a passage with a fine modern sound, speaks to his readers of "the tender sighs of the women and the pitiable cries of the children of those whose labours have suffered from foreign competition."[17] Mun, in *England's Treasure*, offers a dozen rules for maximizing England's wealth and well-being; they include avoidance of "excessive consumption of forraign wares in our diet and rayment. . . . [If consumption must be prodigal], let this be done with our own materials and manufactures . . . where the excess of the rich may be the employment of the poor." Further he advised — and I here paraphrase: always sell dear to foreigners what they do not have, cheap what they can otherwise obtain; use one's own ships for exports (a mercantilist idea that survives powerfully in present-day American legislation); challenge the Dutch more effectively in the fish business; buy cheaply where possible from far countries rather than from merchants in neighboring merchant cities; do not give business to nearby competitors.[18]

But, once again, when one considers mercantilism, it is to the policies and the practice and not to the philosophers, as they have loosely been called, that one looks.

Adam Smith, in history's most climactic assault of ideas on policy, brought the mercantilist era to an end in 1776. Though a strong residue from its attitudes and a strong legacy of its institutions would survive, a reference to mercantilism would thereafter have a connotation of error or reproach. It will now be evident that if such reproach is justified, it should not be aimed at those who

17. Antoine de Montchrétien, *Traicté de l'Oeconomie Politique,* cited in Gray, p. 83.
18. The quotations, as well as the material I have paraphrased, are also in *Early Economic Thought,* pp. 172–174. A slightly indignant survey of Mun's guiding rules is in Gray, p. 86 *et seq.*

expressed the ideas but rather at the circumstances of the time and the interests they served.

We come to Adam Smith in the chapter after next. But first it is necessary to look at the ideas emerging at the end of the mercantilist era in France that served and celebrated not merchants, not manufacturers, but agriculture, the diversely productive farms of France.

V

The French Design

A S THE LONG YEARS just under discussion came to a close, a combination of economic, political and intellectual forces in France served to set this populous, rich and eternally fascinating land ideologically apart from the rest of Europe. Merchant capitalism and the artisan class on which it called for its products and, more recently, a variety of factory establishments like those throughout Northern Europe and England had also appeared in France. Paris had become a city of merchants and their suppliers and workmen; so had Lyon, Bordeaux and the other great French towns. But to a larger extent than any other country in Europe, France had retained a powerful agricultural interest and mystique. At that time, as since, agriculture in France was more than an occupation; it was what with proper solemnity would now be called a way of life. And it was also in no slight measure an art form. French cheeses, fruits and, of course, wines had an accepted personality of their own.

It is true that the government of France had yielded less than had those of other countries to the interests and policies of mercantilism. Louis XIV, if not by himself, had subdued, where he had not destroyed, the independent power of the feudal classes. His urgent and persistent need for revenues for war and an amply supported peace had impoverished them, as had his insistence on their living, at great expense, immediately under his eye. At a minimum, this, in association with the demands of the royal tax farmers and the

46

enforced labor of the *corvée* (the system of obligatory service to the lord and the state), had led the aristocrats to pass their pecuniary needs on to what in later years would be called their sharecroppers or, for they still existed in some parts of France, a smaller number of remaining serfs. Alternatively, the exigent royal levies were imposed in a different form on the independent farmers. All these assaults notwithstanding, agriculture retained its power; the agricultural interest continued to rule France. It was the landed aristocracy that surrounded Louis XIV's successors at Versailles, enjoying social precedence and prestige, its members conceding far less than did their English, Dutch or Italian counterparts to the merchants' purposes and interest. Indeed, one wonders if, being otherwise so occupied with their own enjoyments and their personal associations and rivalries, they gave much thought to the increasing national role of the merchant class.[1]

Yet the landed interest in France was a special case in one important respect. Rarely in history has this kind of community produced a convincing philosophical justification for its own privileges; rather it has usually asserted them as a divine or simply an unchallengeable right. But the assemblage of French aristocracy at Versailles was of no slight artistic and intellectual distinction, and, inevitably, some among them reflected on the source of the ascendency of those so assembled and, in the time of Louis XV and Louis XVI, on the means of their increasingly improbable survival. Uniquely at Versailles, thought intruded on landed wealth and tradition.

From this intrusion — again, as ever, in keeping with the context — came, in the latter half of the eighteenth century, a highly

1. A question that arises, for example, as one reads the memoirs of the Duc de Saint-Simon (1675–1755). See *Saint-Simon at Versailles*, from *The Memoirs of M. Le Duc de Saint-Simon*, selected and translated by Lucy Norton (London: Hamish Hamilton, 1958).

Reviewing the final volume of Fernand Braudel's great trilogy, *Civilization and Capitalism, 15th–18th Century:* Vol. 3, *The Perspective of the World*, translated by Sian Reynolds (New York: Harper & Row, 1984), Christopher Hill recently put the national difference succinctly: "The English aristocracy adapted itself to a commercial society as the French aristocracy never did." (*New Statesman*, July 20, 1984, p. 23.)

innovative French contribution to economic thought. This was in the spirit of the Enlightenment — of the exploratory mood and writings of Voltaire, Diderot, Condorcet and, most of all, Rousseau. It had their vision of change, hope and reform; yet it reflected unmistakably and strongly the principal concerns of the day. Central was the role of agriculture as the source of all wealth. The merchants were accorded their appropriate subsidiary position; agriculture, its ancient eminence affirmed, emerged dominant and triumphant. But at the same time the grave public weaknesses of the current economic and political structure were recognized as matters to be repaired. Affirmation of the traditional values of the land and its associated political power and social precedence was combined with advocacy of reform — reform that was thought essential for the survival of the traditional system.

There has always been a question as to what the members of this school of thought should be called. They called themselves Les Économistes, an admirably modern reference, since economists would not be universally so called until after Alfred Marshall in the late nineteenth century. Adam Smith, who visited Paris and Versailles and the leading progenitors of the school in 1765, refers to their ideas as the Agricultural System.[2] The historians of economic thought, however, settled long ago on the least apt of designations, the Physiocrats — those, roughly, who assert the rule of nature.

The Physiocrats, or Les Économistes, were a closely knit

---

2. In one of his engaging combinations of praise and disparagement, Smith said, in *Wealth of Nations:*

That system which represents the produce of land as the sole source of the revenue and wealth of every country has, so far as I know, never been adopted by any nation, and it at present exists only in the speculations of a few men of great learning and ingenuity in France. It would not, surely, be worth while to examine at great length the errors of a system which never has done, and probably never will do any harm in any part of the world. (Book 4, Chapter 9.)

So many editions of *Wealth of Nations* exist that it seems idle to cite page numbers of any specific one. A very satisfactory modern edition is the one published in 1976 by the University of Chicago Press; it is based on the earlier and in many ways definitive edition of Edwin Cannan of the University of London.

community, and many of their ideas are associated not with an individual but with a common position. Three men, however, stand out. The first, most interesting and most important was François Quesnay (1694–1774), who, a lesson for everyone that life is not soon over, came to economics at the age of sixty-two. By then he was one of the most famous physicians of his day and, by any calculation, the best situated. He had written on the practice of bleeding, the nature and handling of gangrene and fevers, and at an early age had become the secretary of the Academy of Surgery in Paris. Then, in a move that was unquestionably significant for his political and social reputation and position, he became, in 1749, the personal physician to Madame de Pompadour, living thereafter at Versailles and going on, in 1755, to the post of physician to Louis XV himself. No economist since has worked under such favoring auspices.

The second of the group, transcending Quesnay in public service if not in royal patronage, was Anne Robert Jacques Turgot (1727–1781), the son of an affluent tradesman, who was by no means wholly unfaithful to his mercantile antecedents. Because of his plausibly larger view of the merchant interest, he came to be regarded in France as its defender. He achieved public notice as *intendant* of Limoges, then one of the poorer parts of France. There he sponsored a range of reforms designed to encourage agriculture, promote local trade, improve road transportation and limit tax abuse. In 1774, he was brought to Paris by Louis XVI and made comptroller-general and minister of finance, a dual post in which he was to suffer the fate of many reformers. Because he saw the imminent threat of a great revolution, he sought to forestall it with a small one, while his enemies, as so often in history, preferred to risk the greater danger. His support of rigid economy in royal and other public expenditures, tax reform, free trade in grain within France, the abolition of public sinecures and monopolies, the toleration of Protestants and the proposed abolition of the *corvée* united against him a most impressive array of vested interests, ranging from landlords and aristocrats to jobholders with varying claims on the public revenue, grain speculators and priests, on to Marie Antoinette

49

herself. Hurt also by the effects of a crop failure, he was sacked in May 1776 and replaced by Jacques Necker, whereupon he returned to work on the system of ideas by which he and his associates are now remembered.

The third important figure among the Physiocrats may well have had a more enduring practical effect on the American Republic than any other Frenchman of his age, not excluding the Marquis de Lafayette. This was Pierre Samuel du Pont de Nemours (1739–1817), who, after editing a journal on agriculture and writing on political subjects, collected and edited some of Quesnay's works under the title *La Physiocratie*, from which, evidently, came the name by which he and his associates were to be known.

During the French Revolution, du Pont was in hiding for a time, under suspicion of counterrevolutionary tendencies, and in 1800 he immigrated to the United States with his sons, Éleuthère Irénée and Victor. In 1802, Éleuthère Irénée began the construction of a powder mill (an area of knowledge in which he had been instructed by Antoine Lavoisier himself) on Brandywine Creek near Wilmington, Delaware. From these beginnings came one of the largest of American industrial corporations and by a wide margin the most durable of industrial dynasties. The du Pont family was to be secure in both the control and the management of their vast enterprise for the next century and a half.

The Physiocrats were remarkable men. So in many ways was their system, as a set of economic ideas could now, for the first time, be called.

One is reminded again of their pre-eminent purpose: to preserve by reform an ancient society of landed precedence and privilege to which all were committed and to stand off the pretensions and intrusions of merchant capitalism and the unruly, crude and vulgar industrial forces (as they were regarded) that it had spawned.

The first and central commitment of the Physiocrats was to the concept of natural law *(le droit naturel)*, for it was this, they held, which ultimately ruled economic and social behavior. The law of kings and legislators is tolerable only as it is consistent with natural law or as it is regarded as a limited extension thereof. The existence and protection of property are in accordance with natural law; so are freedom to buy and sell — freedom of trade — and the steps necessary to secure the defense of the realm. Wisdom is on the side of leaving things to work out on their own in accordance with natural motivations and restraints. The guiding rule in legislation and in government in general should be *laissez faire, laissez passer.*

These four words, the greatest legacy of the Physiocrats, have different levels of meaning. In later times *laissez faire* would be identified by economists with the achievements of the competitive market — an optimal, if not always agreeable, result to be accepted in preference to any intervention by the state. This may perhaps be termed limited or technical *laissez faire.* But *laissez faire* would also be the rallying cry against government intervention in any form for any social purpose. Leave things alone in the widest conceivable area, national defense aside, and they will work themselves out. This, as it may be called, is theological *laissez faire.* A higher power assures the best possible result. Theological *laissez faire* is a notable force in our own time, not least in the Washington of the 1980s. It is strongly operative in the way numerous modern businessmen view the state, up to the point where threatening bankruptcy, unduly severe foreign competition or some other looming misfortune requires a return to secular state action.

From *le droit naturel* came the case against mercantilism. Obviously regulations on behalf of the merchants — grants of monopoly, the numerous protective restraints on internal trade, the surviving merchant guilds — were all in conflict with natural law. In pointing this out, the would-be saviors of the old regime moved against the more obtrusive privileges of merchant capitalism. Perhaps, as Turgot almost certainly believed, the merchants could thus be freed from a myopic misapprehension of their own long-term interests.

However, another doctrine was even more clearly in opposition to merchant esteem and resulting influence. This was the concept of the *produit net*. In its unadorned form, it held simply that all wealth originated in agriculture, none in any other industry, trade or occupation. Merchants, in particular, bought and sold; it was the same product before and after; nothing was added to it in the process. And the case was, if somewhat ambiguously, the same in industry — in manufacturing. Manufacturing merely added labor to the products of the soil; nothing new emerged. Furthermore, manufacturing was limited in extent by its agricultural source and supply: "To increase the number of cobblers . . . there must first be an increase in the number of cow hides."[3]

Closely associated with the notion of the *produit net* was the Physiocratic class structure. In this there were, first, the landlords or proprietors, who guided, supervised or otherwise presided over agricultural production; to them the *produit net* ultimately accrued and on them fell the social and political responsibilities of the community and the state. Next, there was the productive class, members of which did the husbandry and worked the soil; it was after their reward was paid that the *produit net* went to the proprietors. Finally, sharply lower in status, there were the merchants, manufacturers and artisans — the unproductive class.

From the *produit net* and this view of the class structure came the most unequivocal of the defenses against the merchant intrusion and the strongest of the claims for agriculture and therewith the landed and aristocratic power: it was from agriculture that all accretions to wealth came; from other areas of endeavor came nothing. "Agriculture is the source of all the wealth of the State and of the wealth of all the citizens."[4] Encouragement and support to agriculture was, in consequence, not merely the best but the only avenue to greater national well-being.

It followed that taxes on agriculture should be moderate; the operations of the tax farmers should be neither exploitative nor

---

3. Alexander Gray, *The Development of Economic Doctrine* (London: Longmans, Green, 1948), p. 105. The general position on manufacturing is stated in François Quesnay, *Sur les Travaux des Artisans*.

4. François Quesnay, *Maximes Générales*, cited in Gray, p. 102.

erratic. On such moderation depended the protection of the *produit net* and the prosperity of agriculture and the nation. But as regards taxes there was a more somber companion thought: since those in occupations other than agriculture produced no wealth, it followed, or seemed to follow, that they should pay no taxes. Levies on them, since there was no surplus with which to pay them, would simply be passed back in the form of lower prices or higher costs of farm necessities to be paid for by the agricultural producer from his *produit net* — all taxes would end up on the ultimate source of wealth. And this being so, taxes might better be levied at the outset against the landlord or landowning farmer.

As with *laissez faire*, this, too, was an idea that did not die. The notion that production somehow creates (and conceals) a surplus of revenue — a special largesse — accruing to particular classes was to re-emerge in a different form in the next century. Then it would be the capitalists, not the landowners, who would be thought the recipients of a surplus value — another and different *produit net*. For Marx this would be a special object of revolutionary attention and agitation.

The concept of the *produit net* had a more specific renaissance in the United States in the latter years of the last century. This was in the works of Henry George (1839–1897), the greatly articulate advocate of the Single Tax,[5] to whom I will return in Chapter XIII. George's attention was attracted originally to the wonderful increase in western land values (and the accompanying speculation) that came with increasing population, the railroads and economic development in general. Little, often none, of this largesse could be attributed to any effort by the owner. Since social factors brought the increase, society had a right to that increase. Thus the case for a single tax on land that would absorb all the unearned increment. Though a compelling idea, it aroused no enthusiasm from owners of real estate, who were not a negligible political force. And they

5. Especially in his most widely read treatise, *Progress and Poverty*, which, in various editions and reprintings, had a circulation in the millions and which continues still to attract a small but fervent band of believers.

had on their side the concept of property rights going back to the Romans.

Although George responded initially to his own observations in California and the American West, he found support in his later writing and advocacy from the Physiocrats. The long reach of ideas thus extended from Paris in the latter decades of the eighteenth century to San Francisco a hundred years later.

A more general modern echo of the Physiocrats is in the still frequent assertions of the pre-eminence of agriculture as the ultimate source of wealth and well-being: to this day when farmers assemble for the soothing and warming graces of oratory, they hear, as from François Quesnay, that they and their husbandry are the foundation of all economic progress, all national strength, virtue and excellence.

The Physiocrats also addressed, although casually, the problem of price determination; nothing of value being added by manufacturing, prices were held to reflect the costs of production, an idea that was not helpful without a view as to what had determined the costs. And there were Physiocratic references, made almost in passing, to wages as being at the level that accorded the worker the minimum necessary for subsistence. These questions were to be widely discussed and developed in Scotland and England in the years very soon to come.

There was, however, another Physiocratic contribution, long regarded as an idle novelty, that also has major resonance in our own time. Called the Tableau Économique and conceived by François Quesnay, this was a ingenious design that purported to show how products flowed out from the cultivator to the landlords or proprietors and on to the merchant, manufacturing and other sterile classes, and how money, by several routes, flowed back to the cultivator. Thus it was shown how each part of the economy — each of the major industries or interests — served and was compensated by each of the others. The mechanism of purchase and sale was thus revealed as a complete interlocking system.

At the time, the Tableau seemed a wonderful thing — an insight as from the gods. Victor Riquetti Mirabeau (1715–1789) — Mirabeau the elder, an important figure among the Physiocrats — was perhaps the most extravagant in his comment. He thought that Quesnay's invention, along with the inventions of writing and money, was one of the three great achievements of the human mind. Others, beginning with Adam Smith, were more restrained and more often than not disparaging, and yet later the Tableau was merely dismissed. Alexander Gray, for example, says, "[It was] in its time the crowning achievement of Quesnay and the Physiocratic school, now perhaps better reduced to an embarrassed footnote. . . . It may be doubted whether it will ever be anything but a vast mystification."[6]

In the 1930s, a young Harvard economist, Wassily Leontief (1906–   ),[7] attempted to develop comprehensive tables that would show what each industry received from and sold to every other, and therewith the flow of income through the system and its effects, and they were referred to, sometimes with some slight derision, as Leontief's Tableau Économique. Only with marked difficulty could he raise money to pay for the enormous compilation of statistics required, but in 1973, when he was awarded the Nobel Prize for Economic Science for his work, attitudes became more respectful. Called Input-Output or, more elegantly, Interindustry Analysis, it had become the principal foundation stone for the modern popular and also profitable models for predicting and, on frequent occasion, mispredicting the economic prospect and the effect of changes in prices, wages, interest rates, taxes and demand as these are reflected through to individual industries. Again the long reach of François Quesnay, France and Versailles.

The Physiocrats sought to reform the old system and to defend it at the same time. Superior, as they saw it, to the invading world of mercantilism and of nascent industrial capitalism, it needed, as

6. Gray, p. 106.
7. Who will appear in this history again in Chapter XIX.

Turgot, especially, believed, to rid itself of corruption, extravagance, sinecures, extortion and its other privileged excesses. The question arises and indeed has been asked a thousand times: Had these and companion reforms been made, could they have prevented or forestalled the French Revolution? The query is an idle one. The rich and privileged, when also corrupt and incompetent, do not accept rescuing reform. Lack of intelligence is an undoubted bar; so are pride, righteous indignation and wounded dignity. How could anyone be led to believe that the wealthy are other than the most worthy? There is also the matter of time preference and psychological denial. Why diminish the joys, comforts and contentments of the short run by contemplation of the horrors and disasters of the even modestly longer run? The reforms of Quesnay, Turgot and their *confrères* were a slight puff of wind countering a developing hurricane.

There are revolutions and revolutions in this world. Some, like the American Revolution, leave a social and economic structure wholly in place. Others, as in Russia and China, sweep one away. The French Revolution swept away the world that the Physiocrats had sought to defend and save. Left, however, for generations to come were the idea of an economic system as an interconnected and interdependent structure and a diverse and luminous array of concepts — a controlling natural law in economic behavior, the inherent pre-eminence of agriculture, *laissez faire*, the *produit net*, the Tableau Économique. One can endorse for its time Adam Smith's surprisingly generous summary: "This system . . . with all its imperfections, is, perhaps, the nearest approximation to the truth that has yet been published upon the subject of political economy."[8]

8. In a far from uncharacteristic, elegantly sly comment, he went on to say that "its followers are very numerous; and as men are fond of paradoxes, and of appearing to understand what surpasses the comprehension of ordinary people, the paradox which it maintains, concerning the unproductive nature of manufacturing labour, has not perhaps contributed a little to increase the number of its admirers." Smith, Book 4, Chapter 9.

VI

The New World of Adam Smith

THE INDUSTRIAL REVOLUTION, which came to England and southern Scotland in the last third of the eighteenth century, brought into the factories and the factory towns the workers who previously had been producing goods in their cottages or food and wool on their farms. And it brought others who had been producing very little of anything at all. The capital that once had been invested by the merchants in raw materials sent to the villages to be made into cloth or that had served to purchase the work of independent craftsmen was now in process of being invested in vastly greater amount in factories and machinery or in the far from munificent wages that kept alive, often only briefly, the workers. The dominant figure in this change, and thus increasingly in the community and the state, was not the merchant, whose orientation was to the purchase and sale of goods, but the industrialist, whose orientation was to their production.

There has long been solemn debate among historians as to what initiated these developments. Was it the fortuitous episodes in innovation — the appearance of Watt's steam engine to drive the machines and of the machines themselves, primarily those for textile manufacture, of Arkwright, Kay and Hargreaves and of others less fortunate as to fame? (Cloth, let it be said again, was, along with food and shelter, one of the three requisites that combined to make up the standard of living of the vast majority of the people of

57

the time.) Alternatively, was the Industrial Revolution the product of inspired entrepreneurship? Was it an early step in a long process by which inventions, so far from being an independent innovating force, are the predictable achievement of those who, with brilliance and inspiration, perceive the possibility of change?

The argument need not detain us. Whatever the source of the Industrial Revolution, it profoundly shaped the development of economics. Again it is the context that is important. And from it emerged the two most celebrated figures in the history of the subject, Adam Smith and, three quarters of a century later, Karl Marx. One was the prophet of its achievements and the source of its guiding rules; the other was the critic of the power it gave to those who owned what were to be called the means of production and of the poverty and oppression it thus accorded its workers.

There is as regards Smith a problem of timing. His great tract, *An Inquiry into the Nature and Causes of the Wealth of Nations,* was, as I have noted, published in 1776. By then the shops and mines of the industrial age were already evident in the English countryside and the Scottish Lowlands. According to Paul Mantoux (1877–1956), the great French economic historian, "If we confine ourselves to England, it is certain that from the reign of Henry VII onwards a number of rich cloth merchants in the North and West played the same part then, though on a smaller scale, as our great manufacturers play today. . . . Instead of being mere merchants, buying cloth from the weavers and selling it in markets or at fairs, they set up workshops which they supervised themselves. They were manufacturers in the modern sense."[1]

Yet not much of what came to be called the Industrial Revolution was ever seen by Smith — not the really great factories, not the factory towns, not the regiments of workers gathering for and

1. Paul Mantoux, *The Industrial Revolution in the Eighteenth Century,* translated by Marjorie Vernon (New York: Harcourt, Brace, 1940), p. 33. A classic account of the origins and early years of the Industrial Revolution in England, this was first published in Paris in 1905. A new edition (to which I contributed a foreword) was published by the University of Chicago Press in 1983.

departing their toil, not the politically and socially emergent industrialists. By far the greatest part of the development came after his book was written. Smith describes the work of a pin factory, but one that was far from characteristic of the industrial plants of later decades. It was probably the most famous factory in all the history of economic enterprise, and it had for him, as also for almost all who have written of him, a nearly mystical importance. What captured his attention was not the machinery that characterized the Industrial Revolution but the way the job was divided so that each worker became an expert on his minuscule part of the task. "One man draws out the wire, another straights it, a third cuts it, a fourth points it, a fifth grinds it at the top for receiving the head; to make the head requires two or three distinct operations; to put it on, is a peculiar business, to whiten the pins is another; it is even a trade by itself to put them into the paper."[2] From this specialization, the division of labor, came the great efficiency of contemporary enterprise; combined with man's natural "propensity to truck, barter, and exchange one thing for another,"[3] it lay at the basis of all commerce. But it was not the reality of the Industrial Revolution; had Smith seen the smoking factories, the machines, the massed assembly of workers, as these made their appearance by the end of the eighteenth century, it is by them, and not by the manufacture of pins and the division of labor, that he would have been impressed.

However, though Smith did not see or completely foresee the Industrial Revolution in its full capitalist manifestation, he did observe with great clarity the contradictions, the obsolescence and, above all, the socially confining self-interest in the old order. If he was a prophet of the new, he was even more an enemy of the old. Nor can one read *Wealth of Nations* without sensing his joy in afflicting the comfortable, causing distress to those who professed the convenient and traditional ideas and policies of his time. There

2. Adam Smith, *Wealth of Nations*, Book 1, Chapter 1.
3. Smith, Book 1, Chapter 2.

was much in Smith that prescribed sensibly for the new world of which he stood on the edge; his larger contribution was in destroying the old world and thus leading the way for what was to come.

Adam Smith was born in 1723 in the less than luminous town of Kirkcaldy, a small port across the Firth of Forth from Edinburgh, which became famous in modern times for its linoleum factories and their pervasive smell. His father was the collector of customs, the local manifestation of the protectionist policy and mercantilist faith that his son would so relentlessly attack and so effectively destroy. After the local school Adam Smith went on to the University of Glasgow and then to Balliol College, Oxford, an experience that he celebrates in *Wealth of Nations* with a stern rebuke for the public professors, as they then were called, those whose salary was independent of the size of their classes or the enthusiasm of their students. Thus relieved of incentive, these professors, he alleged, put forth little effort, did little work. Much better, he thought, that they be paid, as he himself would be later at Glasgow, in accordance with the number of students they attracted. Smith's views on this matter would not be well received in a modern American university.

From Oxford Smith returned to the University of Glasgow, where he was a professor, first of logic, then of moral philosophy. Here, in 1759, he published *The Theory of the Moral Sentiments*, a work now largely forgotten and largely antecedent to his interest in political economy. In 1763, he resigned from the university to become the tutor of the young Duke of Buccleuch and to accompany him in travel on the Continent. The benefits to the duke of this tour are lost to history; the experience was to be a most important one for Smith. In Switzerland he visited Voltaire in the handsome château that still stands just outside Geneva in what is now Ferney-Voltaire, and in Paris and Versailles he made the acquaintance of Quesnay and Turgot, among others. A striking feature of *Wealth of Nations* is its cosmopolitan tone; Smith's ideas, observations and information come from far beyond the borders of England or Scotland. For this, these years of travel must receive the credit.

Smith began to write *Wealth of Nations* in France, and he continued to work on it for ten years after his return to Britain in 1766. Its success, when finally published, was immediate; the first two-volume edition sold out almost at once.[4] Smith's friend Edward Gibbon wrote in ecstatic approval to Adam Ferguson, "What an excellent work is that with which our common friend Mr. Adam Smith has enriched the public!" adding that it offers "the most profound ideas expressed in the most perspicuous language."[5] Even this acclaim was mild as compared with that of William Pitt, a decade and a half later, who, speaking in the House of Commons, said of the author of *Wealth of Nations* that Smith's "extensive knowledge of detail and depth of philosophical research will, I believe, furnish the best solution of every question connected with the history of commerce and with the system of political economy."[6] As I have had earlier occasion to observe, "Not since, in the nonsocialist world at least, has a politician committed himself so courageously to an economist."[7]

After the publication of *Wealth of Nations*, Smith was made commissioner of customs in Edinburgh, a sinecure in the mercantilist tradition in which his father had served but one that, in the avowed tradition of his race, he was far too practical to refuse. He died in Edinburgh in 1790; his house and burial place are on the

4. The price was £1,16s, the equivalent, given inflation and the changing exchange rate of the pound, of $50 or $60, perhaps more, today. How many copies were printed is unknown.

In 1973, for the 250th anniversary of Adam Smith's birth, economists from Britain and around the world gathered at Kirkcaldy in celebration. For some of the material offered in this chapter, I have drawn on the paper I gave on that occasion, which was later published in my book *Annals of an Abiding Liberal* (Boston: Houghton Mifflin, 1979), pp. 86–102.

5. Quoted in John Rae, *Life of Adam Smith* (London: Macmillan, 1895), p. 287. Rae's biography is the standard and still almost the only work on Smith's life.

6. William Pitt, speech on introducing his budget, February 17, 1792, quoted in Rae, pp. 290–291.

7. *Annals of an Abiding Liberal* (Boston: Houghton Mifflin, 1979), p. 88.

Canongate there and should be visited by all who profess even a fugitive interest in political economy.

Wealth of Nations is a vast, disorderly treatise, rich in amusement and written in admirable prose but, with the Bible and Marx's *Capital*, one of the three books that the questionably literate feel they are allowed to cite without having read. Especially in Smith's case this is a grave loss. As Gibbon said, the writing itself enchants, and its "curious facts," praised thus by David Hume, are still encountered with pleasure or surprise. Perhaps a short digression may be allowed for a sampling.

For Americans, there is his statement that "the late resolution of the Quakers in Pennsylvania to set at liberty all their negro slaves, may satisfy us that their number cannot be very great."[8] And, in anticipation of Thorstein Veblen, there is his observation that "with the greater part of rich people, the chief enjoyment of riches consists in the parade of riches."[9] And on stockholders and their function or nonfunction no one in the next two centuries was to be more exact: "[They] seldom pretend to understand any thing of the business of the company; and when the spirit of faction happens not to prevail among them, give themselves no trouble about it, but receive contentedly such half yearly or yearly dividend, as the directors think proper to make to them."[10]

Smith's most useful comment, which should always be in mind when national alarm substitutes for thought, is not in *Wealth of Nations*; it was said in response to hearing from Sir John Sinclair that General Burgoyne had surrendered at Saratoga in October 1777. Sinclair expressed the fear that the British nation was ruined, to which Smith replied, "There is a great deal of ruin in a nation."[11]

One learns also from Smith that the expenses of the civil govern-

8. Smith, Book 3, Chapter 2.
9. Smith, Book 1, Chapter 11, Part 2.
10. Smith, Book 5, Chapter 1, Part 3, Article 1.
11. Quoted in Rae, p. 343.

ment of the Massachusetts Bay Colony "before the commencement of the present disturbances,"[12] meaning the Revolution, were about £18,000 a year and that this was a rather sizable sum compared with the expenses of New York and Pennsylvania at £4500 each and of New Jersey at £1200.[13] Also, that after a bad storm, or "inundation," the citizens of the Swiss canton of Underwald (Unterwalden) came together in an assembly, where each publicly confessed his wealth to the multitude and was then assessed, *pro rata*, for the repair of the damage, an early example of a capital levy.[14] And, finally, that by Smith's exceptionally precise calculation, Isocrates earned £3333,6s,8d (well upward of 100,000 of today's dollars) for "what we would call one course of lectures, a number which will not appear extraordinary from so great a city to so famous a teacher, who taught too what was at that time the most fashionable of all sciences, rhetoric."[15] He tells that Plutarch was paid the same. The diversity of Smith's concerns has perhaps been established.

There is much in Adam Smith to seduce the reader away from the hard core of his contribution to the history of economics, and many, over the years, have been so seduced. There are, however, three essentials, matters identified in Chapter I, on which attention must be fixed. The first is a view of the broad forces that motivate economic life and effort — in common reference, the nature of the economic system. The second is how prices are determined and the resulting income distributed in wages, profit and rent. Finally, there are the policies by which the state supports and furthers economic progress and prosperity. Nothing in *Wealth of Nations*, it

12. Smith, Book 4, Chapter 7, Part 2.

13. These and numerous other details on the colonies reflect an interest that John Rae believes was very possibly stimulated by Benjamin Franklin, of whom Smith was an acquaintance, perhaps a friend, in London.

14. Smith, Book 5, Chapter 2, Part 2, Article 2.

15. Smith, Book 1, Chapter 10, Part 2.

must again be emphasized, is as systematic as the foregoing suggests; its author's forgiveness must be asked for suggesting an order that he would have found surprising.

Economic motivation for Smith centers on the role of self-interest. Its private and competitive pursuit is the source of the greatest public good. "It is not," in Smith's most famous passage, "from the benevolence of the butcher, the brewer, or the baker, that we expect our dinner, but from their regard to their own interest. We address ourselves, not to their humanity but to their self-love."[16] He later adds that the individual "is in this, as in many other cases, led by an invisible hand to promote an end which was no part of his intention. . . . I have never known much good done by those who affected to trade for the public good. It is an affectation, indeed, not very common among merchants, and very few words need be employed in dissuading them from it."[17]

The reference to the invisible hand has for many a mystic overtone: here is a spiritual force that supports the pursuit of self-interest and guides men in the market to the most benign of ends. So to believe does Smith a grave disservice; the invisible hand, the most famous metaphor in economics, was just that, a metaphor. A man of the Enlightenment, Smith did not resort to supernatural support for his argument. Later chapters will tell how, in our own time, the market has, indeed, acquired a theological beneficence; Smith would not have approved.

Yet, as a purely secular matter, it was a huge step that Smith here took. The person concerned with self-enrichment had hitherto been an object of doubt, suspicion and mistrust, feelings that went back through the Middle Ages to biblical times and the Holy Scripture itself. Now, because of his self-interest, he had become a public benefactor. A major rescue and transformation indeed! Nothing in all history has so served personal inclination. And so it continues in our own time. As the voice of Physiocracy still rings

16. Smith, Book 1, Chapter 2.
17. Smith, Book 4, Chapter 2.

forth when farmers come together, so the beneficent self-regard of the butcher, brewer or baker and the benign guidance of the invisible hand live again when members of the United States Chamber of Commerce, the Business Roundtable or, as this is written, the Cabinet of President Ronald Reagan gather for mutual reinforcement, rhetorical and oratorical rejuvenation and the consideration of public policy and action.

Value and distribution — prices and who gets the proceeds — were the second of the basic issues of economics that Smith addressed, issues that survive as microeconomics in the textbooks to this day. In identifying them, Smith reflected his aptitude for the time. As workers were assembled in the factories, what determined their pay became highly relevant. As the capitalist assumed control of production, the question arose of his reward, how it was determined and justified. When the tenant farmer replaced the sharecropper or serf, rent became a matter of importance. And prices came to be seen as having an obvious relationship to all these constituents. Adam Smith gave economics its modern structure. But that structure was given to him, in turn, by the earliest stages of the Industrial Revolution.

Though he identified the questions of price and the distribution of proceeds as central to economic understanding, it must also be said that Smith's answers were not durably satisfying. As to prices he was puzzled by the interesting and disturbing circumstance, earlier mentioned, that many of the best or most nearly essential things in life are free or virtually so. Water, even if of indifferent quality in his day, came very cheap or free; diamonds, "the greatest of all superfluities," were then, as now, exceedingly dear. From this came the troubling difference between value in use and value in exchange. As in the case of drinking water, the value in use could be very high, the value in exchange very low. Precious stones were low in use, high in exchange value. The riddle of value in use and exchange would not be solved for another century or more, until, in one of the lesser triumphs of economic theory, the concept of marginal utility was discovered.[18] This would hold that it was the least urgent or marginal need or use that is determining. The utility of water at the margin is diminished, *pro tanto*, by its abundance; that of the diamond is kept high by its scarcity. In a desert with no water, there comes a time when the heaviest and most glittering jewel would be exchanged for a good drink; scarcity does wonders even for the marginal utility of water.

Smith resolved the problem in his time by simply setting value in use aside and asserting a value in exchange that is a version of what was long to be known as the Labor Theory of Value. The worth of any possession is measured ultimately by the amount of labor for which it can be exchanged. "The value of any commodity . . . to the person who possesses it . . . is equal to the quantity of labour which it enables him to purchase or command. Labour, therefore, is the real measure of the exchangeable value of all commodities."[19]

This, however, is not all; in yet other Smithian passages value in exchange comes, seemingly, to depend on all the costs of producing the goods, a solution that requires, as ever, that there be a good explanation of what determines the costs; otherwise the problem of what determines the price is simply transferred from one set of unknowns to another.

The ambiguity in which Smith finally left the question of what determines price has been endlessly debated by scholars. It is an entertainment that need not trouble us. The simple fact is that Smith himself did not decide.

Coming to what determines the shares in income from the sale of the product that should go to the workers, the landlords and the employer-capitalists, Smith again identified the question to be asked and again was ambiguous as to the answer. Wages he regarded

18. Hubert Phillips once explained Smith's dilemma in verse: "The wily bird / Had never heard / Of marginal utility." Quoted in Alexander Gray, *The Development of Economic Doctrine* (London: Longmans, Green, 1948), p. 128.
    There will be more about the concept in Chapter IX.
19. Smith, Book 1, Chapter 5.

generally as the cost of bringing the worker into being as a worker and sustaining him in his job. This, the subsistence theory of wages, would later be converted by David Ricardo into the Iron Law of Wages, which was held to keep the laboring classes to the minimum wage necessary for their survival.

The return to capital and the capitalist — interest and profits were not clearly distinguished — Smith extracted only with some difficulty from a labor theory of value. The quantity of labor and the resulting cost of sustaining it determines price. The return to capital, in consequence, must be an exaction by the capitalist from the rightful claim of the worker whose toil establishes the price and to whom the return from the sale of the product is presumably due. Or it is the appropriation of a surplus value that the worker creates over and above what he is paid and to which, again, he has a seemingly rightful claim. And here Smith left the matter — insofar as his position is clear. This innocently subversive view would also be developed and refined in the next century by Ricardo. And it would become a major source of the revolutionary indignation and agitation of Karl Marx.

Finally, rent. The attention accorded to rent in the writings of Smith, and also later in those of Ricardo and others, has a slightly archaic aspect now. Why so much attention to this particular item of cost and income? We need to be reminded of how significant rent was in a time when agriculture was of central economic importance and the payment by tenants for the use of the land one of the great (and oppressive) transfers of income.

On rent Smith, again, has different and conflicting explanations. After first making it a determinant of price, along with wages and profit, he then makes it a residual from the return from prices after wages and profits are paid. "Rent . . . enters into the composition of the price of commodities in a different way from wages and profit. High or low wages and profit are the causes of high or low price; high or low rent is the effect of it."[20] He then goes on to associate

20. Smith, Book 1, Chapter 11. For a more detailed and most competent discussion

the level of this residual with the quality of the land. "The rent increases in proportion to the goodness of the pasture."[21]

A Physiocratic overtone also enters here; in agriculture, Smith holds, nature labors alongside man, adding something of her own — again a *produit net* — to his efforts. There is an especially troubling contradiction between Smith's view of prices, which are presumed to reflect the cost of the labor incorporated in the product, and his view of the role of land, which "in almost any situation, produces a greater quantity of food than what is sufficient to maintain all the labour necessary for bringing it to market."[22] The solution of this matter is again to leave Smith to those who find scholarly sustenance in his contradictions.

Third and finally, there is Smith on what would now be called public policy — on what stimulates economic growth. Not all of his views on this are original; he is in the debt of such notable predecessors in the attack on mercantile thought as the highly intelligent Sir William Petty (1623–1687). He also draws on the essays of his great Edinburgh friend David Hume (1711–1776). But many of his views are the product of his own observation, his common sense and his already noted pleasure in undoing established belief.

His strongest recommendation as to public policy urges the freedom of internal and international trade. Much, quite possibly too much, of his reasoning derives from his fascination with the division of labor — with the pin factory. Only if there is freedom for barter and trade can some workers specialize on pins, others devote themselves to other requisites and all come together for the exchange that satisfies the individual's several needs. If freedom of trade does not exist, each worker must concentrate incompetently on making his own pins; the economies from specialization are gone. From

---

of Smith on rent, see Eric Roll, *A History of Economic Thought* (New York: Prentice-Hall, 1942), p. 173 *et seq.*

21. Smith, Book 1, Chapter 11, Part 1.
22. *Ibid.*

this Smith concludes that the wider the trading area, the greater the opportunity for specialization — for the division of labor — and the greater, *pari passu*, the efficiency or, as would now be said, the productivity of labor. The division of labor is limited, in another of Smith's famous conclusions, by the size of the market. Thus the case for the widest possible area of free trade, with, in consequence, the greatest possible efficiency of labor.

That the application of power and machinery to production, even in Smith's day, might have been a far greater source of efficiency than the specialized application of workers to a task is more than probable. And it has certainly been the case since. To this day, nonetheless, Smith's division of labor remains a totemic source of efficiency, a cliché in all discussion of international trade policy.

Smith's case for free trade extends to a direct assault on the mercantilist view of gold and silver as the foundation of national wealth and to the belief that trade restrictions can enhance the stock of precious metals. In the very opening words of *Wealth of Nations*, Smith proclaims that it is not its silver or gold that measures a nation's wealth. It is "the annual labour of every nation [that] is the fund which originally supplies it with all the necessaries and conveniences of life."[23] Wealth is enhanced by "the skill, dexterity, and judgment with which its [the nation's] labour is generally applied; and, secondly, by the proportion between the number of those who are employed in useful labour, and that of those who are not so employed."[24]

These, then, are the matters that public policy must address; if they are addressed successfully, prices will be low, supplies of marketable products abundant. Gold and silver will come in from abroad to purchase the products, and the supply of precious metals will take care of itself. Other countries cannot prevent their people from so sending their gold and silver. In what would be a recurring discovery as regards exchange control, he observes, "All the sanguinary laws of Spain and Portugal are not able to keep their gold and

23. Smith, Introduction.
24. *Ibid.*

silver at home."[25] And in a characteristic Smithian thought, he reminds those motivated by a fear that money may become scarce that no complaint "is more common than that of a scarcity of money. Money, like wine, must always be scarce with those who have neither wherewithal to buy it, nor credit to borrow it."[26] In a companion gesture to the Quantity Theory of Money, he observes, "It is not by the importation of gold and silver, that the discovery of America has enriched Europe. By the abundance of the American mines, those metals have become cheaper."[27]

Smith is not, however, rigidly dogmatic on the matter of free trade; he would allow tariffs for industries essential for defense and possibly in retaliation for tariff abuse abroad, and he would be gradual in withdrawing support to protected enterprises and their workers. But not much else. "It is the maxim of every prudent master of a family, never to attempt to make at home what it will cost him more to make than to buy. . . . What is prudence in the conduct of every private family, can scarce be folly in that of a great kingdom."[28]

As Smith was averse to restraints on international trade, so also he was opposed to those on domestic commerce and with colonies. In an age when restrictive preferences, privileges and state grants of monopoly were commonplace, he opposed them all. He also opposed private combinations of producers and workers, although, in a characteristic aside, he noted that there were more laws against combinations by the sellers of labor than against the similar practice by the merchants and manufacturers who employed them. He was not, however, entirely optimistic as to the possibility of contending with private combination. The impulse to such associa-

25. Smith, Book 4, Chapter 1.
26. *Ibid.*
27. *Ibid.*
28. Smith, Book 4, Chapter 2. Again the modern scholar can detect the fallacy of composition. Wise state policy in all its diverse needs and complexity does not necessarily accord with the rules that govern even the wisest and most prudent family.

tion was strong. In another deathless passage he observes that "people of the same trade seldom meet together, even for merriment and diversion, but the conversation ends in a conspiracy against the public, or in some contrivance to raise prices. It is impossible . . ." he went on to say, "to prevent such meetings, by any law which either could be executed, or would be consistent with liberty and justice. But though the law cannot hinder people of the same trade from sometimes assembling together, it ought to do nothing to facilitate such assemblies; much less to render them necessary."[29]

A century later, what Smith thought impossible would, after a fashion, be attempted in the United States, and the effort would continue for another hundred years. The Sherman Act and later legislation would forbid those of the same trade, even when gathered for merriment and diversion, from discussing, much less agreeing upon, prices. The prohibition would encounter not a few of the difficulties that Smith foresaw.

From Smith has come the commitment to competition as a principle in all capitalist societies — competition that is presumed to ensure optimal industrial performance. Considerably less influential has been Smith's warning as to the institution that, along with the state itself, might destroy competition. This was the state-chartered company — in modern terms, the corporation. Where it had monopoly privileges, as in the colonial era, he was especially critical. But he also thought little of its efficiency. Returning today, he would be appalled at a world where, as in the United States, a thousand corporations dominate the industrial, commercial and financial landscape and are controlled by their hired management, something Smith thought especially to be deplored: "Being the managers rather of other people's money than of their own, it cannot well be expected, that they should watch over it with the same anxious vigilance with which the partners in a private copartnery

29. Smith, Book 1, Chapter 10, Part 2.

frequently watch over their own. . . . Negligence and profusion, therefore, must always prevail, more or less, in the management of the affairs of such a company."[30]

There is more on which Smith instructs or for which he pleads. As befits the reputation of his ethnic forebears, he urges parsimony in personal expenditure and extends that advice strongly to the state. He rigorously confines the activities of the state to provision for the common defense, the administration of justice and the provision of necessary public works. His justly famous canons of taxation charge that taxes should be certain, convenient and economical to assess and raise. He endorses, at a minimum, a proportionate income tax: "The subjects of every state ought to contribute towards the support of the government, as nearly as possible, in proportion to their respective abilities; that is, in proportion to the revenue which they respectively enjoy under the protection of the state."[31]

But not everything in Smith can be told here. To try to do so would be to replicate his great book itself and to blur, as does his own love of detail, the central and even vital core of his thought. It is that core which these pages seek to identify.

---

30. Smith, Book 5, Chapter 1, Part 3, Article 1.
31. Smith, Book 5, Chapter 2, Part 2.

VII

Refinement, Affirmation — and the Seeds of Revolt

WITH ADAM SMITH the history of economics took its longest step. As Eric Roll has said of him, "The apostle of economic liberalism spoke in lucid and persuasive terms." He addressed "an audience that was ready to receive his message . . . [and with] the voice of the industrialists who were anxious to sweep away all restrictions on the market and on the supply of labor — the remnants of the out-of-date regime of merchant capital and the landed interest."[1] For the next one hundred years and more, economists in the established tradition would amend and sharpen his conclusions, struggle to resolve his ambiguities and seek otherwise to complete his system.

The obligation that is imposed on the functional historian, the writer concerned not alone with history but with modern relevance, becomes especially complex when he considers economics after Adam Smith. Now to a greater degree than before there is the problem, hitherto noticed, of selecting from a vast mass of material the ideas that are of central and continuing importance. Much in the writing that followed Smith was of purely transitory interest. Ideas were offered, theories proposed, points made in the continuing and sometimes bitter controversies of the time, that did not sur-

1. Eric Roll, *A History of Economic Thought* (New York: Prentice-Hall, 1942), p. 156.

73

vive. There were also eloquent exponents of the established tradition — John Stuart Mill, for example — who were the great teachers of the day but who did not substantially alter the broad current of economic thought. Much of this, the controversies especially, must be passed over; if not, the essential is lost in the mass. Again the test must be not that everything is covered — too many have tried that — but that nothing of continuing importance is omitted.

In the years following Smith's death, three great figures, all very nearly exact contemporaries, one French and two British, emerged to refine and extend his work — Jean Baptiste Say (1767–1832), Thomas Robert Malthus (1766–1834) and David Ricardo (1772–1823). All, but especially Malthus and Ricardo, saw the Industrial Revolution in full flower, and, improving on Smith, they sought to bring economics abreast of this enormous change. With them came the economics of the industrial order.

Jean Baptiste Say was a businessman who, early in life, was concerned in a pioneering way with life insurance. He went on to be a professor, ending his career at the Collège de France. Because he was a Frenchman and not in the then (and henceforth) dominant English-speaking tradition — the tradition that long reflected and spoke for the industrial pre-eminence of Britain — he has received less attention from historians than have Malthus and Ricardo. By some he has been dismissed as the man who, without much contribution of his own, was simply a messenger conveying Adam Smith to the needful French.

In reality, he did much more. It was only part of his task to reduce the disorderly collection of ideas and information in *Wealth of Nations* to the more orderly form of French thought. But he was not in doubt as to the need: in an exceptionally tactful combination of criticism and praise, he said, "The work of Smith is only a confused assemblage of the soundest principles of Political Economy, supported by luminous examples and by the most curious notions of statistics, mingled with instructive reflections."[2] His own major work, *Traité d'Économie Politique,* is a much more concise affair, and both in French and translation it had a wide circulation. The lesser esteem in which it was held as compared with works by other writers of the time has been attributed to its greater readability and popularity. This is ever a danger.

His business background led Say to celebrate the distinctive, even decisive, role of the entrepreneur, the man who conceives or takes charge of an enterprise, sees and exploits opportunity and is the motive force for economic change and improvement. In this his ideas anticipated, among others, those of Joseph Alois Schumpeter of modern times. But Say's major, and for a full 130 years his lasting and exceedingly influential, contribution was his law of markets. To this day reference survives in the textbooks to Say's Law.[3]

Say's Law held that out of the production of goods came an effective (that is to say, actually expended) aggregate of demand sufficient to purchase the total supply of goods. No more, no less. There could, in consequence, be no such thing as general overproduction in the economic system. Put in somewhat more modern terms, from the price of every product sold comes a return in wages, interest, profit or rent sufficient to buy that product. Somebody, somewhere, gets it all. And once it is gotten, there is spending up to the value of what is produced. There can never, accordingly, be a shortage of demand, the obvious counterpart of overproduction. It is, indeed, possible that some people will save from the proceeds of the sale. But having so saved, they will invest so that spending is still assured. Even if they hoard the receipts, this does not change the situation; prices adjust themselves downward to accommodate to the lesser flow of income. There can still be no general excess of goods, no general shortage of purchasing power.

2. Jean Baptiste Say, *Traité d'Économie Politique,* cited in Alexander Gray, *The Development of Economic Doctrine* (London: Longmans, Green, 1948), p. 267.

3. See, for example, Paul A. Samuelson and William D. Nordhaus, *Economics,* 12th edition (New York: McGraw-Hill, 1985), pp. 366–367.

Not everyone accepted Say's Law. Thomas Robert Malthus, as we shall soon see, was, for good reason, doubtful. And in the decades to come there were recurrent and increasingly painful periods of crises and depression, in which goods went unsold and labor, in consequence, went without employment. Surely, it seemed, there was somehow, in some part of the economy, a causative shortage of purchasing power. Economists countered this thought with the concept of a wavelike business cycle that caused temporary dislocation but did not alter the fundamental condition. And so Say's Law survived.

Not only did it survive, but acceptance of it became the index of a decent sophistication in economics. It was the ultimate test by which reputable scholars were distinguished from frauds and crackpots, those of vulnerable mind who could not or would not see how obviously production created its own demand. It was also the indispensable and stalwart defense against those who, by the monetarization and spending of silver, the printing and spending of paper money and government borrowing and spending, would seek to enhance purchasing power in order to overcome a falsely perceived shortage of demand. They prescribed for what could not exist.

Say's Law survived in triumph until the Great Depression. Then it was repealed by John Maynard Keynes, who held and influentially argued that there *could* be (and that there then was) a shortage of demand. There could be a preference for holding and hoarding money — a liquidity preference; prices might not then adjust to the reduced flow of demand; goods generally would go unsold; those who made them would be unemployed. Corrective action could and should be taken by the government through borrowing and spending to supplement the flow of demand. It was the end of the extraordinary reign of Jean Baptiste Say.

It was also the end of a major restraint on economic instruction and scholarly thought and imagination, one that had affected all who studied economics. As long as a sufficient demand for goods was thought to be assured, economic performance was, in a real

sense, optimal; no action by the state or a central bank was needed
to increase or diminish it. With the end of the rule of Say's Law,
the question of the management of aggregate demand — what governments should do directly or through central banks to increase
or diminish income and purchasing power — became an obvious
concern. Value and distribution, prices, wages and the rest suffered
a major diminution in their claim on the economic mind, a diminution symbolized by the modern designation of their study as
microeconomics. The management of demand became the new area
of larger attention and prestige, with the grander title of *macroeconomics*. Macroeconomics was born out of the release from the
long rule of Jean Baptiste Say.

Thomas Robert Malthus, a British clergyman of aristocratic instinct,
was the first of what were to be three important figures in the history of economics to find personal financial support not from university or tutorial instruction, as did Smith, or from business, as
did Say and Ricardo, but from the benevolent employment of the
British East India Company. The others were James and John Stuart
Mill; all served the John Company, as by then it was known, without ever going to India, Malthus as an instructor at Haileybury
College in Hertfordshire, the staff college that trained young men
for service in the company.

Malthus's two books, *An Essay on the Principle of Population*
and *Principles of Political Economy*, cover a wide range of matters,
but to the history of the subject he contributed only two propositions, one of which, rivaling that of Say, has lasted in powerful
form to our own time. The other, lost for a century, was revived by
Keynes, bringing considerable but sadly delayed credit to its original author.

Malthus's supreme contribution — it brought the word *Malthusian* into all modern languages — was the law he saw governing
the growth of population, with further effect on how wages are
determined. To this end, he tapped a most impressive range of
sources, extending from the Greeks and "the wretched inhabitants

77

of Tierra del Fuego [who] have been placed, by the general consent of voyagers, at the bottom of the scale of human beings"[4] to the better-positioned inhabitants of England. Few writers have ever got more information in a single sentence, or in this case three:

> The details of the population of Ireland are but little known. I shall only observe therefore, that the extended use of potatoes has allowed of a very rapid increase of it during the last century. But the cheapness of this nourishing root, and the small piece of ground which, under this kind of cultivation, will in average years produce the food for a family, joined to the ignorance and depressed state of the people, which have prompted them to follow their inclinations with no other prospect than an immediate bare subsistence, have encouraged marriage to such a degree, that the population is pushed much beyond the industry and present resources of the country.[5]

From his observations and some more abstract speculation came Malthus's basic conclusions. First, and rather obviously, population is limited by the means of subsistence; second, population increases when the means of subsistence allows, and does so geometrically, while the best hope for increase in the food supply is arithmetic; third, this asymmetry will persist, with the result that the population will be held in check by the food supply unless prior checks on its increase are operative.

The possible prior checks are moral restraint, vice and misery. Not much can be expected of moral restraint, and virtually nothing after marriage. Vice, the role of which is somewhat uncertain, does not recommend itself to Malthus as a form of birth control. There remain only hunger and starvation, except as these may be forestalled by destructive checks in the form of war, plague or other disease. Malthus did not present a pleasant prospect for mankind.

Nor can it be improved. Were the state or some benevolent and

4. Thomas Robert Malthus, *An Essay on the Principle of Population*, 6th edition (London: Ward, Lock, 1890), p. 15. Malthus supports this rather comprehensive conclusion by reference to Captain Cook's reports on his first voyage.

5. Malthus, p. 259. This, it should be noted, was written some decades before the great famine.

omnipotent benefactor to try to better the position of the masses, their uninhibited procreation would quickly return them to their former condition. Malthus thus provided a powerful case against public or private charity and a greatly serviceable support to those who found it publicly convenient or personally economical to forgo help to the unfortunate. He was not, one judges, an unkindly man, and his mind did turn to ameliorative steps within the controlling authority of his law. He thought that there might be some part of a solution in marriages at a later age. And he wanted the marriage service to include a warning that the young couple would themselves bear the cost and suffer the consequences of their passion.[6] But among the many who sought to put the poverty of the poor on the shoulders of the poor — or remove it from those of the more affluent — none did so more completely than Malthus.

Malthus lives as the prophet of what came to be called the population explosion; by the even less gifted in metaphor, the population bomb. And, indeed, he speaks a grim truth to the poorer agricultural countries of Asia and Africa today, although the rich industrial world, aided by contraceptives and aborted pregnancies, has escaped his grasp.

Malthus's other claim on modern fame was, as noted, his doubt about Say's Law. As just observed, from the proceeds of the sale of goods workers, capitalists and landlords were, according to Say, held to have the wherewithal to buy, *pari passu*, all that they could produce by their combined efforts, and this, inevitably, they would do. Moving on in later years from population to political economy,[7] Malthus held that, in fact, this would not be so. Given the poverty of the workers — they having reduced themselves to the lowest levels of wage or other income by their fecundity — there would be a tendency for more goods to be produced than could be

---

6. As it turned out, not perhaps history's most unpromising form of birth control. In the 1980s, during his first term in office, President Ronald Reagan expressed the thought that population restraint could be left to the market. The practical manifestation of that belief, someone suggested, would be that ardent couples, instead of going to bed, would betake themselves to the nearest shopping mall.

7. In *Principles of Political Economy* (London: John Murray, 1820).

bought and consumed by either these unfortunates or the other, more affluent classes. And this especially would be so as the capitalists or industrialists concentrated their attention in a single-minded way on their business, forgoing, at least to some extent, the pleasures of the consumption they could afford. In consequence, there could be an overproduction of goods. This Malthus saw as being partly ameliorated by the existence of a nonproductive class of consumers — servants, statesmen, soldiers, judges, lawyers, physicians, surgeons and clergymen. These latter, he held, toil not to produce anything useful, but they do consume.

That lawyers, physicians or servants might be useful people for whose services others would gladly pay was a thought that did not appeal to Malthus. But while his distinction between productive and nonproductive occupations has no standing in modern economics, the instinct that there is something peculiarly productive about the creation of visible material goods does survive. The manufacture of boots and shoes and electronic gadgetry continues to be thought more useful, more economically beneficial, than the services of the singer, artist or scholar. When states, cities or chambers of commerce contemplate economic development, it is still of factories making goods of which they think.

In this matter Malthus survives and, more important, in the larger idea that all income might not be spent, that demand for goods might be inadequate, that there could, in consequence, be general overproduction, economic stagnation and despair. "For the first time, in English economic theory at any rate, the possibility of crises arising from causes inherent in the capitalist system was admitted."[8] It was admitted but, alas, not for many generations accepted.

As Malthus wrote on these matters, so, in very nearly the same years, did David Ricardo. And Ricardo rescued Say's Law from Malthus's attack; the flow of income from the production of goods did indeed, he held, create its own sufficient demand. For the next century and slightly more, Ricardo, following the precepts of Say,

8. Roll, p. 224.

was triumphant. As Maynard Keynes said in one of his more resounding observations, Ricardo captured Britain on this issue as the Holy Inquisition captured Spain.

There was a final, if unintentional, Malthusian legacy, one for which he was responsible along with Ricardo. Economics would hereafter be associated with an atmosphere of unrelieved pessimism and gloom, and economists would be given the name and reputation (by way of Carlyle) that survives to this day, that of the "Respectable Professors of the Dismal Science."[9]

David Ricardo is the most puzzling and, in some respects, the most controversial figure in the history of his discipline — puzzling because the nature and depth of his influence on the subject are far from clear; controversial because that influence rendered wonderful service to, as many saw it, the wrong people, specifically to Marx and the Marxists. The mood and style of his writing may, in part, explain the puzzlement. Unlike Smith's prose, which had a certain festive exuberance and clarity, that of Ricardo is grim and difficult. From the demanding exercise in understanding that it imposes, the reader can emerge with some freedom as to what he chooses to believe.

As compared with Smith — or Malthus — Ricardo offered an influential change of method. Smith was empirical and conductive; he proceeded from his own diverse and bountiful observations to his conclusions. Ricardo was theoretical and inductive; proceeding from some evident or seemingly evident proposition, he went on by abstract reasoning to the plausible or, perhaps, inevitable conclusion. It was a method that, in the future, would greatly appeal to economists, for it is economical of information and can, as necessary, be divorced from harsh or inconvenient reality. It served Ricardo well. His method and his conclusions would lead the later defenders of capitalism, its later and most passionate opponents and, above all, Marx to equally firm conclusions.

9. Thomas Carlyle, *Latter-Day Pamphlets*, No. 1 (London: Chapman and Hall, 1899), p. 44.

David Ricardo was the son of a stockbroker of earlier Dutch residence and the Jewish faith. He became a Christian when he married and was detached forthwith from his family. Continuing in the stock market on his own, he amassed a sufficient fortune in around five years to enable him to acquire and retire to Gatcombe Park, a landed estate that was purchased in the 1970s by Queen Elizabeth II to be the country seat of Princess Anne and her husband. At Gatcombe he read and, one can only suppose, wrote with nearly insufferable pain on economics. He was a close friend of Malthus's, and they corresponded at length in wide-ranging and admiring disagreement.[10] He also entered Parliament, where he spoke and did diligent committee service on economic, including monetary, matters. Much of his best work was on issues of contemporary interest and importance in the aftermath of the Napoleonic Wars and is not part of the present account. His most enduring and significant ideas, all in descent from or in intended correction of Smith,[11] can, if at some risk, be made reasonably clear and stated at no undue length.

Ricardo follows Adam Smith in identifying the main concerns of economics but with a certain vehemence in his denunciation of error. Of the factors determining the value or price of a product, he believes that the first must be usefulness, utility. "If a commodity were in no way useful — in other words, if it could in no way contribute to our gratification — it would be destitute of exchangeable

10. As my colleague Robert Dorfman has reminded me on reading these pages.

11. Whom Ricardo warmly acknowledges. "The writer, in combating received opinions, has found it necessary to advert more particularly to those passages in the writings of Adam Smith from which he sees reason to differ; but he hopes it will not, on that account, be suspected that he does not . . . participate in the admiration which the profound work of this celebrated author so justly excites." Ricardo then adds that the "same remark may be applied to the excellent works of M. Say," of whom he says, "All other continental writers taken together" have not done as much to "recommend the principles of that enlightened and beneficial system" originally enunciated by Smith. *On the Principles of Political Economy and Taxation* in *The Works and Correspondence of David Ricardo*, edited by Piero Sraffa (Cambridge, England: Cambridge University Press, 1951), Vol. 1, p. 6. The books, pamphlets and letters of Ricardo were assembled and edited by Sraffa over a period of many years in one of the most distinguished exercises in modern economic research and scholarship. Sraffa was my friend from the years before World War II at the University of Cambridge, and I owe much of my appreciation of Ricardo to him.

value."[12] Here, although there were precedents, emerges in early form the other side of the modern view of price making, the interaction of supply *and* demand.

Having established the need for "exchangeable" products, he then sees their value as coming either from scarcity or "from the quantity of labour required to obtain them." This applies to anything reproducible — anything other than "rare statues and pictures, scarce books and coins, wines of a peculiar quality, which can be made only from grapes grown on a particular soil."[13] Nonreproducible commodities and artifacts are very much a special case; reproducible commodities, governed in exchange value by the labor embodied therein, are the general case. And here he quotes Smith in support of his theory: "It is natural that what is usually the produce of two days', or two hours' labour, should be worth double of what is usually the produce of one day's, or one hour's labour."[14]

As others have noted, Ricardo managed in his later writing to soften positions that were originally very hard, and this has greatly helped many who have sought to find in him what they wished to believe. It is nonetheless his commitment to a wholly firm labor theory of value that is central to the influence he exercised in the years to come.

Responding partly, it seems certain, to his position as a country gentleman, Ricardo next addressed the return to landlords of rent, which he defined in another of the immutable passages of economics as "that portion of the produce of the earth, which is paid to the landlord for the use of the original and indestructible powers of the soil."[15] This return he saw in the controlling context of the Malthusian pressure of population on the means of subsistence; its

12. Ricardo, p. 11.

13. Both quotes are from Ricardo, p. 12.

14. Adam Smith, *Wealth of Nations*, cited in Ricardo, p. 13. Ricardo then adds: "That this is really the foundation of the exchangeable value of all things, excepting those which cannot be increased by human industry, is a doctrine of the utmost importance in political economy; for from no source do so many errors, and so much difference of opinion in that science proceed, as from the vague ideas which are attached to the word value." *Ibid.*

15. Ricardo, p. 67.

effect was to press cultivation to ever poorer land. Such pressure would continue until the increasingly desolate soil returned only the minimum necessary for the lives of those who worked it, and that minimum would then determine in a general way the wages of all workers, certainly of all who worked the land.

From possession of the better land — that back from the margin — would come a surplus over cost. This would be greater in accordance as the land was better and as the general pressure of population on the supply of all land might increase. The owner of good land was thus the beneficiary not only of his own good fortune but also of the increasing misery or poor fortune of all others. It was a very good thing in the Ricardian system to be a landlord, and Ricardo was not troubled by the thought of unearned income or social impropriety. Rent did not force up prices; it was a residual accruing passively from the increase in population and the general progress of the society. "The rise of rent is always *the effect* of the increasing wealth of the country, and of the difficulty of providing food for its augmented population."[16]

Returning to wages, Ricardo, in another of his greatly quoted passages, says that they are "that price which is necessary to enable the labourers, one with another, to subsist and to perpetuate their race, without either increase or diminution."[17] This thought, as the Iron Law of Wages, was to enter into a history extending far beyond formal economics; it established that those who worked were meant to be poor and were not to be rescued from their poverty by a compassionate state or employer or through trade unions or by other action of their own. Later authors and orators made the Iron Law more binding and restrictive than it was in Ricardo's more cautious language. The Iron Law was the natural, or, as would now be said, the equilibrium price of labor — the level to which, all else equal, wages tended to settle. But it included for Ricardo not only the worker's necessities but also "conveniences become essential

16. Ricardo, p. 77. Italics added.
17. Ricardo, p. 93.

to him from habit."[18] Taken together, these are what would now be called a conventional or accustomed standard of living. And the market price of labor in an "improving" — for example, an increasingly capital-rich and technologically advancing — society could be above the market rate for an extended time, "for no sooner may the impulse, which an increased capital gives to a new demand for labour be obeyed, than another increase of capital may produce the same effect."[19] The consequence of this could be strongly ameliorative, for "it is when the market price of labour exceeds its natural price, that the condition of the labourer is flourishing and happy, that he has it in his power to command a greater proportion of the necessaries and enjoyments of life, and therefore to rear a healthy and numerous family."[20]

Though all this was encouraging, there would, alas, also come the deeper tendency: "When, however, by the encouragement which high wages give to the increase of population, the number of labourers is increased, wages again fall to their natural price, and indeed from a re-action sometimes fall below it."[21]

It remains, however, that anyone seeking to protect Ricardo's reputation from the rigor of his conclusions — from the binding rule of the Iron Law — can find support in a certain redeeming instinct. An infusion of capital and technology and the consequent upward effect on the market price of labor could, he believed, continue indefinitely. And this, indeed, has been the wholly plausible course of events. Nonetheless, it was for his controlling law, not the qualifications, that Ricardo was to be remembered and known. And from this controlling law would come his commitment to the inevitable misery of those who live under capitalism and to the futility and error of any corrective action, which he did not hesitate specifically to condemn: "Like all other contracts, wages should

18. *Ibid.*
19. Ricardo, p. 95.
20. Ricardo, p. 94.
21. *Ibid.*

be left to the fair and free competition of the market, and should never be controlled by the interference of the legislature."[22] Misery there must be; the economic law that requires it cannot be contravened. Such is capitalism; such did Ricardo do for its reputation. Let no one doubt that damage can be done by an advocate and friend.

Scholars ever since Ricardo have sought to make sense out of his view of profits. Their problem is partly that his explanation was wonderfully confused; it is partly that he had the greatest difficulty finding room in his system for profits to exist. For if the value of a product is given by the cost of the labor it commands at that margin where there is no rent and the surplus before the margin is rent, then there is nothing left over for a return on capital. Return to a landlord, certainly; to a capitalist, none. But, obviously, there is such return, and Ricardo, with no undue clarity of language, assigns it also to labor. Men have toiled in the past to build the plant and machinery that make up the fixed capital investment and to acquire the goods in process that make up the circulating or working capital. Profit (still including interest) is, according to Ricardo, the deferred payment for this past labor.

There are grave problems with this explanation, not all of them disguised by Ricardo's turgid exposition. But again the central point remains, and it had compelling effect. If profits reflect the return to labor employed in the past in making capital, then any income accruing to the capitalist is an unsubtle form of theft. He has no just entitlement; he is appropriating what properly belongs to the worker. Or so, in any case, it could readily be made to seem. And so with historic effect it *was* made to seem by Karl Marx. Revolutions were to be made on the Ricardian case — supported by the Iron Law and the Labor Theory of Value — that the capitalist, for his return, invades the just return of the worker. Economic justice as identified by David Ricardo, the conservative erstwhile

22. Ricardo, p. 105.

86

stockbroker, later Member of Parliament and landed gentleman, required that this be at an end.

There are scholars — Joseph Schumpeter was one of the most prominent — who have held that Ricardo's influence on the history of economics is exaggerated. Both the rigorous Labor Theory of Value and the companion Iron Law were digressions from a more reasonable, less uncompromising path in the development of economic thought. The point can be argued. But no one can rightly take from Ricardo his role as spark and tinder for the coming assault on the system he sought to describe. "If Marx and Lenin deserve busts [in the gallery of revolutionary heroes], somewhere in the background there should be room for an effigy of Ricardo."[23]

That they were contriving the texts for dissent and revolution, neither Malthus nor Ricardo was, needless to say, aware. The ruling classes, the privileged, always look inward with approval upon themselves, not outward in concern upon those whose anger and passion they may be arousing or could, in the future, arouse. And this was so here. Malthus and Ricardo were spokesmen for the new ruling class in a new economic order. As would generations of economists to come, they spoke to and for their constituency. They did not speak to those who, then or later, might be encouraged to revolt.

But also the new industrial world of which and to which they spoke, if by modern standards a cruel and oppressive one, was still a great step up from all that had preceded it. For thousands of years, as Keynes later pointed out and as there will be occasion to stress, men and women had experienced no basic and continuing change in their living standard — things were sometimes a little better, sometimes worse; there was no fundamental, durable trend. Now with industrialization there *was* improvement in the essentials of life; bad as the factory servitude might be, it was almost certainly better for all save the romantically distracted — Oliver Goldsmith, for example — than the previous life in the villages, endlessly at

23. Gray, p. 170.

the household looms or in lonely, ill-rewarded toil on the farms. In large and, to some degree, still unrecognized measure, it was this older world which would inspire revolution, and it still does. In France, to great extent in Imperial Russia, in Mexico, China, Cuba and now in Central America, there was or would be a far more active anger against the landed aristocrats and landlords than against the industrialists. It is a puzzle, even a paradox, that it was Ricardo's views on industry and capitalism that would eventually help fuel the proletarian revolt; as the author of the greatest tract on the unearned increment of landlords, he should have been the parent of the far more common agrarian revolt.

Be that as it may, in the years to come there would be an increasingly angry division between those who spoke for the system and those who spoke for the masses who were perceived as the victims of the system. From Malthus and especially from Ricardo would come ideas in the service of both sides.

VIII

The Great Classical Tradition, 1

AROUND THE MARGINS

I N THE SEVENTY-FIVE YEARS after the death of David Ricardo, economics underwent a particularly important transformation. It ceased to be a subject for contemplation and discussion by people who were otherwise employed and became instead a profession. Men (and virtually no women) came to make their living as economists, for long calling themselves political economists. Innovation in the subject merged with exposition, instruction and public advice. There were now distinguished political economists who said very little that was new but said better than before what was already believed. Or they said it with greater internal consistency or more persuasive unction. There were also some who owed their distinction to saying more eloquently or repetitively what men of influence rejoiced to hear.

As Britain was the dominant economic power in the world throughout the nineteenth century, so economics was overwhelmingly a British subject. Once again the association we have seen between economic thought and economic life. And despite the professionalization of economics and the vastly extended discussion, more of its substance was constant than was changing. In deeper essentials the ideas — one can now say the system — of Smith, Ricardo and Malthus remained without serious challenge.

This was the classical tradition in economics, a characterization that seems to have been first used by Marx.[1] In its later, more refined and polished form, it would be called the neoclassical system, a designation that survives to describe much of the economics in our own day but one that does not reflect a basic change in substance.

The discussion in the years after Ricardo can be divided into three broad categories. First, there was some systemic dissent, much of it from German, French and American scholars. In their countries economic conditions, philosophical disposition or personal observation denied or seemed to deny the great truths emanating from the British economic scene. Second, and especially in Britain, there was a continuing, sometimes imaginative, effort in these years to find a social and moral justification for the classical system and for the extraordinary differences in the income and enjoyments it accorded to its participants. Third and finally, there were modifications and refinements in the theory of prices and distribution — in how prices, wages, interest, rents and profits are determined. These molded the inferential and sometimes ambiguous ideas of the founders into a firm, intellectually complete and internally consistent whole, one that, as was also first shown during these years, could be given mathematical expression.

Along with the three currents just mentioned and paralleling them in the middle years of the last century went revolt — in particular the strong and pervasive dissent of Karl Marx. As told in the last chapter, this also had roots in the classical tradition — in Ricardo's Labor Theory of Value, in the notion of a surplus value falsely appropriated by the capitalist and the overriding case that to labor belonged all the proceeds from the goods produced. Those who nightly render thanks to the founders of the classical tradition in

1. John Maynard Keynes, in *The General Theory of Employment Interest and Money* (New York: Harcourt, Brace, 1936), p. 4, labeled the ideas with which he would be contending "The Postulates of Classical Economics." This is the title of his second chapter.

economics that explains and justifies their good fortune unwittingly render homage in the same prayerful passage to the authors of the ideas that would expropriate them.

We will now consider the influential criticism of the founding fathers of the classical system by German, French and American economists and their belief, implicit where not explicit, that the classical system may have been too conveniently British. The next chapter will consider the classical tradition at the apogee of high capitalism. Then come the ideas elaborated specifically in its refinement and defense, followed by the powerfully intruding dissent of Karl Marx.

In the early nineteenth century, Germany was still a politically disorderly, economically backward mélange of princely states, each state levying customs duties on the products of the others, each reacting jealously to its own indifferently understood interest, each reflecting in greater or lesser measure the personality and not infrequent eccentricity of its ruler. From this infertile soil came a notably abrupt response to Adam Smith and, by inference, to Ricardo and Malthus. Though there were antecedents going back to the Greeks, there was also initiated here a debate that continues powerfully in our own time, its rhetoric an integral part of American and British election oratory.

It was specific and indispensable to the case of Smith and Ricardo that the state exists for the individual. For what other purpose, as most would now ask in some wonderment. The answer of the Germans early in the last century was that the individual exists for the state. It is the state that accords him protection and the possibility of continued civilized existence. Across the brief, unreliable, often incoherent span of individual human life, the state is the firm bridge from the past to the future. It is not altogether obvious, given the nature and minimal beneficence of the German principalities at the time, why the state should have been accorded this superior role. German philosophical thought and guidance almost certainly had an influence. But here, as ever, economic ideas were in accommodation to what exists and is clearly evident. The state was an omnipresent thing in Germany; the princes did not welcome any denigration of its purposes; the scholars obliged.

The two most important voices in the German response to the British classicists were Adam Müller (1779–1829) and the much more considerable Georg Friedrich List (1789–1846). Müller, ten years the senior of the two, is identified — as List is not — with what came to be called the German Romantic movement. He suffered a century of neglect, which some have thought well earned, until he was brought out of obscurity in the 1920s and 1930s as, in some measure at least, an early affirming prophet of National Socialism. Müller was a conservative defender of the landed and feudal interest; his greatly reiterated argument was that the state "is not merely a fundamental human need; it is the supreme human need."[2] In 1945, as the Russian armies swept across the Oder River and on to Berlin, Adolf Hitler was told of the appalling losses of young German soldiers killed in the futile effort to stem the advance. His comment, a distant echo of Adam Müller, was "What else is youth for?"

But one must, at whatever cost, be fair. Through the last century the followers of Smith and Smithian economics found on going to Germany a great respect for, and reliance on, the state. This reflected the greater prestige enjoyed by German officialdom of all ranks and, quite possibly, its greater competence. Some of Germany's economic strength at the time, strength that still continues today, came, in turn, from the country's being spared the tedious, divisive, progress-resistant debate on the proper and improper roles of government. In Germany, as also in Japan, the way was thus open for timely and intelligently pragmatic discussion and action. Such, in part, was the legacy of Müller. There was more, but it does not survive.

The second German dissenter from the world of Adam Smith was Friedrich List, altogether a more influential figure both in his

2. Adam Müller, *Elemente der Staatskunst,* cited in Alexander Gray, *The Development of Economic Doctrine* (London: Longmans, Green, 1948), p. 219.

own time and later. His early advocacy of liberal trading policies between the German states helped lead to a free-trade zone for all Germany, the eventual Zollverein. It also invited the extreme hostility that so often accrues to those who, even on greatly commonplace matters, are ahead of their time. For his heresy he was thrown into jail, a punishment that some since have wished for those who oppose much wanted tariff protection. After his release, List was forced to take refuge in Switzerland, France, England and eventually the United States. He became a newspaper editor in Reading, Pennsylvania, an ardent advocate of the canal-building boom then under way, and he gave an appreciative ear to the views of Alexander Hamilton on the need and means to encourage national economic development; to those of Henry Clay on the American System; and to those of Henry Carey, the American critic of Ricardo, of whom a later word. He also became a citizen of the United States. Then, in 1831, he returned with his American-nurtured ideas to Germany. It was the earliest manifestation of American influence on European economic thought.

Back home, List, now eminently respectable, became an advocate of tariffs for the Zollverein as a whole, thus seeking for the larger region the protection that he had opposed for the smaller constituent states. In *Das nationale System der politischen Oekonomie*,[3] in what was to be an important tradition in German economic thought, he pictured economic life not as a static norm but as a continuing process that goes through successive stages of development — primitive or savage, pastoral, agricultural and familial, with a combination at maturity of agricultural, manufacturing and commercial activity. The state, he held, had an indispensable role in facilitating the movement from the earlier to the later stages and to the final equilibrium between agriculture, industry and commerce, a goal he felt Adam Smith did not identify properly and pursue.

There was here, in elementary form, the beginning of another de-

---

3. *The National System of Political Economy*, translated by Sampson S. Lloyd (London: Longmans, Green, 1922).

bate that is of the highest relevance in modern times. Is economics a static subject? Do economists, accordingly, seek and find eternal verities as, say, chemists or physicists do? Or are the institutions with which economics deals in a constant process of transformation to which the subject, and more particularly the policies it urges, must be in a similarly constant process of accommodation? Friedrich List was an early prophet of the second view; it is one not without influence in the present volume.

As seen by List, a primary instrument in the accommodation to change was the protective tariff. Its role differed greatly with the specific stage of development. It was not useful for a country in the early or primitive stage and not necessary for one in the final stage. It was, however, essential for a country that had the requisite natural and human resources as it moved toward its final development, and particularly if some other country or countries had got there first. Free trade was for the first arrival, where, as in Britain, it was, indeed, an attractive design for confining the later contenders to their earlier stages of development.

Here was the strongest, most enduring and, for that matter, most nearly irrefutable of arguments against Adam Smith and his followers and their case for free trade: they were not affirming a universal truth; they were simply urging what was indubitably advantageous for the special case of Britain.

The position taken by List would have a strong, if largely independent, reflection in the United States in the same years and for many years thereafter; free trade would there be seen as principally defending the original and still unique advantage of established British industry. List's case for protection would be taken up and become, in the American language, the infant-industries argument: free trade might be right in principle, but there was a valid exception for tariffs that protected and nurtured the development of young and vulnerable industries. No debate in economics would be more durable than that between those who, seeing free trade as a branch of theology, would admit of no sin and those who, seeing the needful case of young firms opposing the old, would plead for a limited absolution. In the end, in all of the aspiring industrial countries, the exception was made: tariff protection was almost everywhere granted to the infant, adolescent or, in any case, newer industry. Adam Smith was still widely celebrated as truth, but in all countries, as they came later to industry, he was accommodated to a seemingly special circumstance.

Friedrich List, were he to return to the United States today, would observe with interest the modern manifestation of his case for protection. The evolutionary process that he described does not end, as he held, with an equilibrium of mature industry and agriculture for which tariffs are irrelevant. There comes at that point an aging process in the more mature countries, and from this comes pressure for protection against newer and more vigorous arrivals on the industrial scene. Thus the present demand in the United States, Britain and variously in Europe for the protection of steel, textile, automobile, electronic and other industries from the superior competence of Japan, Korea, Taiwan and the rest of the newer industrial world. The former infant-industries exception has become the aged- and senile-industries exception. In tactful modern terminology, it is called not protection but an industrial policy.

The response in Germany to Smith and his followers defended the state either romantically or, as in the case of List, with a clear eye on its functional role. In France, with the adverse memory of the state both before and after the Revolution, there was no such temptation. As we have seen, the most influential of French scholars, Jean Baptiste Say, adopted and organized Smith — became, with much else, his French voice. The tendency of Smith's critics in France, one not at all foreign to French intellectual history, was to look at the economic system delineated and urged in *Wealth of Nations* and now early in the nineteenth century showing its reality, including its highly visible social effects, and ask as to the worth and purpose of it all. Was it, indeed, what men and women wanted or should want? It has always been the pride as well as the merit of the French that they seek to savor the quality of life and do not confuse it too easily with quantity, including the quantity of goods. It is not surprising that the first questions as to the beneficence of industrial achievement were asked in France.

The most interesting of the critics writing in the French language was Jean Charles Léonard de Sismondi (1773–1842), who was born in Geneva just three years before the publication of *Wealth of Nations.* Among his later distinctions was a long association with Madame de Staël, which began in 1803 in nearby Coppet. The work of few who were active in her circle, economically concerned or otherwise, ever escaped public attention. Writing then as a relatively young man, Sismondi presented himself as an ardent disciple of Adam Smith; coming back to the subject after some sixteen years, he expressed grave misgivings about his earlier views.

By the late eighteenth century, as already indicated, the profound social effects of the Industrial Revolution were evident. Workers — men, women and children — were massed in the factories of the British Midlands and on north into Scotland. Once in the factory, indeed once in the factory towns, they were subject to the power, were at the disposal, of the employer — the owner of the factory, the capitalist. It was not theirs to protest the wages, the hours, the noisome, stinking factories and houses, the brief and weary lives. Nothing better illustrated the reality than one of the efforts at reform — something visited and observed by nearly all Europeans. This was the New Lanark of David Dale (1739–1806), the Scottish capitalist and philanthropist, who went to the orphanages of Glasgow and Edinburgh, emptied them out and moved their inhabitants to dormitories in his model factory town. There, the children were required to work in the textile mills a mere thirteen hours a day and later, in a breathtaking reform after his son-in-law, the utopian reformer Robert Owen (1771–1858), took over, only eleven. In their *spare* time the boys and girls were given lessons and entertainments. Such was reform in that era.[4]

4. Eventually, it may be added, Owen's reformist instinct and its cost invited the objections of his fellow owners, and he migrated to Indiana, there to found a fully socialist community, which he named New Harmony. It attracted some of the most accomplished malingerers in the American Republic and was a failure.

Sismondi reacted strongly to the dismal social circumstances of the new capitalism, which by the early decades of the nineteenth century were also becoming visible in France. Some of his objections were reminiscent of List: "All the suffering has fallen on continental producers, all the enjoyment has remained with the English."[5] With Malthus, he also thought that modern industry was given uncontrollably to overproduction. An individual producer decided how much should be produced; there was no such judgment by the masses in the factory as to what they needed. He thought that, generally speaking, inventions had adverse consequences. But it was to the workers that his thoughts chiefly turned.

Sismondi's greatest contribution was the recognition and characterization of social classes. He was "one of the earliest economists to speak of the existence of two social classes, the rich and the poor, the capitalists and the workers, whose interests he regarded as . . . in constant conflict with one another."[6]

Here began a debate that, when taken up and intensified by Marx and Lenin, would yield more invective than any other in all history. Smith, Ricardo and Malthus had noted that the employer, or certainly the landlord, was better off than the man or woman who toiled; more precisely, they took this for granted. But the employer — the capitalist or landlord — was not, in their view, the architect of the misfortunes of the poor. The miseries of the workers, the ineluctable slide toward bare subsistence, were their own doing, the result of their uncontrollable commitment to procreation. Now with Sismondi the rich *were* the enemy of the poor, the capitalists of the workers. It was now the function of the state to be the protector of the weak against the strong, "to prevent men being sacrificed to the progress of a wealth from which they will derive no profit."[7]

5. Jean Charles Léonard de Sismondi, *Nouveaux Principes d'Économie Politique,* cited in Gray, p. 211.
6. Eric Roll, *A History of Economic Thought* (New York: Prentice-Hall, 1942), pp. 254–255.
7. Sismondi, cited in Gray, p. 209.

Into the effort to make the poor responsible for their own poverty, to keep their plight off the conscience of the affluent (a matter to which later chapters in this book will return), Sismondi thrust a profoundly jarring note. The poor, to repeat, are not to blame for the fact that they are poor; they are held down by the rich. Class oppresses class. For the next 150 years the fortunate would regret and condemn these ideas. As recently as the American elections of 1984, the Republican vice presidential candidate, George Bush, a man of somewhat flexible syntax, rebuked Walter Mondale, the Democratic candidate for President, for "telling the American people to divide [by] class — rich and poor." The true guilt was not Mondale's; it originated with Jean Charles Léonard de Sismondi.

For the sensitive, however, there is comfort in Sismondi's solution; here again the strong overtones of France and French economic thought. From industrial capitalism there should be a retreat to agriculture and to the independent work of the artisan, who knew, as the factory worker did not, what he himself produced. Accordingly, along with the worker's escape from exploitation, the overproduction that Sismondi thought endemic to the system would be avoided.

Before we leave France on this journey around the margins, notice must be taken of the source of a yet more strenuous dissent. This was Pierre Joseph Proudhon (1809–1865), a near contemporary of Marx, who on numerous matters invited the latter's disdain.[8] Accepting the inevitability of property, Proudhon held the disturbing view that the returns to property — rent, profits and especially interest — were all forms of larceny. From this came the most famous of his assertions: *"La propriété, c'est le vol,"* or "Property, it is theft." His solution, stripped to the barest of essentials, was to abolish interest (and other return on capital) and have property held by worker cooperatives or voluntary associations of workers. These would be financed by a special bank with note-issuing pow-

8. The title of Proudhon's principal work, *Contradictions économiques, ou Philosophie de la Misère,* was parodied by Marx in his *La Misère de la Philosophie.*

ers; the notes thus issued would underwrite the production and purchase of products. In Proudhon's society the state would disappear.

Scholars have regularly assigned Proudhon a position of importance in the history of socialism, syndicalism and anarchism but not in the history of economic thought. It is a distinction without merit. Two ideas of influence can be found in the modern residue of Proudhon's theories. One is the belief, perhaps the instinct, that there is a certain moral superiority in the institution of the cooperative. Or the worker-owned plant. When farmers unite to supply themselves with fertilizers, oil or other farm supplies, and consumers to provide themselves with groceries, the ideas of Proudhon are heard in praise. So also when steel workers come together to take over and run a senescent mill, as at Weirton, West Virginia, in recent times. And Proudhon is one among many parents of the great continuing faith in monetary magic — of the belief that great reforms can be accomplished by hitherto undiscovered designs for financial or monetary invention or manipulation. Proudhon's bank was a dubious imitation of the one with which John Law first astonished, delighted and then ravaged France a century earlier.[9]

There are some economic lessons that are never learned. One is the need for the most profound suspicion of innovation in matters concerning money and more generally the field of finance. The thought persists that there must surely be some as yet undiscovered way of solving great social problems without pain, but the simple fact is that there is not. Ingenious monetary and financial designs, without known exception, turn out to be, if not innocuous, then frauds on the public or, frequently, on their perpetrators themselves. Proudhon was not the first to have faith in monetary magic, but he was an early advocate in an enduring tradition.

The most obvious feature of American economic discussion in the years after Ricardo and Malthus — for a near half century, in fact

9. I deal with John Law in Chapters IV and XII of this history and have written about him in more detail in *Money: Whence It Came, Where It Went* (Boston: Houghton Mifflin, 1975), p. 21 *et seq.*

— was its absence in any formal sense. Or, as will later be urged, the feeling that economics was a subject on which no one needed superior guidance; it was something on which everyone had a natural right to self-expression. This was, as is always true, a reflection of circumstance. For a scholarly discussion of economics, there must be an economic problem, more particularly a recurring scarcity or privation.

Until the Civil War and even after, what distinguished the American scene was a spacious abundance, a prospect of income and opportunity for farmer and worker, as well as businessman and capitalist, unimaginable in England or on the Continent. If the worker could at any moment express his dissatisfaction by deserting to the frontier, there was not much foundation for a theory of wages. If farmers could own and farm their own land, there was no need for a theory of rent. Without these costs there was little chance for a theory of price. There was here the same exception from the central economic problem of value and distribution that slavery accorded the Greeks. Economics may not be, as was held in the last century, a wholly dismal science, but it assuredly does not flourish amidst expanding opportunity and optimism.

One cannot carry the point too far, for even economic opportunity and optimism lend themselves to a measure of literary exploitation. This was undertaken in the early and middle years of the last century by Henry Charles Carey (1793–1879) of Philadelphia, the publisher son of an Irish Catholic immigrant. It was one of Carey's misfortunes that he was a writer of prodigious quantity. Reputation in economics is best assured by one great book — Smith's *Wealth of Nations* or Ricardo's *Principles* — a single volume that scholars will actually read.

In his early work Carey was much attracted to Ricardo and British classical thought. But as he sought to apply them to his American surroundings, he came to have, and comprehensively to proclaim, his doubts. Ricardo had seen increasing population and limited land resources pressing labor to an ever lower marginal return and this, then, becoming the wage for all. Carey saw the same process leading labor to an ever higher return as it moved to ever more productive employments. In the New World, as Ricardo, alas, did not know, settlement had begun on the hilltops, on which forests were less dense and resistant and to which settlers, having observed the tendency of feudal residence in Europe, may have ascribed the greatest value, protection and prestige. Then the pioneers moved to the more fertile, more productive valleys, thus achieving not a diminishing but an expanding return. From the poorest land to better or the best. The same was true when attention turned to the frontier and the great unexploited resources there. As this tendency rejected the views of Ricardo, so it destroyed those of Malthus. An increasing population was dividing not a stagnant or decreasing food supply but one that was rapidly increasing. Henry Carey was not averse to the thought that on some distant day there might be too many people; he even used the phrase "standing room only." But he was content, not unreasonably, to believe that this evil was sufficient unto its own time. God had said, "Be fruitful and multiply." Better God's words than Malthus's "Be not fruitful; do not multiply." [10]

Carey, as already noted, joined his sometime countryman Friedrich List in another concession to circumstance. After first affirming the virtues of free trade, he came to espouse protection. And in a second thought shared with List, he wanted a balance between industry and agriculture. He was also especially struck by the seemingly obvious but by no means certain saving in having industry close to home, thus avoiding the transportation cost from Britain.

The problem of protection is how to accord it intellectual respectability in face of the logically powerful and theologically passionate case for free trade. In this effort, one that would long continue both here and abroad, Henry Carey was an unquestioned pioneer.

As the nineteenth century passed, as the frontier disappeared and

10. Henry Charles Carey, quoted in Gray, p. 254.

as American farmers in particular came to sense their own adversity under the system, economic discussions would enlarge and extend in the United States. Reviving Ricardo, Henry George, earlier mentioned in this history, would observe the pressure on the land supply of rural and urban populations with the resulting increase in land values, and he would, as will be told, see this *unearned increment* as a major social ill, a fortuitous enrichment of the landowner who happened to be in the path of progress, something in grievous conflict with distributive justice. But the broad generalization still holds: the last century did not lend itself to formal economic discourse in the United States, and certainly not in the early decades. As we shall see later, there would be strenuous discussion of banking, currency (notably the Greenbacks and the coinage of silver) and the tariff, but that discussion would be by politicians and the citizenry at large, not by the solemn scholars of the subject. Serious economic discussion, to repeat, requires that there be a serious economic problem.

IX

The Great Classical Tradition, 2

THE MAINSTREAM

THE PRIMARY CONCERN of economics throughout the last century and virtually everywhere in the world was with what were considered — as to some extent they are still considered — the central problems of the subject: how prices, wages, interest and profits are determined. Additionally in these years there was much attention paid to the character of money and the role of banking. Money ceased to be merely a commodity that, in the form of gold, silver and copper, was especially qualified to serve an intermediary role in the exchange of goods. Now because it was deposited in banks, because notes were issued affirming deposits and because these notes and deposits were transferred as a method of payment, money developed a marked personality of its own. Further, as the next chapter will tell, there was the evolving defense, social and moral, of the capitalist system.

The explanation of prices or value and of the revenues proceeding therefrom reflected a single dominant trend in this period, and that trend was from a primary emphasis on the seller to a primary emphasis on the buyer; from a primary emphasis on cost to a primary emphasis on consumer utility; from emphasis on supply to emphasis on demand. And then as the last century came to a close, there was a swing back to a balance of emphasis as between demand

and supply, notably in the work of the great University of Cambridge economist and synthesizer of antecedent ideas Alfred Marshall (1842–1924).

With Marshall the discussion of value and distribution, price and who receives the proceeds, comes into the near present. When studying economics, my generation read Marshall's *Principles*, a massive text that passed through eight editions, and when at Cambridge we went with grave deference to call on Mary Marshall, Professor Marshall's accomplished and highly durable widow and coworker.

But I must go back to earlier times. Ricardo, it will be recalled, had anchored the value or price of any reproducible good[1] firmly in cost; the cost, in turn, was that of the labor going into the product under the least satisfactory circumstances of production. And the price of the labor was the cost of sustaining the laborer. The wages of labor, given the uncontrolled procreative impulse of the masses, were in equilibrium at the level sufficient to maintain life; what was left over accrued as rent to the landlord or, in a considerably less specific way, as return to the producer or capitalist. Nor, as a final point, was there a permissible alternative. Ricardo's commanding sentence may perhaps be repeated: "Like all other contracts, wages should be left to the fair and free competition of the market, and should never be controlled by the interference of the legislature."[2] Here was the point of departure for the further development of ideas on price and the distribution of its proceeds.

First in this development came an effort to improve and refine the elements of cost. That the return to land in the form of rent was a residual deriving from the price and accruing in amount according to the quality and in modern times, most notably, the

1. There was, as has been noted, a Ricardian exception for any wholly unique "non-reproducible" item — a painting by Leonardo or Rembrandt, a gem for which no later mining will unearth a rival.

2. David Ricardo, *On the Principles of Political Economy and Taxation* in *The Works and Correspondence of David Ricardo,* edited by Piero Sraffa (Cambridge, England: Cambridge University Press, 1951), Vol. 1, p. 105.

location of the property gave little trouble. In marked degree, this view of rent survives to our own day as an explanation of real estate values and the return thereon.

A far more serious problem involved the return to capital and labor. In an economy of Robinson Crusoes — not one Crusoe but several, living adjacent to the beach — a labor theory of value would be far from irrelevant. Products would be exchanged in rough accordance with the time and effort going into their cultivation, manufacture or recovery from the sea, although even here a diversity of skills, extraordinary and commonplace, could be a complicating factor. As machinery and other equipment were developed and used, there could hardly be doubt that those supplying these instruments of enhanced productivity would have to be paid. Perhaps it might be argued — as, indeed, Ricardo did argue — that the payment for the machines and the encompassing factory was merely the delayed payment for the labor in *their* manufacture that was embodied therein. But there are limits even in economics to the imaginative reach of subjective thought. All too obviously the owner of the capital equipment did also get paid; all too obviously this payment in interest and profit was often handsomely in excess of past outlays for wages; clearly the excess had something to do with the claims or contribution or power of the owner of the capital.

The first solution to this problem, the service of one of the very earliest professors of political economy, came from Nassau William Senior (1790–1864) and, despite its extreme improbability, had a solid existence for half a century. In addition to the cost of labor going into the capital good, there was, according to Senior, a price in interest or profit that had to be paid to persuade people, including the capitalist, to forgo current consumption. From a forgoing of current consumption there would come the purchasing power to acquire factories, machinery, equipment or, in any considerable manufacturing and trading operation, the goods in process or awaiting sale. It was no slight thing that was so compensated. "To abstain from the enjoyment which is in our power, or to seek distant rather than immediate results, are among the most painful exertions of the human will."[3]

This was the Abstinence Theory of Interest or, more generally, of the return to capital. The cost of winning abstinence from consumption and the cost of labor together made up the cost of production of a good. This cost of production was then the level to which, as a normal, equilibrating tendency, prices returned. Were prices above that level, increased production would bring them back to cost as so determined. The reverse would take place were prices below cost.

The grave improbability in this explanation of prices and the return to capital will be evident. Some people, no doubt, do save — forgo consumption — in order to get interest. But abstinence was singularly unevident in the living standards or spending habits of the great capitalists, who themselves supplied the capital for and from their operations, or, equally, in the spending habits of their bankers and financiers. Especially on the American scene. Cornelius Vanderbilt, Jay Gould, Jim Fiske, even the more sedate first Rockefeller — consumption forgone, indeed! As the century neared its end, abstinence was not the distinguishing feature of Newport, Rhode Island. But no more was it apparent in the England of the new industrial rich; this, too, was a world of exuberant and often ostentatious excess. In face of reality, the word *abstinence* as an explanation of capitalist return disappeared from use,[4] the theory surrendering to extreme implausibility.

Through the last century, in fact, no really acceptable justification for the return on capital appeared, allowing, in consequence, an obvious opening for Marx. Only in the present century did a plausible explanation take form. Profit, now distinct from interest, came to be seen, not altogether unreasonably, as the reward for

3. Nassau William Senior, *Political Economy*, cited in Alexander Gray, *The Development of Economic Doctrine* (London: Longmans, Green, 1948), p. 276.

4. So, later, did Alfred Marshall's semantic substitute. Marshall made interest the reward for *waiting*, for trading a smaller present enjoyment for a larger one in the future.

innovation and for assuming risk.[5] And interest became the equilibrating payment between those blessed with more resources than they needed or could productively use and those who borrowed money because they had less than they needed or could productively use. The absence of a persuasive theory of the return to capital and capitalists was a vulnerable gap in the great classical tradition throughout the nineteenth century.

Another earlier flaw was, however, corrected as the century passed. Attention shifted from cost and supply as a determinant of price to desire and demand as a determinant not only of price, but also of, as they were now being called, the factors of production. This development grew out of the efforts to solve the old and seemingly intractable problem of why the most useful things, like water, have small or no price. The earlier response to this question, it will be remembered, was to distinguish between value in use and value in exchange. This distinction was arbitrary and superficial and too obviously ignored the myriad of shadings between the two. Clothing, at least in a cold climate, has a clear value in use. But at some point some of it surrenders its protective role and becomes mildly precious, like much jewelry. Food is needed and nourishing but can also be rare and exotic; a house is essential as shelter but can be, in location, architecture and history, unique and therefore a luxury. To escape from Smith's unresolved question of value in use and value in exchange became, accordingly, a major preoccupation of economists in the latter part of the last century.

In 1831, Auguste Walras (1801–1866), the father of another notable figure in the history of economics, Léon Walras, had made an attempt to deal with the problem.[6] Cost was accepted as a source of value, and to this he added usefulness or utility. But he believed that a product needed, additionally, to be scarce in order to have

5. See Frank H. Knight, *Risk, Uncertainty and Profit* (Boston: Houghton Mifflin, 1921).

6. In *De la Nature de la Richesse et de l'Origine de la Valeur* (Paris: Furne, 1831).

value; it needed to have what he called *rareté* — to have utility and also scarcity. *Rareté* was something that, in notable measure, water usually lacked.

Others struggled similarly with the question but with no great advance until the breakthrough came in 1871. In that year William Stanley Jevons (1835–1882) in England and Karl Menger (1840–1921) in Austria, followed a few years later by John Bates Clark (1847–1938) in the United States — professors respectively at Manchester and London, Vienna, and Columbia Universities (it was by now the dawning age of the professor) — recognized what the economics textbooks still celebrate. That was the role, although all did not use the term, of marginal, not general, utility.

No one should think marginal utility a difficult concept. It is not the total satisfaction from the possession and use of a product (or service) that gives it value; it is the satisfaction or enjoyment — the utility — from the last and least wanted addition to one's consumption that so serves. The last available scrap of food in a famine is exceedingly valuable and would command a worthy price; in conditions of abundance it has no value at all and goes out with the garbage. Under ordinary circumstances, water, unlike diamonds, is unduly available; the last cup or quart has little or no utility, and its absence of exchange value sets the value for all the rest. At sea with the Ancient Mariner or Captain Bligh, fresh water being indubitably scarce, there was little that, until it rained, another cup would not have commanded in exchange. Thus the proposition that millions of students have since learned, indeed still learn: the utility of any good or service diminishes, all else equal, with increasing availability; it is the utility of the last and least wanted — the utility of the marginal unit — that sets the value of all.

There was something wonderfully neat and logical about the concept of marginal utility; for a time it seemed to solve the whole problem of value or price. The price was what people would pay for the last or least wanted increment. Prices would settle down to this level. When no one wanted more water in the rainy season, its price would settle effectively to zero. But not so on the desert. Who would claim in these circumstances that the cost of production was really relevant?

In fact, the marginality of utility was merely the first step to a further and final formulation. Marginality had relevance not only for utility and demand but also for supply. Goods are produced at different levels of costs; this, Ricardo had already celebrated as regards land. Agricultural production as it is increased presses out to poorer land; labor input or cost per unit of production is therefore increased. But there is a counterpart situation in manufacturing. Different firms in different situations or of different competence produce the same product at different costs. Also an individual firm incurs increasing cost as it seeks to extract more from its plant and labor force. Accordingly, in industry as in agriculture there is an omnipotent and omnipresent law of diminishing returns, which is to say increasing cost. And as relevance rests with utility at the margin, so also with costs at the margin.

Specifically, from the diminishing marginal utility to buyers comes the collectively reduced willingness to pay. Thus was born the relentlessly downward sloping demand curve — the ever lower prices needed to clear ever larger supplies from the market. And from the rising marginal costs of producers and the higher costs of less efficient producers come the rising costs of additional supplies. The more that is sought, the more that must be paid. Thus the ascending supply curve — the ever higher prices needed to cover marginal costs and attract increased supplies to the market. And at the point of intersection of the two curves the supreme achievement, the price. This is the price necessary to induce the supply; it is in equilibrium with the price that the least urgent need commanded.

Born further was the most celebrated of economic clichés, one that even now rarely escapes from everyday conversation for as much as a week, providing as it does the great relief from responsibility: "It *is*, after all, the law of supply and demand." Prices, their basis having moved from cost of production to supply and demand, were now set in an ever moving equilibrium between the two. It was this equilibrium which was established at the end of the century in the teaching of Alfred Marshall; it remains in the conventional instruction to this day.

In the pristine classical world no worker, needless to say, had the power to set his own pay. Nor did any union set it for him. And, the avowedly exceptional case of monopoly apart, no capitalist producer set his own prices or the return on his investment. These also proceeded autonomously from the market.

Here the magic of marginality. Where a homogeneous working force was assumed and differences in skill and diligence were over-looked, as among the untutored masses of the factory, pay was set by the value of the contribution to output and revenue of the last available worker. For any worker to insist on more would mean his retirement from occupation. This being so, no one could ask for more than his or her contribution to the firm at the margin. And taken individually, one at a time, all workers were interchangeable with the worker at the margin. Procreative excess could still act to increase the supply of workers and diminish the marginal return. This could go down to subsistence levels. But the equilibrium wage could be more generous. Labor might not be that abundant; the supply and demand curves for labor could intersect at a level above subsistence.

The return to the capitalist in the form of interest was now sim-ilarly explained: it was established by the last and least rewarding unit of investment. Given its undoubted mobility, capital would move to reduce all return to this level, subject always to a major and generally incalculable allowance for differing risk. The greater the supply of capital emanating from nonconsumption or savings, the lower the return. There would be a balance between the mar-ginal return on capital and the reward necessary to attract the mar-ginal saver. Again supply and demand. (Separate now from interest was profit, that which compensated for risk and rewarded the brave and innovative risk taker.) As the magic of marginality settled the problem of prices and of wages, so now it rescued the rate of interest from its previously improbable antecedents.

There was more, much more, by way of technical refinement. And there also now appeared and was explicitly recognized a major exception in the system, the monopoly. The monopolist extended production not to where an impersonally determined market price just covered marginal cost but to where, in consequence of his reduced price in general, his more rapidly falling marginal return just covered the added cost. That was where profits were maximized. No one could say that this was the socially optimal production and price. Production was at a theoretically smaller output than the competitive equilibrium. The price was higher. Accordingly, it was agreed that although the system generally was benign, monopoly assuredly was not. Monopoly established itself as the single great flaw in an otherwise admirable, even perfect, system.

In our own time, as will later be emphasized, the central concern in all public policy is not in getting goods produced; rather it is in providing employment for all who seek to produce them. The goods are not missed; the employment is sorely wanted. For Ricardo and those who came immediately after him, unemployment was not an issue; workers would always reduce their wages sufficiently to make profitable their employment. But not necessarily as the years passed and conditions changed. By the end of the century in Britain, trade unions were a well-established feature on the industrial scene. They raised the cost of labor at the margin, and in doing so, they reduced the number who were employed or could be employed at a return that covered their wage. Unions could thus be a cause of the unemployment of their own members. And now, on occasion, there *was* unemployment.

Here was the genesis of another idea scheduled for a long life and one that is not yet dead. Unions would eventually be accepted within the classical system, but it would be an uneasy association. Surely there is in the union a monopoly power that removes wages from the free and intelligent operation of the market. And a cause of unemployment; unions reward those with jobs at the expense of those beyond the margin. In the universities in coming decades there would be labor economists who accorded their sympathy and support to the trade unions, but they would be mildly suspect by their classical brethren, for whom unions, like other price-fixing arrangements, public and private, were another example of the flaw of monopoly in an otherwise perfect, or anyhow perfectible, system.

By the beginning decades of the twentieth century, although gaps, especially as in the theory of profits, remained, the essentials of the classical system — or, if one prefers, the neoclassical system — of Alfred Marshall were now in place. Though previously so called, it was now truly a system. In ensuing years there would be, along with the aforementioned technical refinements, some important modifications, especially as regards the view of monopoly and competition. But in what would one day be called microeconomics, the subject matter in direct descent from the classical system, far more would be the same than would be changed.

X

The Great Classical Tradition, 3

THE DEFENSE OF THE FAITH

ANY HISTORY of the classical tradition in economics must, after considering the essential ideas, examine the way it was defended. There is, to be sure, a defense implicit in the explanation of the system itself; economic theory combines interpretation with justification. But there is also an explicit defense, and to both implicit and explicit manifestations we now turn.

In the scholarly writing on the history of economic thought, there is no separate literary tradition devoted to the defense of the system. It was, nonetheless, extremely important, a resort and occupation of some of the most determined minds; it also continues strongly to our own time. Not the least of the factors encouraging it were the approval — and the income — it evoked and still evokes from those who benefited from what was defended. Alfred Marshall observed that there is nothing an economist should so fear as applause, but that is a fear which, over the years, many economists and economic publicists have been singularly able to overcome.

On one important matter, as has been sufficiently observed, the classical tradition required no protection. Goods were produced with such virtuosity in the system it described and affirmed that a highly productive performance was, to some extent, accepted as an economic commonplace. The economy traditionally found its equilibrium with all labor employed, the continuing exception being the insistence of the trade unions on wages in excess of the value of the marginal product. And capital and the savings that provided capital were similarly utilized and rewarded. The tendency was thus to an optimal use of labor and capital, given the state of the industrial art. Then through entrepreneurial profit there was added an appropriate, even generous, reward for improving that art. Perhaps because it did seem such a commonplace, the critics of the capitalist system have persistently underestimated the support the system received from its own productive achievement.[1] Nonetheless, there were points of grave vulnerability and fault for which a specific defense was required, and this need became increasingly evident as the nineteenth century passed.

Among the visible problems, there was, first, the appalling difference between the wages and resulting living standard of the workers and those of the employers or capitalists. We have seen that in the early years of the Industrial Revolution the men and women who flocked to the industrial towns and factories of England and southern Scotland almost certainly had an impression that their lives would improve. The villages and household industry they escaped had advantages of neighborly charm, rural scene, unspoiled vegetation and admirably pervasive fresh air, which were almost certainly more appealing to later commentators than to contemporary participants. (This has often been the case. People who suffer gross deprivation while working outdoors in open countryside — until recent times the poor and black in the American rural South, for example — tend to evoke little sympathy.) With the passage of time, however, the contrast between their former lives and the better existence that brought the early generations to the mills diminished in memory and thus in effect. Instead the focus turned to the huge difference in well-being between those who gave their labor and those who provided the industrial capital and authority. The

1. Marx did not do so; in fact, he strongly affirmed it, as the next chapter will tell.

relevant comparison was now not with what the workers had had before but with what others currently received.[2]

Next there was the unequal distribution of power inherent in the system. The worker — adult or child — was subject to the discipline that came from dependence on the job, if not for the next meal, then certainly for the basic requisites of the next month's survival. These requirements the employer-capitalist could give or withhold at will, and he did. The resulting reference to slavery — the wage slave — was not altogether hyperbole.

The classical tradition was not completely silent as to this grim reality. Adam Smith, it will be recalled, observed that while there were no laws against combinations by merchants or employers to assert their collective strength, there was no such tolerance of combinations by the workers. John Stuart Mill adverted strongly to the relative powerlessness of the workers, a matter soon to be noticed. But generally the classical tradition was reticent on the subject of power — the ability of some in the economic system to command or otherwise win the obedience of others and the pleasure, prestige and profit that go therewith. It is a reticence that persists to this day. The pursuit of power and its pecuniary and psychic rewards remains, as it was then, the great black hole of mainstream economics.

Finally, as the nineteenth century passed and more frequently in the early decades of the twentieth — in 1907, 1921 and, needless to say, in 1930–1940 — there appeared on the scene the phenomenon variously denoted as a panic, crisis, depression or recession, with its associated unemployment and general despair, a phenomenon that was horrifying and theoretically incompatible with the classical system.

Here was a grave conflict with the theory of price and wage determination and with the great central theory of value and distribution — theories that set prices and wages at the margin, which

2. There was a similar change in attitude over time on the part of the workers and their descendants who flooded from the Old World to the mines and steel towns of the United States.

is to say that all products were sold, all workers employed, up to the margin. And here also was a conflict with Say's Law. Unsold goods piled up — not a few items but a broad excess of supply, a general overproduction. For this supply there was a palpable shortage of demand, an obvious and inescapable shortage of purchasing power. Yet Say's Law was a pillar of classical belief.

The uneven distribution of income and of power and the inability of the classical theory to assimilate crisis or depression were the flaws for which a defense was required, and this defense was made urgent because they precipitated the two most important attacks the classical system would suffer. The unequal distribution of income (incorporating the notion that the capitalist enjoyed a surplus rightly belonging to the worker) and the unequal distribution of power, including the power that the capitalist enjoyed in the state, would be the source and substance of the Marxian Revolution. The commitment to Say's Law and the consequent inability of the classical system to contend with the Great Depression would be the conditions that led to what, with some exaggeration, would be called the Keynesian Revolution. But this is to run ahead of the story. It is first necessary to see how the classical tradition itself dealt with inequality and oppressive power.

We have already observed the initial defense postulated for the low wages of the laborer in comparison with the revenues of the employer and landlord: at fault was procreative excess, the abandon with which workers, the lower classes as they then were called, bred themselves to the margin of subsistence. Now thought of as a historical curiosity, at least in the developed countries, this reasoning survived to the middle of the last century and beyond. In his *Principles of Political Economy*, first published in 1848, John Stuart Mill firmly attributed the poverty of the workingman to, on the one hand, an immutable physical law of diminishing returns to labor as more and more workers were added to the productive apparatus, and, on the other, the relentless procreative impulse of the masses. "Little improvement can be expected in morality," he likewise urged, "until the producing large families is regarded with the same feelings as drunkenness or any other physical excess."[3]

Some very plausible evidence reinforced this theoretical argument. In contemporary Ireland and similarly but less notoriously in the Scottish Highlands there was the all too apparent tendency of the inhabitants to breed themselves to the outer margins of subsistence provided by the potato.

In the latter half of the last century, however, the idea that irresponsible sexual behavior was a cause of the workers' poverty declined in influence in the industrial lands. Manufacturing wages rose above subsistence levels, and it became evident in somewhat later times that, with urban industrialization, there was a decline in the birthrate. But in the nonindustrialized countries today, in what has come to be called the Third World, the poor with their procreative impulse continue to bear responsibility for their own poverty. And there is still at least an echo of the theory in the industrial lands, notably in the United States. Excessive procreation as such is not thought the problem now; rather the difficulty is the willingness of mothers to have children in the absence of a man to support them. This explanation is clearly in the great tradition of finding the causes of poverty in the moral deficiencies or sexual excesses of the poor. Ricardo, Malthus and Mill still have more than a fugitive presence in Bedford-Stuyvesant, the South Bronx and the works of the more determined critics of the welfare state.

The second defense of the classical system came from slightly outside the central current of economics. This was Utilitarianism, of which by far the most respected innovative voice was that of Jeremy Bentham (1748–1832). Alfred Marshall thought him "on the whole the most influential of the immediate successors of Adam Smith."[4]

The Benthamite and Utilitarian defense identified happiness or

3. John Stuart Mill, *Principles of Political Economy*, edited by W. J. Ashley (London: Longmans, Green, 1929), Book 2, Chapter 13, Section 1, p. 375.
4. Alfred Marshall, *Principles of Economics*, 8th edition (London: Macmillan, 1920), Vol. 1, p. 760.

utility with "that property in any object, whereby it tends to produce benefit, advantage, pleasure, good, or happiness" or similarly prevents "mischief, pain, evil, or unhappiness."[5] It followed that the maximization of pleasure or happiness could and indeed did come from the maximization of the production of goods, the unchallenged achievement, as we have seen, of the new industrialism. It followed, further, that one should look rigorously at the aggregate effect on such production of any and all economic and political action. What encouraged production was useful or beneficial whether it resulted in incidental suffering for the lesser number or not; the basic rule, which would be endlessly reiterated, was the provision of "the greatest happiness for the greatest number." The unhappiness, even if acute, of the lesser number must, in consequence, be accepted. And, as a matter of practical policy, the Utilitarians and Bentham in particular never doubted, first, that mankind's prime motivation was the pursuit of happiness by the individual and the goods that served that end, and, second, that this pursuit was best served when least hampered by governmental or other social guidance, intervention, inhibition or regulation. Let one steel oneself against compassion for the few — or action on their behalf — lest one damage the greater well-being of the many. There was much more to Utilitarianism, but this was the exceptionally hard core of its defense of the classical system and its hardships.

In the works of James Mill (1773–1836), Utilitarian philosophy had its most relentlessly rigorous expression. And from his oldest son, the powerfully and prodigiously educated John Stuart Mill (1806–1873), came its most wonderfully literate statement. Also from John Stuart Mill, it must be added, came one of the more compelling expressions of doubt as to the unquestionable merit of the classical system.

5. Jeremy Bentham, *An Introduction to the Principles of Morals and Legislation* (New York: Hafner Publishing, 1948), p. 2. This volume, first published in 1789 and with its greatest influence in the century following, fully developed the Benthamite system.

Both father and son, as earlier noted, were employed through much of their lives by the British East India Company. The company, in its combined governmental, military and highly privileged trading functions, was as nearly perfect a denial of the Utilitarian commitment to individual and unlicensed self-interest and *laissez faire* as one could hope to imagine. Neither father nor son seems to have been unduly troubled by this, perhaps partly because neither ever saw the operations of the company at first hand in India, although James Mill, the author of the classic work *The History of British India*, did severely attack the non-Utilitarian tendencies of the Indian caste system, social structure and religion.[6]

A close friend of Bentham's, James Mill held insistently that to the individual belongs his own salvation. From the pursuit of that salvation comes the salvation of all. None can say this view is perfect, but it does come as close to perfection, he believed, as anyone can expect in an imperfect world. Once again — a familiar, perhaps even tedious, point — the modern echoes: "The free enterprise system has its hardships, but it is the price we pay for progress and the general good." The defense of the economic system even today does not involve many new speeches.

It was one of John Stuart Mill's contributions to the history of his subject that he was the author of what could reasonably be regarded as the first textbook in economics, a pioneer step in what was to become a large, highly influential and sometimes remunerative literary tradition. His *Principles of Political Economy* would be so used, and in literary excellence it would not again be approached.

Mill the younger restated the classical system, a more thoughtful and exact version of Smith and Ricardo, and affirmed the Util-

6. As he also condemned the literary quality of the *Mahabharata* — a bold step, for he could not read it in the original, and, at the time, it was not available in English. (He defended his lack of personal knowledge of the country, its customs and literature on the ground that it allowed him to take a larger view.) I have dealt with this in an "Introduction to *The History of British India*" in *A View from the Stands* (Boston: Houghton Mifflin, 1986), pp. 189–197.

itarian defense made by his father and Jeremy Bentham. But he was a sensitive man, open — some thought unfortunately — to a variety of humane influences. These included in later years contemporary socialist thought and the views of Harriet Taylor, *née* Harriet Hardy, who would become his wife in 1851 and who persuaded him to the idea, extraordinary at the time, that women should be enfranchised.

Central to John Stuart Mill's beliefs were the undoubted ability of the economic system to produce goods and the seemingly unquestioned relevance of the Utilitarian defense of that accomplishment. Again, there were, inescapably, those who suffered — who contributed to the aggregate achievement but without personal dignity or reward; here Mill retreated to the supposition that things in the future would be better. It was not to be expected, he held, that the division of the human race into two hereditary classes, employers and employed, could be permanently maintained. And in what would perhaps be the most quoted passage from all his writings, he said:

> If, therefore, the choice were to be made between Communism with all its chances, and the present state of society with all its sufferings and injustices; if the institution of private property necessarily carried with it as a consequence, that the produce of labour should be apportioned as we now see it, almost in an inverse ratio to the labour — the largest portions to those who have never worked at all, the next largest to those whose work is almost nominal, and so in a descending scale, the remuneration dwindling as the work grows harder and more disagreeable, until the most fatiguing and exhausting bodily labour cannot count with certainty on being able to earn even the necessaries of life; if this or Communism were the alternative, all the difficulties, great or small, of Communism would be but as dust in the balance.[7]

Mill, however, was no revolutionary; libraries were not and are not at risk from having his *Principles* on their shelves. His belief

7. Mill, Book 2, Chapter 1, Section 3, p. 208.

was that the classical system was brutally unfair but that, as noted, it would improve. Even capitalists would become more benign. Mill embraced a confining view of wages — a historical curiosity called the Wages Fund Theory, which held that capital supplied a fixed total of revenue for the remuneration of all workers and that there was an inevitable diminution in the share for each as there were more to take part in the division — but he abandoned it in later years. His final conclusion was that there would be a more kindly equilibrium — Mill's stationary state — in which all would survive with some comfort and contentment.

Thus, in summary, John Stuart Mill both advertised dramatically the hardship that the Utilitarians accepted as necessary to progress and, as would many who followed him, appealed for patience and hope to withstand it. This remedy, like the knowledge that one was being sacrificed to the larger good, was never wholly satisfactory, it may be assumed, to those afflicted.

There was, however, an even less appealing defense to come — this one also from outside the main current of economic thought. It was the contribution of the new subject of sociology, and its origins were with the impressively learned and prolific Herbert Spencer (1820–1903). During its half century of influence, roughly from 1850 on, it wonderfully solved the problem presented by the powerless and the poor, and especially those who could not survive industrial employment and its accompanying hardship.

The poor and the nonsurvivors in the Spencerian view were the weaklings; their euthanasia was nature's way of improving the species. "I am simply carrying out the views of Mr. Darwin in their applications to the human race. . . . Only those who *do* advance under [the pressure imposed by the system] . . . eventually survive. . . . [These] must be the select of their generation."[8]

It was Herbert Spencer, not Darwin, who gave the world the

8. Herbert Spencer, *The Study of Sociology* (New York: D. Appleton, 1882), p. 418. Spencer is here noting that his views on this matter in some measure anticipated Darwin.

deathless phrase "the survival of the fittest." It was his further service to insist that nothing should stop or hamper this benign process. "Partly by weeding out those of lowest development, and partly by subjecting those who remain to the never-ceasing discipline of experience, nature secures the growth of a race who shall both understand the conditions of existence, and be able to act up to them. It is impossible in any degree to suspend this discipline."[9]

That the state should not, in this view, intervene to correct the process of natural selection was, needless to say, elementary and agreed; a more difficult question was whether private charity should. Charity also nurtured the unfit and contributed to their antisocial survival, but, in the end, Spencer allowed it. Its effect on social advance was undeniably adverse, but to forbid it was an unacceptable infringement on the liberties of the would-be donor.

One cannot avoid admiration for the comprehensive way in which Spencer and Social Darwinism served the defense of the system. Inequality and hardship were made socially benign; the mitigation of hardship was made socially inimical; the fortunate and the affluent could have no sense of guilt, for they were the natural beneficiaries of their own excellence, and nature had selected them as part of an ineluctable progress to an improved world.

Spencer's views were a major force in their time, and especially so in the United States. In the still young Republic it was easy as well as convenient to believe that someone who couldn't get along was peculiarly unworthy, a blemish on the race, who could, justifiably, be sacrificed. Spencer's books sold hundreds of thousands of copies; his visit to New York in 1882 had some of the aspects of the coming of Saint Paul or of a rock star today. A generation of American scholars echoed his thoughts. One of the most ardent was led to proclaim that "the millionaires are a product of natural selection. . . . the naturally selected agents of society for certain work. They get high wages and live in luxury, but the bargain is a

9. Herbert Spencer, *Social Statics* (New York: D. Appleton, 1878), p. 413.

good one for society."[10] These words came from William Graham Sumner (1840–1910), a Yale University professor and the most eminent of American Social Darwinists. It was, I have elsewhere observed, a rewarding thing when the sons of the affluent could be favored with such ideas.[11]

In the early decades of the present century, Social Darwinism went into decline. It was too obviously convenient for the fortunate; it came to be seen as an excuse for indifference rather than as a fit subject for belief. But it did not disappear, and traces can still be found today. The notion that aid to the poor perpetuates them in their poverty, that it would be better socially to leave them to nature's intended fate, continues to lurk in public and private thought. It is the unspoken excuse (along with personal economy) for passing the beggar with the outstretched hand. Charity is somehow damaging.

The voice of Herbert Spencer is also still heard in powerful resistance to the more generally protective role of the state. Reacting to such diverse governmental intervention as liquor licensing, sanitation controls, education and the like, he warned: "The function of Liberalism in the past was that of putting a limit to the powers of kings. The function of true Liberalism in the future will be that of putting a limit to the powers of Parliaments."[12] Allowing for the changed meaning of the word *liberalism* in the United States, the same thought came a full one hundred years later from Professor Milton Friedman.

There were two further defenses of the classical faith, one now largely gone from sight, the other still influential. Vilfredo Pareto (1848–1923) came from an Italian family with noted political and revolutionary antecedents. He succeeded Léon Walras, the noted

10. William Graham Sumner, *The Challenge of Facts and Other Essays*, edited by Albert Galloway Keller (New Haven: Yale University Press, 1914), p. 90.

11. I have commented on this point, and Sumner's influence generally, in *The Age of Uncertainty* (Boston: Houghton Mifflin, 1977), p. 44 *et seq.*

12. Herbert Spencer, *The Man Versus the State* (Caldwell, Idaho: Caxton Printers, 1940), p. 209. This book was first published in England in 1884.

exponent of the classical equilibrium theory, as professor of political economy at the University of Lausanne; with others they caused that university to enjoy fame as the home of what came to be called the Lausanne School. Pareto's interests ranged widely over economics, sociology and politics, and he amended in no greatly striking way the utility and equilibrium analysis of the economic mainstream. His defense of the classical system, however, was of its view of the distribution of income. Looking at elementary statistical data, including those from early income tax returns, he concluded that in all countries at all times income was distributed in much the same way. The curve showing the shares accruing to the rich and the poor remained basically unchanged. This distribution was far from equal; yet it reflected, in his opinion, the distribution of ability and talent in the social order. Those deserving of wealth were few as compared with the multitude deserving of poverty, and those deserving of great wealth were very few indeed. This was Pareto's law of income distribution. Like Social Darwinism, it was, perhaps, too convenient — or flagrant; as a defense of the classical system, its authority has now largely gone. Among other things, there is evidence that the distribution of income can be made more equitable. But again there are still echoes; there remains the sense that there is a normal inequality in the system that is justified by initiative and talent.

The final defense of the faith is more influential in our time than Pareto's law. It does not concern the ideas of economists; rather it removes from them any sense of social or moral obligation. Things may be less than good, less than fair, even less than tolerable; that is not the business of the economist as an economist. Because of the claim of economics that it should be considered a science, it must separate itself from the justice or injustice, the pain and hardship, of the system. The economist's task is to stand apart, analyze, describe and where possible reduce to mathematical formulae, but not to pass moral judgment or be otherwise involved.

Already in the first half of the last century this point had been made strongly by Nassau Senior. As navigation is separate from astronomy and astronomers do not offer advice on guiding a ship, so, he held, the science of political economy has no concern for practical or moral issues, and economists need not or should not offer advice or criticism thereon.

In later decades this rejection of practical questions and judgments was strongly affirmed. An influential voice in doing so was that of William Stanley Jevons, who in *The Theory of Political Economy* was moved to declare "Economics, if it is to be a science at all, must be a mathematical science."[13] From a mathematical science moral values are obviously extruded.

The detachment and the justifying commitment to scientific validity as opposed to social concern are especially influential in our own time. When acting in his professional role, the economist does not contend with the justice or benignity of classical or neo-classical economics; to do so is to deny scientific motivation. To proclaim economic injustice or failure, to pass qualitative judgment on economic performance or to prescribe too freely for its improvement is, scientifically speaking, off limits.

Perhaps, as a practical matter, it is well that all economists do not address social and moral concerns or involve themselves in practical issues. The result could well be a deafening clamor of voices. But the history must not be denied: the pretension of economics that it is a science is firmly rooted in the need for an escape from blame for the inadequacies and injustices of the system with which the great classical tradition was concerned. And it continues to serve as the defense for a quiet, noncontroversial professional life even today.

13. William Stanley Jevons, *The Theory of Political Economy*, 5th edition (New York: A. M. Kelley, 1965), p. 3.

XI

The Grand Assault

THE CENTRAL CURRENT of economic ideas as it developed after Ricardo and Malthus, along with the defense it engendered, was a powerful thing. Whether because of specific instruction or from the general wisdom of the time, it was the accepted vision of economic life and of the public action and private aspiration appropriate thereto. In all the industrial countries there was, to be sure, criticism of the industrial system as it appeared to the observant eye, and there was dissent from the ideas by which it was interpreted and defended. Some of this dissent was from socialists, as they had come to be called, men who questioned the power and human motivation and behavior associated with the private possession of property and the pursuit of wealth. In France, especially, there was such an attack, one led by Claude Henri Saint-Simon (1760–1825), Charles Fourier (1772–1837), Louis Blanc (1811–1882) and Pierre Proudhon. A little later in Germany Ferdinand Lassalle (1825–1864) and Ludwig Feuerbach (1804–1872) were heard in similar criticism. But it was the fate of all these men, some of them of no slight interest and eloquence, to be swept into the shadows by one overpowering personality, that of Karl Marx (1818–1883).

Others — Adam Smith, David Ricardo, Thomas Robert Malthus — shaped the history of economics and the view of the economic and social order; Karl Marx shaped the history of the world. The classical economists wrote, urged and advocated; Marx founded and gave leadership to a political movement, one that is the major source of political tension within and between countries to this day. There is no common reference to Smithians or Ricardians; Keynesian is only a mildly descriptive term. To be a Marxist in the Western industrial countries, and notably in the United States, is, even in the late twentieth century, to be excluded from reputable concourse.

In dealing with Marx as part of the history of economics, as later will be the case with Keynes, one must be rigorously, even brutally, selective. Marx spent much, perhaps most, of his adult life in economic, political and social study and in writing; the Reading Room of the British Museum was his refuge and workplace for many years. He was also a journalist; for the financially difficult period he spent in London he was sustained by *The New York Tribune,* parent of the later *New York Herald Tribune* and champion of high Republicanism — a matter of which all decently ardent members of the modern Republican Party should be appropriately aware. He was also an active and voluble revolutionary. But it is with Marx's economics or political economy alone we are here concerned and not with all the rest. As noted, the controlling and enduring ideas must be extracted from the mass. A word must first be said, however, on the sources of Marx's thought and the experiences by which it was shaped.

Karl Marx did not become a dissident and revolutionary in reaction to the hardships and privation of his youth. Modern disciples who make a pilgrimage to his birthplace in Trier, at the head of the Moselle Valley in Germany adjacent to Europe's most beautiful countryside, find a pleasant, exceedingly spacious residence. It is superior in elegance to the ones from which, in all but the rarest cases, they themselves come. Marx's father, Trier's leading lawyer and an officer of the High Court, was a member of an old Jewish family. At the time of his son's birth, he had recently converted to Protestantism, but spiritual belief is not thought to have been involved in his conversion; in his official position in Prussia he could not easily be a Jew. Karl Marx's associations as a youth were with the local social elite; his eventual marriage to Jenny von Westphalen, the daughter of Baron Ludwig von Westphalen, the first citizen of the town, was in keeping with his position, and the von Westphalen family was one with which he had established a close, affectionate relationship. Marx's early years offer no portent of the fierce revolutionary dissent that was to follow.

This dissent was first nurtured during his college days, when, after some romantically feckless years at Bonn, he went on to Berlin, there to fall under the influence of Georg Wilhelm Friedrich Hegel (1770–1831). From Hegel, or more precisely from the formidable, often appalling, aggregation of Hegel's thought, came an idea of the utmost importance, one we have already encountered in very elementary form in the work of Friedrich List. It is the belief that economic, social and political life is in a process of constant transformation. As one social structure or institution assumes authority or eminence, another rises to challenge it. And from the challenge and conflict come a new synthesis and a new power, these to be challenged in turn. The obvious flesh-and-blood example of this superb abstraction was the way the capitalists — the new industrialists — were challenging the old landed ruling classes. And it required only a slight stretch of imagination to see that the new bourgeoisie, having suitably reduced the power of the old aristocracy and having achieved a new synthesis, would, in turn, be challenged by the workers they had amassed in their service.

The classical tradition, we have seen, had posited an equilibrium; this would come to be called equilibrium economics. The basic relationship between employer and worker, between land, capital and labor, never changed. There could be change in the supply of labor and capital, but change there only brought a new and similar equilibrium. Identification and study of that final equilibrium was the substance of economic science. Marx, proceeding on from Hegel, was conditioned to reject the most fundamental of the assumptions of classical economics. The equilibrium was not the end for him; it was an incident in a far larger change, which altered the whole relationship between capital and labor.

There is here the basis for the most important single difference in modern economic attitudes. For economists of classical or neo-classical disposition there is still a fixed, unchanging norm. To this, economic life, whatever the interim disturbances and interferences, has a controlling tendency to return. Economic science refines and improves knowledge of basic institutions and relationships that are constant. Opposing this view is the belief in a continuous change to which economists and economic ideas must adapt, the legacy of Hegel and of Marx. Economic institutions — trade unions, corporations, the economic manifestations and policies of the state, class conflict — are all in movement or are a source of movement. The cost of believing in equilibrium — of seeing the study of economics as a search for improved knowledge of a fixed and final subject matter and thus as a hard science like physics or chemistry — is to be in an ineluctable march to obsolescence.

In the United States, as will later be told, economics divides today as between classicists (the overwhelming number) and institutionalists, between those committed to the inevitable and constant equilibrium and those who, with much less claim to scientific precision, accept a world of evolution and continuing change.[1] One source of the institutionalists' ideas is Germany in the world of Hegel — and of Marx.

Hegel did place Marx in opposition to the most fundamental assumption of classical economics by making him accept the idea of change, including revolutionary change, but the practical experience of life also helped make Marx a revolutionary.

The events that influenced and controlled his thinking followed his departure from Berlin in 1841. From there he went to Cologne, where he became the highly successful editor of the *Rheinische Zeitung*, the well-financed organ of the new industrialists of the Ruhr — not, seemingly, a voice of sedition. Marx was to make it

1. The latter are represented in the Association for Evolutionary Economics, which publishes a dissenting journal, the *Journal of Economic Issues*.

so, at least by the remarkably sensitive standards of nineteenth-century Prussia. He supported the right of the people to go into the forests and pick up dead wood, an ancient privilege but now, as wood had become valuable, an intrusion on the rights of private property. He also criticized the Czar of Russia at a time when it was forbidden in Prussia to criticize royalty of any kind or any country, and he urged free discussion of the problems of the wine growers of the Moselle Valley, who were suffering from competition as the result of the Zollverein — the common market that the German states had recently adopted. And he proposed a more secular approach to the problem of divorce. For these heresies he was peremptorily sacked and the paper suppressed.

More frustration followed. He went to Paris and sought to publish there for an audience in Germany; the censors intervened and confiscated the only issue of the *Deutsche-Französische Jahrbücher* ever printed. He settled down to reading and started a new publication, *Vorwärts*, for the sizable German refugee community in Paris. This brought a complaint to the French authorities from the Prussian police: harboring Marx was considered an unfriendly act. He had to move on to Belgium. In 1848, the Belgians, too, became uneasy about his presence, but in that year of revolutionary mood — and freedom — he was allowed to return to France and from there to go briefly back to Germany. Then in the counterrevolution he was again expelled, and this time he went to Britain. He thought of immigrating to the United States but lacked the money for the passage; a great current of history would perhaps have been altered in an interesting way by a few dollars or pounds. To the continuing attention of the police in these years one must accord credit for the cultivation of Marx's increasingly revolutionary mood; anyone regarded as that dangerous must feel compelled to live up to his image.

Marx was still young enough to be influenced by their attention; when at last he found refuge in London, he was only thirty-one. By then, however, he had already produced, with Friedrich Engels (1820–1895), the most celebrated — and most energetically denounced — political pamphlet of all time. This was *The Communist Manifesto*, which addressed the widely felt discontent expressed in the revolutionary movements of 1848.

The association with Engels had begun with a meeting in Paris some years earlier and was to last throughout Marx's life. Also a German, a member of a family of textile manufacturers in the Ruhr, Engels headed the family enterprise in Manchester, England. To him Marx would look for intellectual guidance, editorial assistance and, especially during the early poverty-ridden days in central London, financial rescue. (Marx's later years in a pleasant house in Hampstead were far from uncomfortable.) Engels edited for publication the first volume of Marx's *Capital*[2] and, from notes and portions of manuscript, completed and published the last two volumes after Marx's death.

As earlier in Cologne, Marx's personal intellectual debt was not to the workers whose case he urged but to the bourgeois employers whose exploitation he condemned. Nor is it without relevance that it was Britain, the leading country in capitalist development, that gave him shelter and accorded him freedom of expression. The liberal ideas that allowed capitalism to flourish in independence from the state also protected capitalism's most effective critic and antagonist.

Of Marx as an economist and scholar, Joseph Schumpeter, who was decidedly no disciple, wrote that he "was first of all a very learned man," adding that "the cold metal of economic theory is in Marx's pages immersed in such a wealth of steaming phrases as to acquire a temperature not naturally its own."[3] In these steaming phrases his readers have found an endless opportunity for argument as to Marx's meaning and an equal possibility of finding what they themselves wished to believe. As would later be the case with

2. A modern edition is *Capital: A Critique of Political Economy* (New York: International Publishers, 1967), Vol. 1.

3. Joseph A. Schumpeter, *Capitalism, Socialism, and Democracy* (New York: Harper & Brothers, 1942), p. 21.

Keynes, the ensuing debates as to what Marx truly intended attracted followers and added enormously to his influence. From the steaming mass, however, four hard criticisms of the classical system stand out; with great precision, they assail capitalism as it existed in Marx's time and the ideas by which it was interpreted and defended.

Marx did not at all question the productive achievements of the system; to these, indeed, as has already been noted, he gave his strongest praise: "During its rule of scarce one hundred years, [it] has created more massive and more colossal productive forces than have all preceding generations together."[4] As a subsidiary achievement, it "has created enormous cities, has greatly increased the urban population as compared with the rural, and has thus rescued a considerable part of the population from the idiocy of rural life. . . . The cheap prices of its commodities are the heavy artillery with which it batters down all Chinese walls."[5] Workers were also reminded that the *first* object of their revolutionary attention should not be the great capitalists who were the source of this productive power but rather "the remnants of absolute monarchy, the landowners, the non-industrial bourgeois, the petty bourgeoisie,"[6] who are the enemies of capitalist power and achievement. It was part of the genius of Marx that he deployed his weapons in the primary instance not against strength but against weakness.

The vulnerable points in the capitalist system and its interpretation were, as he saw them, first, the distribution of power — which had been effectively and almost universally ignored by the classical economists.

Second, there was the highly unequal distribution of income — which the classical tradition explained but for which it had never found a wholly compelling justification.

Third, there was the susceptibility of the economic system to

4. Karl Marx and Friedrich Engels, *The Communist Manifesto* (New York: Modern Reader Paperbacks, 1964), p. 10.

5. Marx and Engels, p. 9.

6. Marx and Engels, p. 17.

crises and unemployment — in modern terms, to depression — something that, if recognized by the classical economists, was nowise integrated into their theory. The tendency of the economy, as classically perceived and earlier noted, was to the full employment of its productive resources, including its supply of willing and eager workers, the last such willing worker setting the wage.

Finally, there was monopoly, a flaw that was conceded by the classical tradition. But for Marx this was not an isolated phenomenon; it reflected a basic tendency, one that would be decisive in the final fate of capitalism.

For Marx power was the inescapable fact of economic life; it proceeded from the possession of property and thus was the natural, inevitable possession of the capitalist. The capitalist "strides in front . . . the possessor of labour-power follows as his labourer. The one with an air of importance, smirking, intent on business; the other, timid and holding back, like one who is bringing his own hide to market, and has nothing to expect but — a hiding."[7] Less metaphorically, the worker, including in Marx's repeated reference the child, comes to the factory with nothing but his physical effort to sell and with no alternative save to be there. Thus the power and authority of the capitalist, the powerlessness of the worker. But this is not an unequal distribution of power that is original to capitalism. As noted, Marx stressed the earlier association of power with the feudal, aristocratic and landowning classes. Nor did he think the household industry that preceded capitalism an economic Elysium. "This exploitation is more shameless in the so-called domestic [that is, household] industry than in manufactures, and that because the power of resistance in the labourers decreases with their dissemination; because a whole series of plundering parasites insinuate themselves between the employer and the workman."[8] He hinted at the possible corrective role of the trade union or workmen's association, but for Marx the essential fact remained:

7. Marx, p. 176.
8. Marx, p. 462.

power in capitalism resides with the capitalist; it is the natural attribute of the productive property he owns. The payments proceeding therefrom command the obedience and submission of people who have no property and thus no alternative income.

Nor is the power of the capitalist confined to the enterprise. It extends to the society and the state: "The executive of the modern State is but a committee for managing the common affairs of the whole bourgeoisie."[9] And, an especially poignant thought, it even extends to the economists and political theorists who describe and interpret the system, to the classical tradition in economics itself. "The ruling ideas of each age have ever been the ideas of its ruling class,"[10] in Marx's time the capitalists and those who tell of their system. Thus economics and economists were swept under the authority of the ruling power.

In the Western industrial world in our day, and especially in the United States, the label of Marxist is, to repeat, one of heavy opprobrium. Nevertheless, two of Marx's propositions as regards power survive this hostile climate: that modern governments serve the interests of corporate or business power and that orthodox or accepted economic thought is in keeping with dominant economic interest are the stuff of everyday, wholly commonplace, political comment. On these matters more people speak in the voice of Marx than most, themselves, ever imagine.

With the greatly unequal distribution of power goes a greatly unequal distribution of income, the second point in Marx's critique. This thought Marx derived from Ricardo, but he added refinements, much technical persiflage and no slight subjectivity, with a result that has puzzled and entranced his followers for a century. The worker at the margin receives payment in wages reflecting his added contribution to the total revenue of the enterprise. That contribution, by the ineluctable operation of the law of diminishing returns, diminishes as workers are added. And the marginal wage sets the

9. Marx and Engels, p. 5.
10. Marx and Engels, p. 37.

wage for all. But those back from the margin, though paid the marginal wage, contribute more, and perhaps much more, to earnings than their wage. They are in the infra-marginal, more fruitful stages of diminishing return. This is surplus value they create, and this surplus value accrues, alas, not to those who earn it but to the capitalist. It rightly belongs to the worker, but the capitalist intervenes to appropriate it. Marx notes that while there are laws of production that are given by nature, such as the law of diminishing returns, the laws of distribution are given by man, and there is no overriding reason that the workers must surrender to such man-made arrangements.[11] The notion that workers earn more than they get — and that corrective action lies in their hands — was also to have a highly influential future, although it would be going too far to ascribe all of it to Marx. It is an idea that would strongly invade the minds of workers and trade union leaders on its own.

The third point in Marx's assault was the capitalist crisis. This, again, had no clear presence in the classical tradition; Marx made it an inherent characteristic of capitalism.

His explanation of the crisis is now a historical curiosity: the productive power of capitalism that Marx so fully respected would press its goods relentlessly on markets, and as the labor supply became fully employed, wages would inevitably rise. The result would be a falling rate of profits, a loss and retrenchment by the producing firms, an imbalance in the productive process. Balance would be restored in practical effect only as diminished production, unemployment and falling wages allowed production to be profitable once more. It was an important point for Marx that the system is stable only when wages are held down by a reserve of unemployed workers — his industrial reserve army of the unemployed. Full employment was a possible but unstable condition.

Although Marx's explanation is no longer believed, even by most

11. This, it is perhaps worth stressing, is an exceedingly hard — and succinct — summary of a matter with which Marx deals at length and with, to repeat, some qualification and no slight obfuscation.

Marxists, he identified what would come to be recognized as capitalism's greatest point of vulnerability when he saw the capitalist crisis as an inherent feature of the capitalist system. Not the unequal distribution of power, not the unequal distribution of income, but the disposition to depression and unemployment would be the greatest threat to capitalism's survival. It would also, in the next long step on from the classical system, be the flaw that Keynes, like Marx before him, would see and address as an inherent part of the system.

In the classical tradition, as we have seen, monopoly was a flaw, one that especially impressed itself on the American mind and psyche. But even to the classicists it was the exception to the competitive rule, and it presented no threat to the system as a whole. For Marx, on the other hand, it was much more than a flaw; the increasing concentration of economic activity in the hands of ever fewer capitalists was an organic tendency of capitalism, one that proceeded with irresistible force. In association with the increasingly sophisticated, socialized character of the workers as they came increasingly to understand capitalism and their role therein, this concentration would contribute immutably to the collapse of the system. Here is the dénouement in Marx's words. An often tedious writer, he had his great moments; few passages in the history of economics have been more quoted.

> One capitalist always kills many. . . . Along with the constantly diminishing number of the magnates of capital, who usurp and monopolise all advantages of this process of transformation, grows the mass of misery, oppression, slavery, degradation, exploitation; but with this too grows the revolt of the working-class, a class always increasing in numbers, and disciplined, united, organised by the very mechanism of the process of capitalist production itself. The monopoly of capital becomes a fetter upon the mode of production, which has sprung up and flourished along with, and under it. Centralisation of the means of production and socialisation of labour at last reach a point where they become incompatible with

their capitalist integument. This integument is burst asunder. The knell of capitalist private property sounds. The expropriators are expropriated.[12]

Thus, according to Marx, the economic system celebrated by the classical tradition would come to an end, an end brought about by characteristics, some of the most important of which had already been identified by Ricardo and the classical economists themselves.

But the Marxian system itself had obvious points of vulnerability, and these were to prove serious and decisive. There was, first of all, the threat posed to it by reform, the possibility that the hardships of capitalism would be so mitigated that they would no longer arouse the revolutionary anger of the workers. Of this danger Marx was aware, but he could not easily condemn or resist specific reforms that would serve the interests of the workingman. *The Communist Manifesto* did not; it urged, along with much else, a progressive income tax, public ownership of railroads and communications, free education, abolition of child labor and jobs for all. Liberal reformers in the twentieth century are companionately in step with much of *The Communist Manifesto*.

There was also the possibility that trade unions might develop and strengthen, receive public protection and ease or reverse the progressive immiseration of the workers that, with growing population and the continuing decline in the marginal return to labor, the Marxian system foresaw. And this has happened.

Also intensely damaging to the Marxian system would be anything that lessened the impact of the capitalist crisis.

In an extraordinarily logical response to Marx, the later development of the welfare state, the support for mass education, the abolition of child labor and the Keynesian attack on the capitalist crisis would all address the points of capitalist vulnerability he identified. All of these steps against Marx, it might be added, would

12. Marx, p. 763.

in their time be accorded a measure of condemnation as being themselves Marxist!

Two other things were potentially adverse to Marx. Along with the counterrevolutionary reforms that Marx was required to advocate even in his own time, reforms that included welfare (income from outside the production system) for the old, the unemployed, the handicapped and the young, there could be the larger effect from the enormous productive power of capitalism, a power that Marx himself so frequently emphasized. This could lead to a great outpouring of goods, spreading onto the working masses and acting as a blanket over misery and complaint.

Further and finally, a thought that Marx did not harbor and certainly did not voice: perhaps capitalism might itself change; perhaps there might be capitalist transformation along a different line; perhaps the relentlessly aggressive capitalist might give way to mellower, more compromise-minded organization — to a corporate bureaucracy. The ruling power would then be not the capitalist but the technocrat and the organization man.

All of these things have, in fact, happened; the development of economic society has not been kind to Marx. The advanced industrial countries have proved themselves largely immune to his revolution. Reforms, welfare measures, government macroeconomic policy, the rise of the bureaucratic corporation and the organization man have all tempered, even destroyed, the Marxist thrust to revolution. Where the Marxist ideas have succeeded, it has not been against capitalism but against the remnants of feudalism in Russia and China in the context of war and anarchy. There, as also in Cuba and now in Central America, landlords and their governing agents, not industrialists or capitalists, have inspired the deprived to revolutionary fervor. In so doing, they have been far more influential than the capitalists.

Marx's critique failed in another respect. He thought that the state, after it was taken over by the proletariat, would eventually wither away. Instead, in massive operational form, the modern state has retained its power under socialism, and this has led to the bureaucratic problems with which the modern Marxists in positions of authority now contend. They struggle also with the closely related difficulty that the socialist apparatus has with production. Marx saw the productive powers of high capitalism being carried over, more or less automatically, to socialism. It was not to be so easy.

Yet a word of caution is in order. Telling how Marx was wrong is more than a literary effort; it is, and long has been, a small industry in the service of those for whom Marx continues to be a glowering threat. We shall greatly underestimate his historical power if we do not see that, on many matters of everyday thought and expression in the nonsocialist world, he is a major influence and force.

XII

The Separate Personality of Money

I T IS NECESSARY now to step back a little to consider the sources
of what some would hold to be the principal subject of modern
economic discussion and policy: the role of money and its
management, the origins of what is known today as monetarism.
More than in any other aspect of economic history, the institutions and experience surrounding money, not the formally expressed
ideas about it, are important, and to these we now turn.

The earliest history of money — the probable innovation in China,
the coined money of the Lydians — has already been indicated. Also
Gresham's Law and the Quantity Theory of Money developing out
of the inflow of silver and gold into Europe from the New World.
In the beginning, to remind, money was a commodity like any other,
save that its physical characteristics allowed of its being divided
into parts of varying but specified weight, and it had high enough
worth in small enough bulk so that it could be readily carried around.
Thus it served as an intermediate step in exchange, eliminating the
inherent awkwardness of barter, the need to search for someone
who had the product sought and who wanted the product prof-
ferred. And it was a convenient way of holding wealth — a store-
house of value.

Even in the earliest times, however, when something like silver
or gold was used as money, what was so used developed a modest
personality of its own. Thus it was soon learned that a little of the
metal could be shaved off the coin or a little of a lesser metal intro-

duced into its manufacture. The debased coin could still, it was hoped, pass as before, and the metal saved could be spent for other needed things. No other economic practice, it might be added, was ever universally so condemned. The phrase "debasement of the coinage" became synonymous with public depravity; its practice in the later centuries of the Roman Empire was taken as typical of the moral decay that led to the decline and fall.

But in major measure the separate identity of money, its personality, was discovered with the establishment of banks; through banks the supply of money could be increased or, on occasion, sharply diminished, and this, more or less, at will. The funds thus made available could be used for investment, necessary or frivolous consumption or the needs of the state.

The roots of this discovery, or in any case its earliest modern development, were in Italy in the thirteenth to the sixteenth century — first in Venice and, a little later, in the cities of the Po Valley.[1] So close was the identification of banking and moneylending with Italy that the street in London where, in the course of time, these activities were eventually housed was called Lombard Street.

All history, however, accords a major pioneering role in these matters to the Bank of Amsterdam, which from 1609 on took the variously minted and thoughtfully debased coin of the time, weighed and ascertained its true content and worth and gave the owner an honest rendering as a deposit. Other guardian banks in other Dutch towns — Rotterdam, Delft, Middelburg — were soon established, and, as time passed, so were similar banks in other countries.

At first the Bank of Amsterdam was simply a place of deposit; the exact weight of honest metal was stored there on the depositor's behalf. When he asked that the deposit be transferred to a creditor — used as a means of payment — the coin was moved to

1. See Charles F. Dunbar, "The Bank of Venice," *The Quarterly Journal of Economics*, Vol. 6, No. 3 (April 1892), pp. 308–335, and Frederic C. Lane, "Venetian Bankers, 1496–1533: A Study in the Early Stages of Deposit Banking," *The Journal of Political Economy*, Vol. 45, No. 2 (April 1937), pp. 187–206.

the creditor's place of storage. The total of the money available for transfer and payment thus did not exceed the amount of the original deposit.

But not for long. Men came to the bank not only to deposit money but to borrow money. Borrowing and then depositing the proceeds, they also had an account; from this account, backed now not by a specific but by a general claim on the metal, they could make payments, spend money. As the new deposit could be spent, so could those already existing. Money had been created, and not less so than when dug by brutal toil from the ledges at Potosí. As an added benefit from this notable act of creation, revenue accrued as interest to the bank. The creation of money was no disinterested act; it was now a very rewarding thing.

The borrowing and the resulting act of money creation had another very early form as well. Instead of a deposit subject to transfer by order — that is, written instruction or check — the borrower could take his loan in bank notes. These affirmed that he had the metal on deposit, and the receiver of the notes could then go to the bank and command it. Or, more probably, he could pass the notes on to yet another supplier or creditor. Meanwhile the original metal remained in the bank vaults and could also be lent. As with the deposits, so with the notes: again, money had been created.

Together, the deposits and the notes were in excess of the value of the metal on which they were based. This, however, was entirely safe and acceptable for so long as everyone — original depositors, borrowers, note holders — did not come at the same time for the hard money. Unless there were fear, panic or spreading rumor and unease about the competence and solidity of the bank — all by no means negligible possibilities — this would not happen.

Given the profits possible from this manufacture of money — the return in interest for an effortless act of lending — the temptation to overdo a quite wonderful thing was obvious. Out of this temptation were born the central banks and much of the structure of modern bank regulation. In return for various privileges, including in later times the exclusive right to issue notes, central banks came into existence, the Bank of England as the most significant example in 1694. They then proceeded to regulate the lending and money creation of the lesser banks, which they did in an inconvenient disciplinary way by returning to the smaller banks their notes for payment in metal and by enforcing minimum levels of reserves against deposits. Of this more later.

The final great step in according money its separate and distinctive personality was the realization by kings, princes and parliaments that the creation of money could be used as a substitute for taxes or as an alternative to borrowing from unduly stiff-necked or reluctant financiers. There were elements of this discovery when the Roman coinage was debased to permit a larger volume of payments from a given supply of metal, this as an alternative to tax levies for the needs of Emperors and the Empire. But for modern purposes the discovery came with the general use of paper notes. Then, in a manner not different from that described for the banks, the state acquired hard coin, stored it in the state treasury and issued notes that constituted a claim on such coin. Or a bank did so on behalf of the government. Once this seemingly innocent step had been taken, it was again all but inevitable that the notes put in circulation would exceed the metal on which they were based. In normal times it could be assumed that, with the note issue subject to reasonable restraint, not all depositors would come for their hard money at once. But there was an ever present temptation to pay in paper for current or compelling state needs instead of resorting to the grim and often impossible alternative of raising taxes. Need, not caution, would be the ruling force.

Sometimes, as indicated, notes were issued by a government-sponsored or central bank. In Britain such note issue by the Bank of England helped finance the wars against Louis XIV in the last decades of the seventeenth century. Similarly in France from 1716 to 1720, when John Law, perhaps the most innovative financial scoundrel of all time, rescued the fiscally strapped and otherwise incompetent regent, Philippe, Duc d'Orléans, with the notes of the

Banque Royale. But a central bank was not essential; the paper money of the American colonies before the Revolution, the *assignats* that helped finance the French Revolution, the Continental notes that paid Washington's armies and the Greenbacks of the American Civil War were all issued by governments on their own. And when the volume outstanding could no longer be sustained by the state from any available metal, conversion of the notes back into hard coin would be suspended. To the economic lexicon was then added a new phrase: "They have gone off the gold standard."

Once the several manifestations of the separate personality of money are recognized — something that has only rarely happened — the economic thought and controversy that money has evoked are readily understood. Thus all modern revolutions — American, French, Russian — have been paid for by issues of paper money. The revolutions themselves, notably those in France and the United States, are much celebrated and admired, while historians have not yet ceased to deplore the paper notes by which they were financed.[2]

Controversy over the use of paper money as a substitute for taxes began in America, in fact, well before the Revolution. Nearly all of the colonies, in greater or lesser measure, were given to the practice. The Middle Colonies (Pennsylvania, New York, New Jersey, Delaware and Maryland) issued paper to pay bills with general prudence and restraint. Rhode Island, South Carolina and Massachusetts acted with considerably less discretion; Rhode Island, in fact, with uncomplicated abandon. Rhode Island notes were regarded with disdain, perhaps alarm, even in Massachusetts.

In the Middle Colonies, as indeed some recent scholars have come

---

2. Similarly deplored, as was earlier told, has been the role of the banks in the creation of money, at least in the more extravagant cases. In 1720, the Prince de Conti, losing confidence in the notes of Law's Banque Royale, sent in a sheaf of them for redemption. According to a highly questionable legend, three wagons carried back the gold and silver. The prince was then ordered by the regent to return the metal to the bank. He and some thousands of other holders of the notes were soon to lose munificently. For the next century, in consequence, banks were regarded with extreme suspicion in France.

to agree,[3] a moderate issue of paper served also to stabilize prices and stimulate economic activity. Here was the early source of a controversy that would enliven and at times dominate American politics for the next 150 years. Emergency need apart, should money be called into service deliberately to affect — that is, improve — prices and provide for capital needs? On the frontier and in agricultural regions, this effect was especially sought. Money created by the banks could buy land, livestock and farm equipment; paper money or freely coined silver could improve prices and ease debt repayment. Established centers of commerce and industry, supported eventually and strongly by the best economic opinion, powerfully resisted such action. Money should be neutral in its economic effect. More particularly, it should be kept scarce and valuable, as those already possessing it had every reason to wish. In the history of economics it is the conservative view that has always had nearly universal approval.

The frontier perception of money as a stimulating force did not prevail in the colonies; indeed, it did not prevail even when graced by the approval of so great a figure as Benjamin Franklin. In 1751, the Parliament in London, expressing the reputable view, forbade the issue of further paper money in New England and a decade or so later extended the ban to the other colonies. Until very recent times, this was regarded by economists as an act of wise and needed restraint. In 1900, Charles J. Bullock, one of the most respected authorities on colonial (and also contemporary) public finance, referred to the colonial monetary experiments as a "carnival of fraud and corruption" and a "dark and disgraceful picture." He thought the action of Parliament in controlling them "wholesome."[4] Davis Rich Dewey, another highly respected monetary expert of the same generation, noted that "there was a substantial element of the population, particularly in the larger cities in the East, which stood

---

3. In particular, Richard A. Lester in *Monetary Experiments: Early American and Recent Scandinavian* (Princeton: Princeton University Press, 1939).

4. Charles J. Bullock, *Essays on the Monetary History of the United States* (New York: Macmillan, 1900; Greenwood Press, 1969), p. 43 *et seq.*

aloof from the revolt against England, not so much out of opposition as because of the fear that independence would bring excessive issues of paper money with all its consequent derangement to business affairs."[5] Independence was one thing; conceding to those who saw money as an instrument to be used to their personal advantage was something else again.

The Continental notes that financed the American Revolution, serving as they did as a substitute for taxation, or perhaps one should say a tax system, invited a similar rebuke; they placed permanently in the American language the expression of abrupt and total condemnation "not worth a Continental." Similarly the Greenbacks, which Secretary of the Treasury Salmon P. Chase used, by no means recklessly, to help pay for the Civil War.[6] The word *greenback* continues to denote something deeply disreputable to this day. Few writers have come forward to tell of Chase's alternatives.[7] Nor were the Civil War results devastating. That a country could be torn apart, endure four years of terrible conflict and experience a mere doubling of prices in the process was, at least by modern standards, something of a miracle.

The resort by the Confederacy to paper money was, needless to say, even more vigorously condemned. The most eminent of the American historians of his time observed without surprise that "Northern writers of an economic turn of mind have oftentimes attributed the collapse of the Confederacy to its paper money, over-issues of bonds, and the impressment."[8] Even in our own day a

5. Davis Rich Dewey, *Financial History of the United States,* 10th edition (New York: Longmans, Green, 1928), p. 43.

6. An action of less than impeccable constitutional probity. The Constitution, reflecting the reaction to colonial excess and revolutionary need, had forbidden the issue of paper money by the states and also, alas, by the federal government.

7. An exception should be made for the distinguished economic historian Chester Whitney Wright, who, however, can hardly be said to exculpate the Greenbacks. "The outstanding mistakes in financing the war were the failure to tax promptly and vigorously, the use of paper money with all its attendant evils." *Economic History of the United States,* 2nd edition (New York: McGraw-Hill, 1949), p. 443.

8. Edward Channing, *A History of the United States* (New York: Macmillan, 1925), Vol. 6, p. 411. I have dealt with these attitudes at more length in "The Moving Finger Sticks," in *The Liberal Hour* (Boston: Houghton Mifflin, 1960), pp. 79–92.

recurrent warning is issued against the financing of the public deficit "by the printing of money." In all this we see again how deeply rooted in history are present-day attitudes and expression.

As civilization proceeded south and west in the United States in the early decades of independence, the settlers in what were to become the border states and the Middle West were, as noted, enthusiastically devoted to the creation of banks and by them of money. The loans so made and the money so created put farmers into production and merchants into trade. Such banks the states could charter and amply available private initiative could supply. In response to this demand, every location large enough to have "a church, a tavern, or a blacksmith shop was deemed a suitable place for setting up a bank."[9] "Other corporations and tradesmen issued 'currency.' Even barbers and bartenders competed with the banks in this respect. . . . Nearly every citizen regarded it his constitutional right to issue money."[10] These relaxed attitudes, as might be expected, collided violently with conservative belief and interest. Money, it was now evident, had a dual personality, and the two parts were in violent conflict.

The focus of the struggle soon became the two institutions called the Bank of the United States, the First in existence from 1791 to 1811, the Second from 1816 to 1836. These were privileged competitors of the casually created state banks; they were also the financial agents of the federal government and the fortunate holders of its deposits. But, more important, as agents of the conservative eastern establishment they were the highly unwelcome disciplinarians of the state-chartered banks. They accepted the notes only of those smaller banks which redeemed them in specie. On receipt of the notes, the Bank of the United States then insouciantly returned them for redemption, the very redemption that

9. Norman Angell, *The Story of Money* (New York: Frederick A. Stokes, 1929), p. 279.

10. A. Barton Hepburn, *A History of Currency in the United States* (New York: Macmillan, 1915), p. 102.

the creators of money traditionally hope and intend to avoid, at least partially. Accordingly, and not surprisingly, the existence of the two banks became the major political issue of the time. And as population and the weight of political power moved westward, the opposition to them increased. With the election of Andrew Jackson in 1828, a President strongly faithful to the western scene, their fate was sealed. Limited war would continue between the President and Nicholas Biddle, the head of the Second Bank, but the political opposition to the banks, reinforced by the objections of some lax eastern bankers who also found the discipline inconvenient, was decisive. And the suspicion of such institutions would remain. Not for another eighty years would political opinion in the United States allow of a third try at establishing a disciplinary force, in this case the Federal Reserve System.

As noted, the era of free banking and its relatively relaxed aftermath were strongly favorable to economic development. Farmers and small businessmen on the frontier got loans and acquired livestock, equipment and other capital that otherwise they would not have possessed had lending and money creation been under more severe constraint. But this the reputable classical thought has not conceded even to the present day. Free banking is considered a dark chapter in American economic history, and Andrew Jackson, whatever his other qualities, a financial aberration. Stemming from the period of free banking are modern attitudes on bank regulation. On other industries the hand of government is believed to rest with unnecessarily heavy weight, but banking, most agree, is a special case that requires sterner measures.

Two further precipitating factors shaped American attitudes on money in the last century; they were the Greenbacks and silver. Though the Civil War had brought the Greenbacks and the associated aura of monetary irresponsibility, it had also taken from Washington the financially relaxed statesmen from the South and the southern Mississippi Valley. So, during the war and after, the casual issue of bank notes was brought to an end. In the case of the state banks, such notes were made subject to punitive taxation; note issue was allowed to new national banks only as it was covered with government bonds deposited firmly in the Treasury. Steps were then taken in 1866 to retire the Greenbacks in an orderly way — ten million in the first six months, thereafter at a rate of four million a month. Finally, in 1873, in a further and what seemed at the time innocuous action, the country returned to the gold standard. The coinage of silver, with a minor exception for the trade with the Orient, was also abandoned.

Silver had traditionally been scarce in relation to gold. For 23.22 grains of gold it had been possible to get a dollar at the mint; for the 371.25 grains of silver that it took to get a dollar at the mint, it had been possible to get more than a dollar by selling the metal to a private buyer. The accepted though not ancient ratio of 16 of silver to 1 of gold had been adverse to silver; now with silver's new abundance from the mines in the western United States, it was unduly favorable. Thus the elimination of silver from the monetary system. It was too abundant. In 1879, as a final step in returning American money to a solid footing, the remaining Greenbacks were made fully convertible into gold.

Meanwhile in these years prices, and particularly farm prices, were falling — from an index level of 162 in 1864 (1910–1914 equals 100) to 128 in 1869 to a withering 72 in 1879.[11] In consequence came a further and highly charged debate over the appropriate personality of money. The problem was no longer its use as a substitute for taxes or its creation by banks for the benefit of business and agriculture on the frontier; the controversy was over its role in raising or lowering the price level. (Some of the debate was occasioned, as eventually would be recognized, by the unique competitive vulnerability of farm prices.) This last controversy would be in many respects the most vigorous of all.

To the retirement of the Greenbacks and their convertibility into gold was attributed the decline in prices; more Greenbacks, it was

11. U.S. Bureau of the Census, *Historical Statistics of the United States, Colonial Times to 1970, Bicentennial Edition* (Washington, D.C., 1975), Part 2, p. 201.

held, would put prices back up. The Quantity Theory of Money had reached the American prairie and plains not as espoused by economists, not as taught in school, but as the result of practical instinct. In 1878, the Greenback Party, which opposed total withdrawal of the notes and urged that more be printed instead, polled more than a million votes in sixteen states and elected no fewer than fourteen congressmen. Never before in history had monetary policy brought forth such a political force. The expansion of the Greenback circulation sought by the Greenback Party was not conceded, but further withdrawal of the Greenbacks was halted and notes worth around a third of a billion dollars were left in circulation, where they remained until after World War II.

But this was only the beginning. Monetarism, which had created a political party, now went on to capture one — through William Jennings Bryan, the Democratic Party itself.

Because silver was now cheap and available, free coinage of it — to use the urgent slogan of the time — would add munificently, it was thought, to the money supply. More money in circulation would raise prices in general and farm prices in particular. Meanwhile debt and interest charges would remain as before; as compared with farm prices, the price of things purchased would rise less. So to the advocacy of the silver miners was added the far more powerful pleading of the farmers.

Heard for both was the voice — the *silver* tongue, no less — of William Jennings Bryan. Three centuries after silver had brought the price revolution of merchant capitalism, it was hoped that this metal would work the same wonder again. It is not on record whether Bryan or the other advocates of the free coinage of silver and the rescue of the nation from what was to become famous as the cross of gold had full knowledge of how much in the great current of monetary history they really were.

Silver was eventually purchased as a concession to the farmers and silver miners, but Bryan and his party were three times defeated in national elections. The combination of established economic interest and what was deemed to be sound economics triumphed again. And in the histories written of the time it still does: there William Jennings Bryan survives, as does Jackson, as an irresponsible, economically unacceptable figure, a vagrant voice speaking for the unknowing masses. It could be argued that no politician ever better represented the economic interest of his constituency.

The money wars of the last century in the United States were, as noted, fought without the benefit of economists or much academic commentary. The great struggles just described are not mentioned even now in histories of economic thought.

However, by the end of the century, as professional economists were making their way into American universities, they were being heard on the issues here under discussion. They did not march with William Jennings Bryan. For them, wise management of the political economy and sound gold-backed money were identical. No one who spoke well of Greenbacks or the free coinage of silver could be thought fit to teach the young. In these years President Charles Eliot of Harvard University was given a sum of money in the name of David A. Wells, an economic scholar of consequence in taxation and other matters in the latter half of the last century, to reward the author of an essay on political economy and to pay for its publication. The Wells Prize remains to this day a signal honor, with insignificant monetary reward, for authors of doctoral theses in economics at Harvard. When it was funded, specific directions were given that no award should go to any work favoring the depreciation of the currency. No one seems to have objected to what was thought so reasonable a stipulation.

In these same decades there was, however, the opening of what would later be a truly major breach in the classical orthodoxy — in the view that money, if not quite another commodity, was passive and certainly unmanaged in its role in facilitating exchange. A decisive step was the appointment in 1898 of Irving Fisher (1867–1947), then thirty-one years old, as professor of political economy at Yale. Besides being an economist, Fisher was a mathematician; the inventor of index numbers and of a card file system, which he sold remuneratively to Remington Rand; a pioneer econometrician, which is to say an early practitioner of the measurement of economic phenomena; a eugenicist; an ardent advocate of Prohibition, which he saw as a compelling design for enhancing labor productivity; and, not least, a personally disastrous stock market speculator. (In the autumn of 1929, he averred that stocks had achieved a new high plateau and, acting on this assumption, lost, it is said, between $8 and $10 million in net worth.)[12] There is no question that with Thorstein Veblen, who preceded him by a few years as a student at Yale, Irving Fisher was one of the two most interesting and original of American economists.

In 1911, in *The Purchasing Power of Money*,[13] Fisher published his deathless contribution to economic thought, his equation of exchange. He held that prices would vary with the volume of money in circulation, with due allowance for its velocity or rate of turnover and the number of transactions in which it served. In the equation, which, let it be emphasized, should discourage no one,

$$P = \frac{MV + M'V'}{T}$$

P is prices, M the amount of ordinary, hand-to-hand currency, V its velocity or rate of turnover, M' bank deposits subject to check (that is, in use as money in banks), V' the rate of turnover of these checking deposits and T the number of transactions or, roughly, the level of economic activity. Implicit here is the thought that the rate of the spending of money is more or less constant and that the volume of trade is relatively stable in the short run. So an increase or decrease in M or M', magnitudes subject presumably to public action and control, directly affects the level of prices.

No other mathematical formulation in economics, perhaps no other in history save that of Albert Einstein, has enjoyed a greater

12. Irving Norton Fisher, *My Father Irving Fisher* (New York: Comet Press, 1956), p. 264.
13. (New York: Macmillan.)

vogue, and this continues without diminution to our own time. With it and from Fisher himself came the seriously seditious thought that varying the supply of money in the equation of exchange while other things, specifically velocity and the volume of trade, remained the same could raise or lower the level of prices. Upward movements could be arrested by reducing the money supply; more urgently in Fisher's day, prices could be raised by increasing the money supply. With the equation of exchange, the theoretical apparatus of monetarism — the subject of the most intense economic debate of the 1970s and 1980s — was born.

This was a major, even awe-inspiring, step in the history of economics. Previously it had been the instinct of the community that the colonial monetary experiments, the Jacksonian note-issuing banks, the Greenbacks and the free coinage of silver had had an effect on prices. Now Fisher made that instinct respectable, if not yet quite official, and with it the thought that the state or some delegated authority should deliberately and forthrightly take responsibility for managing the money supply, thus regulating the price level. Later, in the early years of the Great Depression, Fisher and his disciples would be at the center of policy; they would urge and, in some measure, create a plan to arrest the punishing price deflation of the time.

With Fisher the long history of money is brought into the modern era. The equation of exchange is the basic frame for the highly influential advocacy of Professor Milton Friedman, of later note in this history. Take firm hold of the supply of money, allow it to increase only as T, the volume of trade, expands and prices will be stable — or in a few months will so become. In the years that followed, there would be a problem as to what in the modern world of banking really is money; savings deposits subject to check, the purchasing power back of credit cards, unused lines of credit, would all so function, along with hand-to-hand currency and checking deposits. And there would be a more serious question as to whether what was defined as money could, in fact, be controlled. Finally there would be concern as to whether an attempt to reduce or control the supply of money would, instead, have a powerfully adverse effect on T, more poignantly on industrial output and employment. But all these refinements came later; with Irving Fisher and the equation of exchange the lengthy preoccupation with money and particularly the powerful American preoccupation come fully into the present.

XIII

American Concerns

TRADE AND TRUSTS;
ENRICHED AND THE RICH

I N THE LAST CENTURY the United States, as has sufficiently
been said, was a world of improving land, life and well-being.
Civilization and population growth pressed cultivation not to
worse land but to better. The forested valleys of New England were
more fruitful than the hills to which the settlers had first repaired,
and so was the deep, black soil of Ohio, Indiana and beyond. Here
was an economy not of increasing misery but of manifest improvement; to this more optimistic world the economic dynamics of the
Old World did not apply.

One would expect that in so different a context there would be a
new and more hopeful economics, but, as we have seen, the more
exact truth is that through nearly all of this period there was not
very much formal American economic comment of any kind. Suitably inspired scholars have tried in a determined fashion to dis-
cover a uniquely American system, but little of a comprehensive
sort has been found. Again the point: the study of economics
responds well to visible misfortune and despair; success, self-
approval and satisfaction provide no similar inspiration.

There were other reasons for the lack of what might be considered truly American economic thought. The United States was,
at the time, a country of owner-operated farms. Holdings were of a

highly agreeable size; the 160 acres that had been accorded by the Homestead Acts of 1862, in keeping with the general estimate of what was adequate to support a family, were vast by European or, indeed, any other standard. And no other economic design has ever been viewed with such nearly universal approval by both participants and outside observers as the revered family farm. This social approval further reduced the need for economic discussion.

As, until the Civil War, did the plantation system and slavery in the South. Wages and wage costs were excluded from consideration because of slavery, as they had been in Aristotle's time, and, just as in ancient Greece, the fact of slavery greatly focused attention on such ethical and moral issues as emancipation rather than on economic ones.

While there was little concern in the United States for the central themes of classical economics or for the Marxian and other assaults thereon, there was an ardent discussion of a range of eminently practical economic topics. These included the tariff, monopoly, the social behavior and defense of the very rich and, most urgently of all, as the last chapter has told, the diverse questions pertaining to money.

Toward the end of the century universities established professorships in political economy, soon to be called economics, but their occupants largely confined themselves to taking over the current British orthodoxy. There were American textbooks, but they were derived, as a matter of course, from their English counterparts and were not wholly accepted. The American Economic Association, formed in 1885, was initially a protest against the highly conservative support accorded industrial capitalism by the accepted classical theory and the companion commitment to *laissez faire.* Over the century as a whole, as Professor Robert Dorfman has observed, every man was his own economist in the United States. Economics combined indiscriminately with politics, philosophy and also theology: "You shall not press down upon the brow of labor this crown of thorns. You shall not crucify mankind upon a cross of gold."[1] Only at the end of the century did two distinctively American economic figures emerge — Henry George and Thorstein Veblen. About these there will be more later. First we must look at the earlier preoccupations.

Next to banks and money and their proper character and control, the most ardently discussed economic subject over the whole of the nineteenth century was the tariff. The debate began with Alexander Hamilton's *Report on Manufactures*, "perhaps the most able presentation of the case for protection ever written."[2] In the debt of Adam Smith on many matters, Hamilton departed sharply from him on the virtues of free trade where the interest of a young country in competition with the industry of an older country such as Britain was concerned. In the next generation Henry Clay's advocacy of the American System, a euphemism for industrial development under tariff protection, added to the case. As did the voice of Henry Carey, who, as earlier mentioned, urged that manufacturing should be encouraged in balance with agriculture and that the infant industries of the United States, a greatly durable designation, should be protected.

These attitudes prevailed in the northern states, but the South was against a protectionist policy, for it wished to have its products go freely to Europe and to bring back inexpensive goods in return. Possibly also there was some instinct that advised the plantation owners that if factories were built in the slave states, slavery would not long survive. It is the singular and not always noticed feature of early industrial development that nowhere did it rely, in any consequential way, on slave labor. Slavery was an agricultural institution.

The other problem with tariff protection — one that calls for an engaging reflection in our own times — was the tendency for the

1. William Jennings Bryan, speech to the Democratic National Convention in Chicago, July 8, 1896, in *Speeches of William Jennings Bryan* (New York: Funk & Wagnalls, 1909), Vol. 1, p. 249.
2. Ernest Ludlow Bogart, *Economic History of the American People* (New York: Longmans, Green, 1930), p. 388.

tariff, then the principal source of public revenue, to produce embarrassing surpluses in the federal Treasury. In the quarter century following the War of 1812, such excess was endemic; in eighteen of the twenty-one years between 1815 and 1836, the budget was in surplus, and by the last year the federal debt had been wholly extinguished. The surplus from the tariffs was deemed an urgent problem, the critical question being whether to return funds to the states or to spend them, many thought unwisely or unconstitutionally, on internal improvements.[3] Short-term relief was provided fortuitously if not painlessly by the depression or recession, as it would now be called, of 1837, which, along with another recession twenty years later, sharply diminished customs revenues. Nonetheless, the problem of an excess in the Treasury was a persistent force against the tariff in those years, as, in milder measure, it was to be when, improbably, a surplus recurred in the 1880s.

At midcentury, however, the Civil War removed both of the major resistances to the tariff. The southern senators and representatives were no longer in Washington to offer opposition; the surplus revenues gave way to an urgent wartime need for money. For the next seventy years the pro-tariff forces would have things their own way. Expanding manufacture and the domestic production of minerals and materials would serve to increase their power, and the culmination of their efforts would come with the Smoot-Hawley Tariff Act of 1930, when tariffs would be in the range of 40 to 50 percent of import value.

There were eloquent economic rationalizations in support of this policy. The infant-industries argument gradually — very gradually — faded from use, as did Henry Carey's proposal to save transportation costs by local manufacture. Instead it was said that the American standard of living had to be protected; also, and urgently, that the wages of the American worker were endangered by low-cost imports, although it might be observed that no similar concern

3. See Catherine Ruggles Gerrish, "Public Finance and Fiscal Policy, 1789–1865," in *The Growth of the American Economy*, 2nd edition, edited by Harold F. Williamson (New York: Prentice-Hall, 1951), pp. 296–310.

had been voiced when these wages were being set or negotiated. "Scientific" tariff making now required that there be a careful equalization of American and foreign production costs. In fact, as came intuitively to be accepted, protection was a manifestation of industrial influence impelled by comparatively unclothed greed.

When, at the century's end, formal consideration of economic issues finally arrived, American economists, not surprisingly, addressed the question of protection more fully than any other; indeed, it became a major preoccupation. But whereas the prevailing economic interest spoke for high tariffs, the economists, exceptionally, took an adverse position. As already noted, the British classical orthodoxy and its case for liberal trade policy had come over the Atlantic in force and unimpaired; the leading American textbook of the time held that, with free trade, "goods are imported which were formerly made by protected industries. . . . The eventual result, says the free trader, is that more workmen will be turned to the advantageous industries, and more goods will be exported in exchange for more imports; there will be higher wages . . . resulting from the more productive direction of its labor.

"In all this reasoning, the free trader is right."[4]

As time passed, economic orthodoxy came also to prevail in the formulation of policy. In 1930, under the leadership of Clair Wilcox, a much beloved professor of economics at Swarthmore College, an ardent defender of liberal trade regulation and later a principal architect of the General Agreement on Trade and Tariffs (GATT), 1028 economists united in an unsuccessful plea to President Hoover to veto the Smoot-Hawley Tariff bill. In the ensuing years the Roosevelt administration, led on this matter by Secretary of State Cordell Hull, reversed the thrust to higher tariffs through the reciprocal trade agreements program. Henceforth the United States would surrender advantage as and to the extent that others

4. Frank W. Taussig, *Principles of Economics* (New York: Macmillan, 1911), Vol. I, p. 515. Professor Taussig of Harvard University was, by a wide margin, the most influential American teacher of economics in the early years of the century and from 1917 to 1919 chaired the newly formed United States Tariff Commission, with, however, no enduring effect on trade policy.

did. Thus began a thirty-five-year-and-more movement toward lower tariffs, a movement that found nearly unanimous support in American economic thought.

It also reflected a renewed unity of such thought with the dominant economic interest. American industry and agriculture in those decades — the 1930s through the 1960s — were, with exceptions, effectively competitive on world markets. And there had been a major institutional change: American transnational or multinational corporations that were engaged in moving materials, components and products between different plants and markets in different countries in search of the lowest production costs were now dominant, and they considered tariffs, in major measure, a nuisance.

However, it has been sufficiently established that nothing in economics is forever. In the 1970s and 1980s, the rise of Japanese, Korean and Taiwanese industrial competition has substantially weakened the American commitment to free or liberal trade. There has been a renewal of the call for protection — protection of now aged and ailing American industries from the younger industries abroad. And with this has come a partial and, as will be expected, predictable accommodation in economic thought. Economists of reputable view now stress the need for an industrial policy, a euphemism, as noted, for protection either by tariffs or quotas or by some form of subsidy to domestic industry. To these matters I will return in a later chapter.

While at the end of the last century the classical orthodoxy crossed the Atlantic, the Marxian response to it did not. There were, however, three other, very specific responses in the United States. These were a determined action against monopoly, the already discussed appropriation to American use of Social Darwinism and a highly specific attack by Henry George and Thorstein Veblen on those whom the system greatly enriched.

The strongest of these responses was to monopoly — in the American language, to the trusts. In the years following the Civil

War there had been a spectacular exfoliation of designs for control-ling competition, which was something strongly urged in principle but often deeply regretted in actual practice. The trusts included informal combinations; pools to which diverse producers surren-dered control over output and prices and then shared in the profits; trusts to which stockholders or owners of hitherto competing com-panies surrendered their stock and control; and holding compa-nies, a later development, by which formerly competing companies were brought under the common command of a superior company that held a majority stock interest or one sufficient for control.

These abridgments of competition could not be reconciled in any plausible way with classical theory, which, we have seen, judged monopoly to be a grave flaw while at the same time holding it to be exceptional. With monopoly, consumers had to pay not the optimal price at which marginal costs were just covered; they had to pay the higher price for the suboptimal output that maximized monopoly profits. So great in the 1870s and 1880s in the United States was the attention accorded the combination movement, as it came to be called, that monopoly, not competition, seemed almost the norm. The spectacular case was Standard Oil. Not only did the company bring about a major consolidation of previous competi-tors in 1879, but it did not hesitate to lower kerosene prices and take local losses to eliminate local unaffiliated firms. These gone, it then raised prices to recover its earlier losses. And it negotiated transportation terms exceptionally favorable to itself, one reward-ing feature being rebates not only on its own freight charges but on the oil carried for its competitors as well.

These aggressions against both the public and would-be compe-tition led to the passage of the Interstate Commerce Act of 1887, which sought to prohibit the more painful manifestations of com-bination and resulting price fixing as practiced by the railroads, and three years later to the immortal Sherman Act, which affirmed in legislation the common-law disapproval of monopoly and provided that "every contract, combination in the form of trust or other-wise, or conspiracy, in restraint of trade or commerce among the several States, or with foreign nations, is hereby declared to be illegal." Later came more specific regulation of the railroads and, under Woodrow Wilson, further and more specific strengthening of the antimonopoly laws by the Clayton Antitrust and the Federal Trade Commission Acts.

The Sherman Act and its supplements seized the interest and imagination of American economists as did no other legislation and held that interest for well on to a century. The reason is not in doubt: support of the classical system had therewith been united with a seemingly strong commitment to the public interest. And reform had been proposed, the relevance of which no friend of the classical system could deny and the need for which conservatives could not readily oppose.

The antitrust legislation also invited the support of consumers and even more of smaller businessmen and farmers — those who used the railroads or who suffered from the aggressions of the great combines.[5] The advocate of the antitrust law could see himself as protecting both the public interest and a substantial business interest as well. But, above all, he could see himself as a defender of the classical orthodoxy. The antitrust laws addressed the one conceded flaw in an otherwise perfect system. Friends and supporters of big business might prefer silence, but because of their beliefs they could not complain. Rarely has economic activism had such a secure and respectable base.

In the years following the passage of the Sherman Act, the major law cases affirming, controlling or limiting its enforcement — Trenton Potteries (1927), the breakup of the Standard Oil and Consolidated Tobacco trusts in 1911, the failed cases against United Shoe Machinery Company (1918) and U.S. Steel (1920) — became an integral part of economic instruction in the United States. The antitrust laws also became a major source of income to lawyers, and a modest revenue flowed through to economists when they testified from allegedly expert knowledge as to whether there was

5. On this see Joe S. Bain, "Industrial Concentration and Anti-trust Policy," in *The Growth of the American Economy*, pp. 616–630.

or was not, had or had not been, an exercise of monopoly power.[6] Antitrust enforcement acquired during this period the status of a general therapeutic in American economic thought. Any seemingly adverse exercise of economic power — prices asked too high, prices paid too low, output and employment too small — called for a resort to the antitrust laws. Having so urged, economists often felt themselves relieved of any further responsibility.

Faith in the efficacy of the antitrust laws managed to survive the increasingly visible fact that they seemed not to have much bearing on the concentration of economic activity. But apart from some pale reflections in Britain and Canada and some legislation in Germany and Japan inspired by American economists and antitrust lawyers after World War II,[7] the American commitment to antimonopoly policy was not emulated; it was unique. In spite of that commitment, there is no ground for thinking that economic development in the United States has been different from that in other parts of the world. Here as elsewhere the larger dynamic of industrial concentration has been unimpaired. Perhaps there has been less horizontal combination in the same line of business, more conglomerate association, than would otherwise have been the case. But the overall concentration in the United States — two thirds of industrial production in the largest one thousand or so corporations — has been similar to that in the other industrial countries. It is still said by some more than adequately romantic American economists that, by stern antitrust enforcement, this concentration could have been forestalled, an irrefutable expression of a durable faith.

Along with later developments in classical theory the idea of monopoly became generalized as the years passed: both small

6. At Princeton University in the early part of the present century, Frank A. Fetter, one of the most distinguished economists of his time, laid down the rule that any economist who testified for a private concern in an antitrust case should not be accorded academic promotion or tenure in his department.

7. A few of whom attributed some of the German and Japanese acquiescence in and even encouragement of aggressive behavior and the war to the influence of the cartels in Germany and the *zaibatsu* in Japan.

numbers in the market or oligopoly and special characteristics of a product or service that were original or endowed by advertising and salesmanship became forms of monopoly. This generalization, together with the concentration of production, made monopoly no longer the exception, perhaps in some degree the rule. An attack on it could thus be seen as an attack on the system, and not many would expect such an attack to succeed or wish that it might. The antitrust laws still exist; students still read of the evils of monopoly; the old enthusiasm has, however, dimmed. Of this, also, more later.

As the classical ideas came to the United States, so and even more spectacularly did one great theory in their defense. That was the already discussed Social Darwinism of Herbert Spencer. It came and was accepted and urged as, in some degree, a biblical revelation, with which its advocacy was regularly associated. A word must now be added on its peculiarly American form and on those associated with its American exegesis.

By showing that the rich were the naturally selected products of the Darwinian process, Herbert Spencer, it will be recalled, had relieved those so endowed of all sense of guilt and made them understand that they were, instead, the incarnation of their own biological excellence. And he had also removed all feelings of obligation and concern as regards the poor. However cruel their euthanasia, it served the higher purpose of human improvement as a whole. Among the influential American voices that spread his message was that of Henry Ward Beecher (1813–1887), a member of one of the most talented of American families in the last century and pastor in Brooklyn of one of the most affluent congregations in the Republic. Beecher, in a not uncharacteristic American union of economics, sociology and theology, bridged the seemingly unbridgeable chasm between Darwin, Spencer and evolution on the one hand and biblical orthodoxy as to man's origins on the other. This he accomplished by urging a distinction between theology and religion, the first being evolutionary by nature, the second,

God's word in Genesis, being immutable. It is not a distinction that anyone has since claimed to understand, but it allowed Darwin and therewith Spencer to enter American churchly precincts. And on one vital point Beecher was wholly clear: Spencer was simply giving a form of expression to divine will — "God intended the great to be great and the little to be little."

Previous mention has been made of Spencer's most famous American disciple, William Graham Sumner, professor of political and social science at Yale. Sumner had studied at Oxford and, as had others of his generation, in Germany.[8] Fully steeped in the larger British classical system, he was nonetheless known for his commitment to Social Darwinism. Sensing the political pressures and the compassion that would one day lead to the welfare state, he stood doggedly against both. The middle-class virtues of thrift, hard work and sound family life must be protected and rewarded. Those so exercising diligence and reaping reward owe nothing in the way of help to the racially or mentally ill-adapted, whom society is acting to inhibit and extrude.

Sumner did not think everything the state did in defense or promotion of social well-being was wrong; he was strongly in support of education and libraries as instruments of public enlightenment. But he opposed anything that subtracted from the income of the rich or preserved or uplifted the poor. Sumner was mentioned by Richard T. Ely, the leading figure in the founding of the American Economic Association, as the kind of economist he would not wish to see join.

In Europe the division between privilege and impoverishment was by classes; in the United States it was by individuals — the rich and self-reliant and below them the ragged fringe. There could be a Darwinian selection of individuals, a Darwinian euthanasia of the fringe, but not so obviously of an entire class. This was another reason for Spencer's peculiar appeal to Americans.

8. Where they sought out the great German historical scholars — Wilhelm Roscher (1817–1894); Bruno Hildebrand (1812–1878); the already mentioned Gustav Schmoller; Karl Knies (1821–1898); Hermann Schumacher, the father of the even more distinguished E. F. Schumacher of "Small is beautiful."

In time, nonetheless, enthusiasm for his views diminished; as the present century passed, a reference to Social Darwinism came to have, as I have already suggested, a note of distaste. But Sumner's case against the welfare state — that it was inconsistent with and destructive of the family virtues of thrift, self-help and the will to win — strongly survives. And the more general need to find formulae for getting the poor off the individual and public consciences continues in our time and remains one of the constants in social and economic history.

Spencer and his prophets were the supreme achievement in the defense of the great American rich in the years after the Civil War. Heard in criticism and attack on these views were such influential tracts as Edward Bellamy's *Looking Backward, 2000–1887* (1888) and Henry Demarest Lloyd's wonderfully titled *Wealth Against Commonwealth*, published in 1894. Interest in these great books has not, on the whole, survived. However, two works from this time have continuing significance. One, the bible of a small but articulate group of true believers, is Henry George's *Progress and Poverty*, published in 1879 and already mentioned in this history; the other, squeezing barely into the last century, is Thorstein Veblen's *The Theory of the Leisure Class*, published in 1899, which remains to this day one of the best-read American economic and social tracts.

In his time and even into the 1920s and 1930s, Henry George was the most widely read of American economic writers both at home and in Europe. He was, indeed, one of the most widely read of Americans.

He was born in Philadelphia, but his effective years were spent in San Francisco, where he pursued a financially perilous newspaper career and a uniformly unsuccessful political one. (Later, in New York, he did very nearly become mayor.) He was also an early but lasting demonstration of the fact that no journalist can ever be taken quite seriously as an economist. His *Progress and Poverty*, its continuing social influence notwithstanding, receives only passing mention or none at all in the standard works on the history of economic thought.

Henry George's principal idea, to which earlier reference has been made, centered on the accidental and unjust enrichment that came from the ownership of land and the further meaning this had for the financing of the modern state. From personal observation and from Ricardo, George had learned how an expanding population pressed out to ever more distant, if not necessarily poorer, land and the deprivation that accompanied that process. But from the vantage point of San Francisco, amidst the burgeoning population and economic life that followed the gold rush of 1849, he saw another aspect of Ricardian development in a much stronger light. That was the wonderfully lush enrichment of landowners as the frontier moved forward, the population increased and, as would now be said, economic development proceeded. The resulting contrast between wealth and misery he condemned as intolerable, the denial of anything that could be called progress: "So long as all the increased wealth which modern progress brings goes but to build up great fortunes, to increase luxury and make sharper the contrast between the House of Have and the House of Want, progress is not real and cannot be permanent."[9]

From this followed the remedy he prescribed and for which he became famous: it was to tax away the unearned gain in land values that did not derive from the effort or intelligence of the owner but came in effortless fashion from the general advance of population and industry. The revenues thus collected, George believed, would more than cover the expenses of the state; all other taxes would be redundant, unnecessary. Thus the name of his great reform, the Single Tax, and to it his devoted followers accorded their political advocacy and agitation.

There were several problems with his formulation, and they may perhaps account for some of the disdain of the professional economists. Increasing land values were far from being the only fortuitous

9. Henry George, *Progress and Poverty* (New York: Robert Schalkenbach Foundation, 1955), p. 10.

form of enrichment. Many others besides landowners, not excluding passive investors in all manner of industrial, transportation, communications and banking enterprises, were similarly enriched and had similarly a free ride. Why single out the owners of land as uniquely culpable? The view from California of rising land values had, one could feel and argue, carried Henry George away.

Nor should the return from the increased value of the land be confiscated after the fact. Had the United States or, better still, the colonies been blessed by Henry George from the beginning, perhaps a tax might have been possible, one that rose with increasing rents and revenues and thus kept land values constant as settlement and development proceeded. But to come later and by taxation reduce, even confiscate, the property values of those who had bought land as distinct from those who were investors in railroads, steel mills or other appreciated property was surely discriminatory. There was also solemn discussion and some calculation as to whether Henry George's tax would, indeed, pay all the costs of the modern state.

A final and most considerable difficulty went largely unmentioned: that was the very large number of landowners, rich and less rich, and their certain, strongly motivated and decisive political opposition.

Around Stockholm there is a perimeter of publicly owned land that denies to private owners the unearned increment of metropolitan growth. The London Greenbelt does the same, although it is privately owned. In 1901, Thomas L. Johnson was elected mayor of Cleveland on a Single Tax platform, and in 1933 Pittsburgh elected William McNair as a Single Tax mayor. Neither had a sufficient mandate to initiate the tax. A band of the faithful, a presence in New York and elsewhere, continues to promote the ideas and remedies of Henry George and keep his book in print. But now, like Spencer's, his beliefs can be found less in formal conscious thought than in the social subconscious. The real estate developer, encouraged by and encouraging an increase in land values, is, quite possibly, the least praised of American entrepreneurs. The real estate speculator is deemed inherently less reputable than the man or woman who profits from buying and selling stocks, bonds, commodities or options. The property tax, if not loved, is thought socially superior to the sales tax and possibly even to the income tax. In all these attitudes Americans continue under the distant influence of Henry George.

And there is a more specific legacy. With Canada and the Soviet Union, the United States shares a deep commitment to the public ownership of land — the public domain.

> This public domain . . . [Henry George said] has been the great fact that, since the days when the first settlements began to fringe the Atlantic Coast, has formed our national character and colored our national thought. . . . The general intelligence, the general comfort, the active invention, the power of adaptation and assimilation, the free, independent spirit, the energy and hopefulness that have marked our people, are not causes but results — they have sprung from unfenced land.[10]

An overstatement, no doubt, but one that, in both spirit and practical political effect, has kept American eyes on the still vast public estate and its protection. Socialism is not strongly avowed in the United States, but, thanks to Henry George, let no one question its virtue where the national parks, forests or public lands are concerned.

South from Minneapolis and St. Paul in Minnesota, the gently rolling landscape nurtures some of the best-endowed farms on the American continent, even in the world. One has a sense of a broad, rich stream flowing on to the horizon or, more precisely, to the Iowa border. Just south of the small city of Northfield are the 290 acres of deeply fertile land to which one Thomas Veblen came and on which, in 1868, he built with his own hands the house that

10. George, pp. 389–390.

stands to this day.[11] There his son Thorstein Veblen (1857–1929) spent his childhood — he had been born on an earlier Veblen farm in Manitowoc County in Wisconsin — and from there he went on to study at Carleton College, Johns Hopkins University and at Yale, where among his principal mentors was William Graham Sumner.

It is central to the Veblen myth that he was a poor farm boy, from his youth emotionally and intellectually at odds with the greater affluence of the world to which he was later exposed. In more somber fact, the Veblens were people of thrift but also of substance, as members of the family were angrily to affirm in later years, and Thomas Veblen certainly had no doubt as to his good fortune as compared with that of the people he left behind in Norway. The Veblen children's education was paid for by the farm, although, in a characteristic step, Thomas Veblen built a house on the edge of Northfield to shelter his offspring while they were attending Carleton, a sensible way of keeping down living costs. More probably, Thorstein Veblen's later writing derives its character — and animus — from the position of his ethnic group in the Minnesota community. The Norwegian farmers were responsible, diligent, economically effective but socially inferior to the local Anglo-Saxon establishment of the towns. Social inferiority can, on occasion, be accepted; intellectual superiority that goes unrecognized, as in the case of the Veblens, is a source of more acute resentment. It seems plausible that from this came Veblen's lifelong assault on those presuming to social excellence.

After Yale, where he wrote his doctoral thesis on Immanuel Kant for the philosophy department, and some years of unemployment and reading back in Northfield, he studied economics at Cornell and then went on to faculty positions at Chicago, Stanford and Missouri Universities, ending his career at the New School for Social Research in New York. An earlier generation of writers and critics have made much of Veblen's relaxed views on marital and sexual

11. Some well-motivated men and women at Carleton College in Northfield, where Thorstein Veblen was a student, have, with other Minnesotans, taken steps in these last years to rescue and preserve the Veblen homestead.

matters as the reason for some of his moves.[12] Those views would not now attract even passing comment.

To the history of economics Thorstein Veblen was to make many contributions of continuing influence, one or two of them of major importance.

Veblen established himself, first of all, as a critic of the classical system; this he did in a series of short papers published just before and just after the turn of the century.[13] In these he held that the central ideas of the classical system did not reflect a search for truth and reality; rather they were and are a celebration of approved belief. Any society has a system of thought founded not on what is actual but on what is agreeable and convenient to the influential interest. The carefully calculating, pleasure-maximizing economic man in classical economics is an artificial construct; human motivation is far more diverse. Economic theory is an exercise in "ceremonial adequacy," timeless, static in tendency and universally and continuously valid, as is religion, but economic life — a familiar point — is evolutionary. Economic institutions change; so does or should economic subject matter; there can be understanding only if one is in tune with change.

From the foregoing came a new, persistent and even obligatory skepticism as regards the classical system. To be too committed to these ideas was to be no longer in touch with truth, or rather, as Veblen put it, it was to accept an anthropological tendency to liturgical celebration. Such is classical theory. This irreverent, almost agnostic, mood came to characterize one not wholly negligible

12. A Harvard legend tells of Veblen's being invited to the university by President A. Lawrence Lowell to be considered for an appointment as a member of the department of economics. After being entertained by fellow economists, he had a last-night dinner with Lowell, who used the occasion to bring up, in a suitably careful way, Veblen's most noted academic drawback, which was then being much discussed.

"You know, Dr. Veblen, if you come here, some of our professors will be a little nervous about their wives."

To which Veblen is said to have replied "They need not worry; I have seen their wives."

There is, I believe, no truth to the story.

13. Collected and republished in *The Place of Science in Modern Civilisation* (New York: B. W. Huebsch, 1919).

branch of American economic thought. Accepted ideas were suspect; motives were meant to be questioned; public action, even from seemingly the best of intentions, should be viewed with skepticism. Thorstein Veblen was an avowedly destructive figure who rarely if ever descended to practical recommendation. The conscientiously critical attitude that lurks in some American economic comment to this day owes much to him.

A further Veblen contribution, one most effectively presented in *The Theory of Business Enterprise* (1904), identifies a powerful conflict in the modern business organization between the engineers and scientists — professionals of great skill and productive potential — and the profit-oriented businessmen. The businessmen, for good or ill, keep the talents and tendencies of the scientists and engineers under control and suppress them as necessary in order to maintain prices and maximize profits. From this view of the business firm, in turn, comes an obvious conclusion: somehow release those who are technically and imaginatively proficient from the restraints imposed by the business system and there will be unprecedented productivity and wealth in the economy.

A conflict between the engineers and the price system, to recapture one of Veblen's titles, might exist. Things might be invented or produced that could not profitably be sold. Nonetheless an arrangement for determining what part of this effort should be encouraged and what part suppressed was still necessary. This brought his engineers back either to reliance on the market or to subordination to some overriding authority, perhaps an engineer-dominated planning apparatus. The first meant no change; the second required a revolution. To neither solution was Veblen committed. As noted, he eschewed such practical questions.

For a time in the 1930s, however, a Veblenian political movement founded on these beliefs flourished under the leadership of Howard Scott. This was Technocracy, an economic and political design that would have given free rein to the productive energies of the engineers and other technicians while diminishing the importance of the business interests. It did not survive.[14]

Veblen's views on two possibly lesser matters also call for mention. One is his emphasis on the ordinary worker's or artisan's artistically motivated concern for the quality of his performance — "I take pride in my work." This is found in *The Instinct of Workmanship* (1914) and is something which, when once identified, is happily evident every day. Another is his wonderfully acid examination of the academic world in *The Higher Learning in America* (1918), a volume not uninfluenced by his own peripatetic experience and the evident desire of university administrators to have him teach somewhere else. American colleges and universities in his time were kept on a close rein by the business interests ruling through the boards of trustees. The views of teachers were closely examined for possible heresy, which was defined as anything opposed to perceived business need. This, Veblen strongly and very effectively assailed. Although matters have much changed, there is still an echo of these once dominant attitudes in the belief, continuing today, that the ultimate guidance of the academy must be by businessmen, now corporation executives, with a proper background in practical management. Professors, it is admitted, can be successful in public affairs; they should not be trusted with responsibility for the finances or other business aspects of the university.

The Instinct of Workmanship and *Higher Learning* still inform and also amuse. And on a final and vital matter Thorstein Veblen remains a uniquely resonant voice nearly a century after his most important book was published. That is his superb examination of the manners and motives of the rich in *The Theory of the Leisure Class*, which can be and is still being read with pleasure, intellectual reward and even delight. After doing so, no diligent reader ever again sees the economic world in quite the same way.

14. Although publications on the subject still emanate from Continental Headquarters, Technocracy, Inc., in Savannah, Ohio.

The subject of the book is the American rich, who in the 1880s and 1890s were the most ostentatious phenomenon on the American and, increasingly, the European social scenes. Americans in Paris or on the Riviera at that time were what the Golden Greeks, the Iranians and the Arabs in St. Moritz, Gstaad and Marbella were later, in passing sequence, to become.

Even before Veblen, the rich of the Gilded Age, to which they gave the name, had not gone without attack, as we have seen. They were vulnerable as probable monopolists, although well within the classical system. But such criticism they could endure, for they could still believe their good fortune to be the reward of unusual initiative or a reflection of the biological excellence accorded by Spencer. Envy was to be expected. So were political voices appealing compulsively and mindlessly to the masses, even the voice of Theodore Roosevelt in Provincetown, Massachusetts, in 1907, when he spoke of "malefactors of great wealth." What could not be endured was ridicule, and certainly not when it allowed impecunious intellectuals to feel socially superior to the man of means.

This ridicule Veblen accomplished in *The Theory of the Leisure Class,* the term "the leisure class" as he used it being synonymous with the rich. The tone of the book is rigorously scientific, rather more so than the method. The rich are an anthropological phenomenon; they are of a piece with the primitive tribes that Veblen describes and, on occasion, accommodates to his need, and they are so to be studied. "The institution of a leisure class is found in its best development at the higher stages of the barbarian culture,"[15] and the tribal rites of the latter have their counterpart in the dinners, dances and other entertainments at the great houses in New York and Newport. Both in Papua and on Fifth Avenue these are exercises in competitive display. "Costly entertainments, such as the potlatch or the ball, are peculiarly adapted to

15. Thorstein Veblen, *The Theory of the Leisure Class* (New York: The Modern Library, 1934), p. 1.

serve this end."[16] The tribal leader in both Papua and New York sets great store by the adornment of his women. In the one instance, breasts and bodies undergo painful tattooing and mutilation; in the other, the women are subject to the more or less equally painful constriction of corsets. However, the modern leisure class has moved on a little from its purely barbarian forms: "As the latter-day outcome of this evolution of an archaic institution, the wife, who was at the outset the drudge and chattel of the man, both in fact and in theory — the producer of goods for him to consume — has become the ceremonial consumer of goods which he produces."[17] On none of these matters does Veblen allow himself a word of criticism or regret; his only interest is the objective depiction of the evident, even obvious.

A superior example of Veblen's method is his analysis of the relation between dog and master. It is worth quoting at some length.

> The dog has advantages in the way of uselessness as well as in special gifts of temperament. He is often spoken of, in an eminent sense, as the friend of man, and his intelligence and fidelity are praised. The meaning of this is that the dog is man's servant and that he has the gift of an unquestioning subservience and a slave's quickness in guessing his master's mood. Coupled with these traits, which fit him well for the relation of status — and which must for the present purpose be set down as serviceable traits — the dog has some characteristics which are of a more equivocal aesthetic value. He is the filthiest of the domestic animals in his person and the nastiest in his habits. For this he makes up in a servile, fawning attitude towards his master, and a readiness to inflict damage and discomfort on all else. The dog, then, commends himself to our favour by affording play to our propensity for mastery, and as he is also an item of expense, and commonly serves no industrial purpose, he holds a well-assured place in men's regard as a thing

16. Veblen, p. 75. But celebrations were not the only source of high repute. "Drunkenness and the other pathological consequences of the free use of stimulants therefore tend in their turn to become honorific, as being a mark, at the second remove, of the superior status of those who are able to afford the indulgence." Veblen, p. 70.

17. Veblen, p. 83.

of good repute. The dog is at the same time associated in our imagination with the chase — a meritorious employment and an expression of the honourable predatory impulse.[18]

However, it was not alone through wonderfully contrived and adept argument and illustration that Veblen had his greatest effect. This was also achieved to an extraordinary degree through his use of the language, and through two phrases in particular, "conspicuous leisure" and "conspicuous consumption." Exemption from toil and thoughtfully ostentatious expenditure were for Veblen's rich the frequently flaunted badges of superiority: "The only practicable means of impressing one's pecuniary ability . . . is an unremitting demonstration of ability to pay."[19]

The two phrases, and especially "conspicuous consumption," have entered the American language and culture. They have affected the economic and social attitudes and behavior of countless thousands who have never heard of Thorstein Veblen. In consequence, leisure for the affluent in the United States, men certainly but even women, has come, in a favorite Veblenian phrase, "to lack repute." No one is spared the question "What do you do?" And, more specifically, no entertainment and no house, if sufficiently expensive or grand, is safe from the denigrating description "conspicuous consumption." Consumption had been the highest purpose of classical economic life, the supreme source of Bentham's "happiness," the ultimate justification of all its effort and toil. With Veblen it became in its fullest development a vacuous thing, a service to puerile personal aggrandizement. Is this what the economic system is really about?

One practical consequence of Veblen has been the change in contemporary attitudes toward architecture and the use of personal wealth. Income after taxes now exceeds anything known in Veblen's day, but it no longer builds great houses on Fifth Avenue or in Newport. The ostentation it sustains in Beverly Hills is adequate

18. Veblen, p. 141.
19. Veblen, p. 87.

but by no means the equal of that of the Gilded Age. The corporate jet and the lavish festivals associated with business conventions must now be under the functional protective cover of corporate service or need. Only rarely does wealth countenance the nonfunctional ceremonies and celebrations of earlier times.

There are, to be sure, other influences that repress the joyful expenditure of money: it is not thought politically wise that personal wealth be unduly flaunted; servants and other subordinates are no longer willingly available. But of unquestioned importance is the legacy of Veblen, with his amused smile at the barbarian culture and conspicuous consumption.

His influence is also evident in the contrast between social attitudes in the United States and those in Europe. The Riviera, Paris, Switzerland, were all spared the Veblen touch. There consumption at the highest level still remains reputable; there the American rich can still go for the unconstrained enjoyment of wealth and its associated display that are denied them at home because of the deft ridicule of Thorstein Veblen.

XIV

Completion and Criticism

A LL OVER the industrial world in the first decades of the
twentieth century the classical ideas could scarcely have
looked more secure. Marx was long gone from the scene;
his eloquent and politically more successful heir, Vladimir Ilyich
Ulyanov, known as Lenin (1870–1924), was still a distant figure,
at first in Russia, later in exile in Cracow, which was then in the
Hapsburg Empire.

Disturbing ideas would emanate from Lenin. One was that the
great industrial powers of Europe owed their economic success and
well-being to the imperial domains they had carved out or seized
in Africa, Asia and the Pacific. They, and notably also their workers, lived on the backs of the deprived masses of the colonial lands.
However, the economics of imperialism was not central to classical thought; it had not been a matter on which even the Mills,
father and son, had reflected strongly, although they lived, by way
of the East India Company, on the revenues of the India trade. Nor,
before Lenin, was it a compelling socialist concern; Marx had gone
so far as to say that the British in India were a progressive force.
However, it would eventually enter the political attitudes of leaders in the colonial lands, where, more than incidentally, it still
strongly remains. And in time it would become a part of the political consciousness of the liberal left in the industrial countries,
helping, along with declining economic interest, to motivate the

inevitable thrust to decolonization. This, however, was still in the future.

Coming also from Lenin, as earlier from Marx, was the notion that the working class of the industrial countries knew no fatherland. The state was the instrument — the executive committee — of the capitalist class. The workers had no allegiance to it and need not therefore be fodder for the guns of their oppressors in another war. As the threat of hostilities moved up on the horizon, this was, at least for some, a disturbing thought. It was also one that disappeared promptly on the outbreak of the First World War in 1914. The socialists in Germany, the most sophisticated, disciplined and politically influential in Europe, voted in the Reichstag for the war credits and, along with the proletarians of the other industrial countries, marched cheerfully to their own slaughter. The supranational commitment of the working class proved to be a shallow myth.

As to the classical tradition itself, the instruction of Alfred Marshall, in person at the University of Cambridge and widely through his *Principles of Economics*, was now above any challenge in England. And his influence directly or by way of such disciples as Frank W. Taussig (1859–1940) of Harvard was scarcely less in the United States. Prices adjusted to marginal costs; costs, including that of labor, adjusted downward as necessary to ensure the employment of available plant, materials and, above all, workers. Say's Law ruled. Demand was adequately sustained by what was paid out in wages, interest and profits; prices moved to accommodate to any interruption in the return flow of purchasing power.

Money was still seen in these years as a largely neutral intermediary that facilitated the exchange process. Much of it was paper; more was in the form of checking deposits, but these were interchangeable with gold. And the central bank, the most elegant example being the Bank of England, stood by to rein in any unduly liberal lending and deposit creation that might jeopardize the ability of the individual bank or banks in general to redeem their deposits in gold. If lending and resulting money creation seemed too liberal, government bonds from the portfolio of the central bank could be sold. This would have the effect of bringing the cash from the purchases into the central bank from the subordinate banks. The latter would then be forced to restrict their loans and perhaps to borrow from the central bank at what would, today at least, be only very slightly punitive rates. If money seemed insufficiently plentiful, interest rates too high, the whole process could be put in reverse.

The monetary and banking mechanism just described was, however, no longer only a British institution. In 1913, after nearly eighty years, it had become possible, as already indicated, to face down populist suspicion in the United States and establish a central bank, although the spirit of Andrew Jackson could not yet be ignored. Not one bank was created but twelve; these were scattered generously over the country with, as originally conceived, a rather minor coordinating committee in Washington. A thoughtfully decentralized central bank. The eastern financial establishment was still suspect on the prairie and the plains.

Almost immediately the Federal Reserve System and its guiding authorities were endowed with prestige and mystery in the economic world. Nothing so enhances a reputation for economic perception as association, however theoretical, with large sums of money. Appointment to the Federal Reserve Board, later the Board of Governors of the Federal Reserve System, was to bring marvels of personal transformation to some of the more intellectually absent participants on the American political scene. They would promptly be assumed to have the financial sophistication and insight that would win for their exquisitely conventional observations a respect verging on wonder. Economics would henceforth deal with the Federal Reserve System and its operations in equally respectful detail. Money and banking would become a course of study in its own right, much of it concerned with the highly synthetic mysteries of Federal Reserve policy.

*

Although Alfred Marshall ruled in these years, his system did receive two influential amendments, one just before the First World War, another some twenty years later. The first was from the previously mentioned Joseph A. Schumpeter (1883–1950), Austrian finance minister in the unrewarding postwar years, when he presided over the great inflation; successively professor at Czernovitz, Graz, Bonn and Harvard; and, by a wide margin, the most romantic and dramatic figure in economics in his time. In *The Theory of Economic Development*,[1] originally published in 1911, he added a major dimension to the Marshallian equilibrium. This came from the central figure of Schumpeter's system, the entrepreneur, also already discussed, who, aided by bank credit, challenges the established equilibrium with a new product, a new process or a new type of productive organization. The tendency then is to a new equilibrium — a new stability in what Schumpeter saw as a circular flow, production moving in one direction, money in the other. This new equilibrium would inevitably be disturbed and broken by the next innovator, the next change in the productive process. And so economic life would continue and enlarge; this is the nature of economic development.

The entrepreneur did — and still does — much for economics. He glows in the somber company of laborers, white-collar workers, solemn executives and assorted corporate bureaucrats. Unlike the capitalist, the entrepreneur carries no burden of Marxian guilt. His distinction, which continues with no slight nimbus to the present day, is the major legacy of Schumpeter.

Schumpeter also, though less successfully, attempted to take some of the curse off monopoly, which was redeemed in his view by innovation. Innovation, the contribution of the entrepreneur, was best financed, encouraged and rewarded when the innovator was

1. Translated by Redvers Opie (Cambridge: Harvard University Press, 1934). Schumpeter was also the author of two other important works, *Business Cycles* (New York: McGraw-Hill, 1939) and *History of Economic Analysis* (New York: Oxford University Press, 1954). The latter was edited by his widow, Elizabeth Boody Schumpeter, and published posthumously while still somewhat incomplete. I reviewed it on publication, and its general influence I gratefully acknowledge.

free from the threat of imitation and competition, and such freedom was most possible given monopoly. The competitive world,
by contrast, was, creatively, relatively sterile. This argument, however plausible, was not widely influential. The classical system was
too ingrained. Monopoly was wicked; it could not be redeemed.
The textbooks cite Schumpeter's case for monopoly, but it is not
seriously accepted.

Another view of monopoly, one that broadened it and made it a
potentially much larger part of the classical system, is, however,
accepted. This was the second amendment to the Marshallian system. Though long in the making, the relevant ideas were finally
and fully crystallized in 1933 in the work of two economists working separately, one in each of the two Cambridges. They were Edward
H. Chamberlin (1899–1967) of Harvard and Joan Robinson (1903–
1983) of the University of Cambridge.[2] Edward Chamberlin, a
somewhat tragic figure, remained rather exclusively with his
impressive contribution for the rest of his life, while Joan Robinson was for another fifty years a powerfully motivated critic of the
classical orthodoxy and a dominant — and formidable — presence
in the English-speaking academic world. She rarely looked at a
commonly applauded proposition in economics without taking
exception to it.

Chamberlin and Robinson both arrived at the thought that
between the general case of competition in the classical system,
where no producer influenced or controlled his price, and the
exceptional case of monopoly, where a single seller could so set his
price as to maximize return, there was an array of intermediate
possibilities. The seller might have a distinctive brand for which
there could be no exact substitute. This gave him a limited but not
necessarily insignificant ability to control his price. This freedom
he could enhance by advertising, thus deepening brand loyalty. The
location of his place of business, quite possibly even his personality,

2. See Edward H. Chamberlin, *The Theory of Monopolistic Competition* (Cambridge: Harvard University Press, 1933), and Joan Robinson, *The Economics of
Imperfect Competition* (London: Macmillan, 1933).

might also differentiate his product or service and accord him a similar measure of power, slight or not so slight, over what he was able to charge. All this was monopolistic competition, as it was denoted.

But more important as an intermediate case between pure competition and monopoly was that of small numbers of participants in the same industry. This was oligopoly, a term that promptly entered the language of economics. The American automobile industry with three major performers, and the petroleum, steel, chemical, rubber tire, machine tool and farm equipment industries with a few giants in each, were cases in point. The intelligent oligopolist — and intelligence had surely to be assumed — would, in setting his price, give thoughtful consideration to what would be most advantageous for all; so would the others in his industry. Subject to some minor adjustments, a price and profit would thus be arrived at that were not significantly different from those of monopoly. Alternatively, initiative might be left to one recognized leader, who would identify the most profitable price for all. Oligopoly, to repeat, would require intelligence and also restraint. It would not, however, need any of the direct communication so starkly forbidden in the United States by the antitrust laws.

In consequence of Chamberlin and Robinson, there was now, instead of the presumption of competition in a large sector of the modern, increasingly concentrated economy, the presumption of monopoly or something approximating monopoly. No longer could the socially optimal price and output of the competitive market be assumed.

The concept of oligopoly, and with lesser effect that of monopolistic competition, entered classical or, as it was now being termed, neoclassical thought with great, almost astonishing, celerity. They became fixtures in economic teaching and writing, and they so remain. Only the most determined of the defenders of the classical orthodoxy — for a time in the United States economists associated with what came to be called the Chicago School — resisted them.

Some scholars did see in oligopoly the case for a much more energetic enforcement of the antitrust laws. In the depression years there was also a significant current of thought that held oligopoly and its associated restraint on prices and output responsible for the all too evidently suboptimal performance of the economy. But there were practical problems in totally condemning it. The large modern corporate sector of the economic system where oligopoly ruled was the dominant sector, and, monopoly or not, one could not declare it illegal. Also, while oligopoly was, in principle, socially iniquitous, in actual performance — in supplying automobiles, rubber tires, gasoline, cigarettes, toothpaste, aspirin — it aroused no great consumer resentment. Wrong in principle, it was acceptable in practice. So economists came to view it with theoretical concern but to dismiss the necessity for practical action in dealing with it. Monopoly was still deplored; oligopoly was accepted. This remains the solution in the modern textbooks.[3] And for purposes of technical and mathematical exercise, the case of pure competition can still be assumed; the competitive market can still remain the central subject of instruction. What seemed to some a grave threat to the classical tradition — a general rule of monopoly or crypto-monopoly — has been survived.

Also influencing the history of economics in these years was the enormous, even traumatic, convulsion in Russia — the October Revolution of 1917. As earlier told, this was not the kind of revolt that socialists had envisaged, one led by the workers against capitalist power and exploitation.[4] As was to be the case later in simi-

3. See Paul A. Samuelson and William D. Nordhaus, *Economics*, 12th edition (New York: McGraw-Hill, 1985), pp. 541–542, and Campbell R. McConnell, *Economics*, 9th edition (New York: McGraw-Hill, 1984), pp. 532–534. These, the leading economics textbooks of the present day, both view oligopoly with reserve, seeing it as an obstacle to optimal output, but they retreat from any policy seriously adverse to it. Both derive a modest measure of comfort from the views of Joseph Schumpeter cited above and some of my own arguments as to technical advance under oligopoly and the tendency of any position of economic power to generate a neutralizing development of countervailing power.

4. Although, as we have seen, Marx did consider the sweeping away of ancient feudal remnants the first task of revolution.

lar uprisings in the Far East and Central America, the one in Russia was against an archaic and repressive agricultural system and a government that reflected that interest despotically as well as corruptly. Agriculture and landlords, not industry and capitalists, were the relevant precipitating causes of revolution in this century. And in Russia, as also later in China and Vietnam, the revolution was in large part successful because of the disorganization, disorientation and hardship brought on by war. Given peace, even the czars and their regime would have remained, at least for a time. It should be a matter for reflection by all conservatives that war is the one thing an economic system is least likely to survive. And there should be further thought that those who most earnestly portray themselves as conservative defenders of the *status quo* are the ones who are most disposed to accept the risks of war.

After 1917, the new fact in economics was the existence of an alternative: now, besides the classical system, there was also socialism. In 1919, Lincoln Steffens, a prolific commentator of his day on the abuse of economic power as well as the related issues of urban politics and corruption, returned from a visit to Russia to tell Bernard Baruch, in a carefully rehearsed outburst of spontaneity, "I have been over into the future, and it works."

In the bitter aftermath of war and revolution in Russia, Steffens's comment was, without doubt, a considerable exercise in exaggeration. Nonetheless, who could tell but that the new system might work? And in consequence of a truly monumental change. Private property for productive purposes (and much personal property as well) had ceased to exist in Russia; a chain that stretched back to Rome and Roman law had been broken. The market no longer decided what was produced; instead, a presumptively wise and concerned central authority would assess the needs of the people rationally and proceed to fill them. And men and women would no longer work in response to the unworthy prospect of pecuniary reward, the banal hope of self-enrichment; they would toil for the common good. A higher manifestation of the human spirit would be called upon and released.

Impressive difficulties were inherent in this vision. It would eventually become known that this superior manifestation of the human spirit might be lacking. Also, as was already evident to Lenin even in his short period of leadership, the bureaucratic structure that was needed to manage the process was heavy and could be inert and depressing, a problem that survives in the Soviet Union to this day. Further, it might be intellectually and administratively possible to plan and guide production in an economy where food, clothing and shelter were the primary and near total needs of the people, the special problems agriculture poses for socialism apart; but such planning would prove far more difficult for a society with a rising and increasingly diverse standard of living. And there would be Josef Vissarionovich Stalin, whose exercise of power would place a worldwide blight on the very word *socialism* — or *communism* — and who would, in the end, be repudiated by the people and system he had governed and oppressed.

But all this was in the future. At the time of the Russian Revolution, and especially with the arrival in America and Europe of the Great Depression thirteen years later, the new Soviet alternative seemed plausible, even a pillar of hope. It was especially so for economists.

In England at the University of Cambridge, Maurice Dobb (1900–1976) of Trinity College, much of whose teaching was adamantly Marshallian, formed a lifelong affiliation with the British Communist Party. And John Strachey (1901–1963), an influential figure from outside the academic community, heralded the coming revolution in a series of widely read volumes, most notably *The Coming Struggle for Power*.[5] In the United States there was no senior economic scholar of great note who joined the cause, but younger economists, especially in the 1930s, did. The Soviet example was the obvious and available alternative to the miseries of the Great Depression — to the palpable failure of the capitalist system. An

5. (New York: Covici Friede, 1933.)

economist should come to terms with the obvious. For a time doing so also ensured social and intellectual respectability in the contemporary academic, New York or other intellectual environment. For some, however, it was to mean grave trouble in the great Red hunts of the 1950s.

There would be a further effect of the Russian Revolution on economic attitudes and policy. The downfall of Imperial Russia was the warning that revolution could occur. Henceforth in the established economic world there would, in consequence, be a sharp and at times grim and angry cleavage. Some would see modification and reform of the classical system, the correction of its more obvious flaws, the tempering of its more evident cruelties, as a step *away from* revolution. Better that old-age pensions, unemployment compensation, support to trade unions, a minimum wage and much more be provided. Standing against this view were those who saw such reforms as a step *toward* the Soviet reality, one long stride down the road to an allegedly similar serfdom. This conflict would continue a full seventy years, into our own time.

In the two decades after the climactic events of 1917–1918, there was another important Central and Eastern European influence on the modern history of economics, this one from Poland, Hungary, Austria and Romania. It was the migration from these countries, some to Britain and some to the United States, of the economists who were to take a considerable part in and, to some extent, dominate economic discussion in the English-speaking world in the years ahead. All were, at least partially, responding to the world they had left. Those who had experienced conservative repression, as in Poland or Hungary, were strongly critical of the classical orthodoxy. Those who had had experience of socialism, as in Austria between the wars, devoted themselves to a defense of the classical system.

From Poland came the two leading socialists of their time, both of whom would return home after the Second World War to serve and, in some measure, suffer the revolution there. Oskar Lange (1904–1965), a calm, gentle but determined scholar, came to the University of Michigan and then went on to the University of Chicago, the center of market orthodoxy but, as it happened, a not wholly inhospitable environment. It was central to Lange's thought that socialism could, at its best, replicate the theoretically perfect response to the exercise of consumer choice and the productive efficiency of a perfectly competitive system but without its monopoly, exploitation, recurrent unemployment or other flaw. Two of his distinguished colleagues at Chicago, Frank H. Knight (1885–1972) and Henry C. Simons (1889–1946), were the best-known American proponents of the classical orthodoxy at the time, Simons detailing in these years the stern public policy, including the strong antitrust enforcement, that would ensure the best working of the free, unmanaged market.[6] The notion that socialism could take the market as its model was in some measure an acceptable thought at the University of Chicago.

Michal Kalecki (1899–1970), unlike Lange a perpetually tense and angry figure, was a man of remarkably diverse and inventive mind, the acknowledged and frequently unacknowledged source of ideas for numerous of his colleagues and friends at the University of Cambridge and later in New York.[7]

Both Lange and Kalecki returned, as noted, to important positions in post–World War II Poland, Kalecki for a time to have charge of long-range planning, Lange eventually to be chairman of the Polish State Economic Council. Neither Lange during the Stalinist years of Bolesław Beirut nor Kalecki in later times found daily

6. In *A Positive Program for Laissez Faire.* Public Policy Pamphlet No. 15, edited by Harry D. Gideonse (Chicago: The University of Chicago Press, 1934).

7. None of his work decisively altered the main currents of economic thought, but many of his ideas, including the notion of increasing risk as a constraint on the size of the entrepreneurial firm, became revealing amendments to the central core of both orthodox and socialist thought. See his *Theory of Economic Dynamics* (New York: Rinehart, 1954).

existence to be without tension. Toward the end of his life, Lange told Paul M. Sweezy, the most noted American Marxist scholar, that during this period he did not retire for the night without speculating as to whether he might be arrested before the dawn.

To Britain from Hungary and from Nowosielitza near Czernovitz in Austria (later part of Romania) came the three scholars who would most strongly urge the reform of the capitalist system as an alternative to its self-destruction. They were Nicholas Kaldor, later Lord Kaldor (1908–1986); Thomas Balogh, later Lord Balogh (1905–1985); and, a rather more accommodating voice, Eric Roll (1907–   ), later Lord Roll of Ipsden. Kaldor and Balogh, both from Hungary, combined relentless attacks on the classical orthodoxy in the country of their adoption with active participation in, and support of, reform. Initially at the London School of Economics and for long a professor at the University of Cambridge, Kaldor was a leading participant in the preparation of the Beveridge Report, the great postwar design for the British welfare state. He was also, along with much else, a persistent advocate of progressive tax policy, including the taxation not of personal income but of personal expenditure — the expenditure tax — which has the effect of exempting savings and investment from levy. He urged it with special vigor on countries in the early stages of industrialization because they have a special need for savings and capital formation.

Thomas Balogh of Balliol College, Oxford, and an influential (and by conservatives strongly reviled) adviser of Labour governments, was a ruthless critic of the classical orthodoxy and, together with Kaldor, of the eventual fascination with monetarism. He was also a strong advocate of an incomes and prices policy instead of idle plant capacity and unemployment as a check on inflation. On the classical system he was adequately explicit: "The modern history of economic theory is a tale of evasions of reality."[8]

8. Thomas Balogh, *The Irrelevance of Conventional Economics* (London: Weidenfeld and Nicolson, 1982), p. 32.

The third of these figures, Eric Roll, has committed the largest part of his life to government service, with special attention to international economic policy. He had a central, perhaps the central, role in the negotiations leading to the Marshall Plan and Britain's entry into the Common Market. He has also been a trusted and influential participant under Labour governments in the movement away from classical rigor in economic policymaking.[9]

The Polish and Hungarian economists, as noted, were in retreat from the right-wing and crypto-fascist governments in their native countries in the years between the wars, and with dialectical precision they turned to the revolutionary or reformist left. During these same years, from postwar Austria and its socialist and working-class orientation came the profession's most committed exponents of the classical orthodoxy in its purest form. They were Ludwig von Mises (1880–1973), Friedrich A. von Hayek (1899–   ), the more pliable Fritz Machlup (1902–1983) and, a lesser figure, Gottfried Haberler (1900–   ).[10] All arrived eventually in the United States, some by way of Geneva or London, as had their fellow countryman Joseph Schumpeter by way of Bonn. All, but especially Mises and Hayek, were dogmatic in the view that any departure from classical orthodoxy was an irreversible step toward socialism. Socialism, if one considers the variety of human wants and the complexity of the capital and labor structure for satisfying them, is a theoretical (and practical) impossibility. And it is intrinsically in conflict with liberty. Unemployment compensation, old-age pensions and help to the poor lead to socialist repression and the resulting degrada-

9. And he wrote, among other books, including his memoirs, *A History of Economic Thought* (New York: Prentice-Hall, 1942). The frequent citations in these pages attest my indebtedness to this indispensable work.

10. Mention should also be made here of one distinguished Hungarian scholar, William J. Fellner (1905–1983) of Yale University, who was equally firm in the classical faith and who served on the Council of Economic Advisers under Presidents Nixon and Ford from 1973 to 1975.

tion of the human spirit. The capitalist system would not be saved by such reform; it would only be destroyed. And, in the Mises-Hayek view, it was on the way to being destroyed. There had to be no compromise with classical perfection. Monopoly, a preoccupation of the American economic mind, was a largely irrelevant thing, which did not justify the greater evil of government intervention, although some restraint might be called for in the case of the unions. Mises, the most ruthless of purists, even took occasion to condemn intervention with the drug traffic as an unwarranted interference with market forces and the associated freedom of the individual.[11] And when his colleagues in the orthodox faith gathered on Mt. Pelerin in Switzerland for discussion and mutual admiration, he was said, perhaps apocryphally, to have caused considerable dissent by suggesting that all national navies should be returned to private enterprise.

Austria, in the decades since World War II, has been a model of successful economic performance: prices have been relatively stable, the currency hard, employment full, social tranquillity great. Much has been attributed to a good welfare system, a balance between publicly and privately owned banks and other enterprise and the Austrian Social Market Policy, which, as the defense against inflation, calls for carefully negotiated wage and price restraint instead of harsh monetary and fiscal policy and unemployment. None of this, alas, would have been possible had the great figures of Austrian economics in the 1920s and 1930s remained in commanding influence in their fatherland.

The Central and Eastern European migrants to the West were by no means the sole source of the ideas supporting revolution, reform to forestall revolution and rigorous resistance to reform because it

11. See *Human Action: A Treatise on Economics* (New Haven: Yale University Press, 1949), pp. 728–729. Friedrich von Hayek's views are most fully expressed in his widely read tract of the time, *The Road to Serfdom* (Chicago: University of Chicago Press, 1944).

was a step toward revolution. But these distinguished scholars had a marked clarity of view and a truly notable vigor of expression. Certainly no one was more severe — or influential — in his criticism of classical orthodoxy and the need for ameliorating reform than Kaldor or Balogh. No one spoke for intransigent resistance to reform so powerfully as did Friedrich von Hayek — or on occasion still does as this is written.

XV

The Primal Force
of the Great Depression

A SINGULAR and significant feature of the classical system was the lack of a theory of depressions. Nor is this surprising, for, as we have seen, it excluded the relevant causes by its nature. The equilibrium to which the economy adjusted itself was one of full employment; that was the result to which movements in wages and prices inevitably led. And there was Say's Law. A depression, more than obviously, is a time when goods pile up for the want of buyers; workers, in consequence, remain idle because, with numerous goods in more than adequate supply and inventories replete, who needs to make more? But a want of buyers is a shortage of demand, and Say's Law specified in the clearest terms that this could not occur. Only the untutored and — a grim but frequent word — the crackpots believed otherwise. All reputable economists knew that from production comes at any time the flow of purchasing power that is by its nature sufficient to buy what is produced. In one way or another, that flow is spent — directly on consumers' goods or, if saved, then on investment in capital plant and working capital.

From all this there was a further obvious consequence: there could not be a remedy for a depression if depression had been ruled out by the theory. Physicians, even of the highest repute, do not have a treatment for an illness that cannot exist.

This is not to say that in the years before the Great Depression the business cycle was not studied. It was. But neither its study nor instruction about it was part of the central core of economic thought. It was a separate line of inquiry and teaching called Business Cycles — or just Cycles. And there was no agreement on the cause of business fluctuations. In one not wholly plausible argument they were attributed to sunspots operating either directly, if somewhat mystically, on the economy or indirectly through their effect on the weather and hence on agricultural production. Or they were brought about by other cycles in the weather. Or, more probably, the cause was the recurring speculative episodes of the previous century — periods of expansion based on easy borrowing from the unduly accommodating banks of the time, with the inevitable contraction when loans were called or when notes came for redemption in the hard money that was not there. Or there were waves of growth of different and immutable length and more than slightly mysterious origin. Finally, poor times were associated with astringency in the money supply and the associated deflation in prices, as after the adoption of the gold standard in 1873.

The most competent, indeed brilliant, study of the business cycle was by Wesley C. Mitchell (1874–1948), early of the University of California and for much more of his career at Columbia University and the National Bureau of Economic Research. A scholar with no confining classical ties, Mitchell concluded that every business cycle was a unique series of events and had a unique explanation because, as he said, it was the outgrowth of a preceding series of events likewise unique.[1] About sunspots or weather an economist could expect to do little in a remedial way. Or about financial crises recognized, as was the tendency, after the fact. And if, as Mitchell held, depressions were caused by different and disparate events, there could be no generally applicable design for their prevention or cure.

*

1. See Wesley C. Mitchell, *Business Cycles* (New York: National Bureau of Economic Research, 1927).

The consequence of the foregoing when the Great Depression struck after the stock market crash in October 1929 was that economists in the classical tradition, which is to say nearly all economists, stood aside. This was something to be waited out. Two of the leading figures of the time, Joseph Schumpeter, by now at Harvard, and Lionel Robbins of the London School of Economics, came forward to urge specifically that nothing be done. The depression must be allowed to run its course; this alone would effect its cure. The cause was an accumulating poison in the system; the resulting hardship was what extruded the poison and put the economy back on the way to health. Recovery, Joseph Schumpeter avowed, was something that always came by itself. And, he added, "this is not all: our analysis leads us to believe that recovery is sound only if it does come of itself."[2]

Through what remained of the presidency of Herbert Hoover, until March of 1933, the economic policy of the United States followed the classical design. Recovery was expected and compulsively predicted, so compulsively that the stock market tended to fall following official predictions, and a chairman of the Republican National Committee was led eventually to charge a Democratic plot in Wall Street. However political its auspices, such prediction was, to repeat, wholly grounded in classical theory; the full-employment equilibrium was an inherent feature of the system; it ruled, so recovery was inevitable. There was no need for action to advance the inevitable. Herbert Hoover, a maligned figure in economic history, was, in fact, in complete accord with the accepted economic ideas of his time.

With Franklin Roosevelt came at last major departures from the classical orthodoxy, although they were far from promised in his 1932 election campaign. The depression had three visible features. The first was the relentless deflation in prices, with its bankrupting effect on industry and agriculture. The second was unemploy-

2. Joseph A. Schumpeter, "Depressions," in *The Economics of the Recovery Program* (New York: Whittlesey House, McGraw-Hill, 1934), p. 20. Lionel Robbins commented similarly in *The Great Depression* (London: Macmillan, 1934).

ment. The third was the hardship depression brought for especially vulnerable groups — the old, the young, the ill and the ill-housed, along with the unemployed. The first broad line of Roosevelt's policy addressed the problem of prices; the second sought to aid the unemployed by providing them with jobs; and the third attempted to mitigate the hardships of the vulnerable. In this last line of policy was the genesis of the welfare state, which had come earlier to Europe and was now on its way in the United States. To the efforts at price enhancement, as inspired or viewed by economists, we come in this chapter. The direct attempts to provide employment may be passed over; seen as emergency measures, they did not greatly engage the attention of the profession. The emergent economics of welfare is taken up in the next chapter. Then attention will be turned abroad to Keynes and to the attack not on the manifest effects and hardships of depression but on the whole tendency to depression itself. But first a word on the participation of economists in the government, a matter now taken for granted but in the 1930s distinctly an innovation.

In Roosevelt's gubernatorial years a small group of scholars had rallied to his support. They were immediately denoted the Brains Trust (later the Brain Trust), the word *trust* still being highly evocative in the American language. According to the disposition of the speaker, the connotation could be appreciative, irreverent or adverse, but no presidential candidate of any moment would be without his coterie of such advisers in the future.[3]

Two members of the Roosevelt Brain Trust, Rexford Guy Tugwell (1891–1979) and Adolf A. Berle, Jr. (1895–1971), were figures

3. Not always with benign results. In April 1936, the Republican National Committee recruited an economic brain trust, on the Roosevelt model, that consisted, appropriately, of several of the most distinguished conservative — which is to say, rigorously classical — scholars of the day. There is a story, possibly improved in the telling, of one of them, Thomas Nixon Carver of Harvard. Unaware that on his appointment his words would, somewhat exceptionally, be noticed, he spoke publicly of the desirability of sterilizing all paupers in the United States so that they could not breed and perpetuate their kind. A pauper he defined as anyone earning less than $1800 a year, a category that then embraced around half of all the families in the country. The Republican brain trust was quietly but firmly set aside.

of particular distinction in economics. While a junior professor at Columbia University in the 1920s, Tugwell had persuaded a group of young economists of his acquaintance and generation to contribute to a volume that he planned to edit called *The Trend of Economics*.[4] He thought, and hoped, it would be "a sort of a manifesto of the younger generation," noting that it could be said of the contributors "that none of us has published a book of the traditional sort called *The Principles of Economics*."[5] A central point of emphasis in the book was the need for an examination of economic institutions — business firms, government, interest groups — and of "non-commercial" as well as pecuniary incentives. All these were to be seen as they occurred in the real world rather than as they were accommodated to the needs of classical economics. The book also urged the statistical measurement of economic phenomena, an inconvenience to which the classical system did not, in general, descend.

Tugwell's *Trends*, as it came to be called, was a pioneer document in a distinctive American economic tradition that derived from Veblen; it looked anthropologically on the accepted economics, and, being unconfined by classical rigor, it was open to pragmatic reform. Eventually such reform would be called institutional economics or institutionalism and its adherents the Institutional School.

Rex Tugwell, as universally he was known, was a key participant in the pre-election Brain Trust and later in the administration. With his academic credentials he was in an admirable position to persuade Roosevelt that he could break with the classical orthodoxy, no slight risk at the time.

The second economic figure in the Brain Trust was Adolf A. Berle, Jr., also of Columbia University. A lawyer, not an economist, by profession, he was, nonetheless, the author, along with Gardiner C. Means (1896–   ), a young Columbia economist, of an attack of major importance — and great potential influence — on the clas-

4. (New York: Alfred A. Knopf, 1924.)

5. Both quotations are from the Introduction to *The Trend of Economics*, p. ix.

sical system. That it was not immediately so recognized is attributable partly to the fact that Berle, as a lawyer, was not taken too seriously by the reputable economic establishment on a matter of major economic moment. Partly Berle and Means's work was simply too damaging to the classical system; better that it be ignored.

Their study, *The Modern Corporation and Private Property,*[6] was of the management and control of the modern large enterprise, and it told with compelling statistical force[7] of the current concentration in American industry: the two hundred largest nonbanking corporations were estimated to possess close to one half of the nonbanking corporate wealth of the country, almost one quarter of the total national wealth. And, an equally urgent point, in half of these firms, the stockholders had ceased to have any significant role. Power, for all practical purposes, had passed, and irretrievably, to the management, which was responsible, if at all, to a board of directors of its own selection.

Here was subversion indeed. Given this concentration, not competition but oligopoly was the norm. The trend thereto, as foreseen by Marx, had obviously been proceeding in a relentless fashion. But there was worse yet to conclude. Not Marx's capitalists but the professional managers were now extensively in control. There now existed power without property.[8] The corporate bureaucrat, not the greatly celebrated entrepreneur. Bureaucracy, not entrepreneurship. All this being true, would the managers maximize revenues for the owners they did not know, or would they maximize revenues for themselves? Or, perhaps, would they have other and conflicting goals; would they encourage the size of the enterprise, the objective that most enhanced their own prestige and power, not profits for the unknown stockholders? Dismaying questions. In the

6. (New York: Macmillan, 1932.)

7. Although their work as a whole was not immediately criticized, there *were* strenuous attempts to undermine their statistical evidence. The leadership in this effort was assumed by a Harvard statistician, W. Leonard Crum, who, on meeting his colleagues over a period of some months, always told of new flaws he had found in the Berle and Means calculations.

8. The title of a later book by Adolf A. Berle, Jr. (New York: Harcourt, Brace, 1959).

imperfect or monopolistic competition of Joan Robinson and Edward Chamberlin, the capitalist or entrepreneur still ruled and profits were still maximized — or such was the effort. The results were not socially optimal, but they could be accommodated to classical thought. The views of Berle and Means could not. The best solution, accordingly, was to ignore them, and this in very considerable measure was done.[9]

Following Roosevelt's election to the presidency, Berle, though soon to be an influential figure in Washington, did not immediately take a government post. Tugwell did, as did Gardiner Means, of whom a later word. They and other later arrivals would pioneer the role of economists in American public life. The response was not one of great enthusiasm: cartoonists of the time would celebrate their presence in the nation's capital by making an academically robed figure of highly undignified aspect a symbol of the New Deal.

The most ardently debated intervention by economists in the first year of the first Roosevelt administration was not, however, a gift of the original Brain Trust; it had different sponsors and, in the oldest of American traditions, centered on money.

By the time Roosevelt came to office in March of 1933, prices, industrial and especially agricultural, had been in a devastating three-year slump. And from across the country had come Bryanesque appeals for monetary action to reverse the trend — pleas for the abandonment of the gold standard, for recourse to a new issue of Greenbacks (which was authorized but not compelled by the Agricultural Adjustment Act of the early days of the new administration) and for the remonetarization of silver. Nor were the demands confined to the farmers and the West, the traditional sources of soft-money agitation; respectable businessmen, even some bankers, joined in the cry.

9. To some extent Berle is still ignored. In the index of *Economics*, 9th edition, by Campbell R. McConnell (New York: McGraw-Hill, 1984), his name does not even appear. In *Economics*, 12th edition (New York: McGraw-Hill, 1985), however, Paul A. Samuelson and William D. Nordhaus do acknowledge appropriately the influence of Berle and Means's "classic study."

In 1921, Irving Fisher, with the support of Wesley C. Mitchell and other dissonant economists, along with future Secretary of Agriculture and Vice President Henry A. Wallace and John G. Winant, later governor of New Hampshire and ambassador to the Court of St. James's, had formed the Stable Money Association. It was devoted to the proposition that the supply of money in Fisher's equation of exchange should be so increased or decreased as to give a stable price level — this, instead of the instability, especially the seemingly deflationary tendencies, of the gold standard. Now in early 1933, there emerged the formidably named Committee for the Nation to Rebuild Prices and Purchasing Power, with Fisher as one of its advisers. It was headed by Frank A. Vanderlip, the former president of the National City Bank, and it included among its members the heads of Sears, Roebuck, Remington Rand and the Gannett newspapers. Managed money, monetarism no less, had penetrated, even if it had far from captured, the high corporate establishment.

In the first days of the New Deal, Roosevelt ordered the suspension of gold payments by the banks and forbade the hoarding, which is to say the private possession, of gold. Not only was the gold standard thus suspended but also the holding of gold in anticipation of its appreciation in dollars. Though commodity prices stirred upward briefly in the summer of 1933, there was nothing in the President's action that added appreciably to purchasing power and demand. And the new administration, in a companion exercise in orthodoxy, initiated substantial cuts in government wages and other expenditures as a more than symbolic display of fiscal conservatism. In the late summer and early autumn, prices, especially those of farm products, sagged miserably again, and the monetarists came to the rescue.

At Cornell University, not in the then adequately classical economics department but on a hill above the lovely campus in the College of Agriculture, were two agricultural economists, George F. Warren (1874–1938) and Frank A. Pearson (1887–1946), who were professionally concerned with the punishing effect of the price deflation on farmers. They had charted the relationship between commodity prices and the price of gold over many decades. When the price of gold rose, so did the price of commodities, a not wholly surprising correlation. When the Continental currency and the Greenbacks had been issued to help finance the Revolution and the Civil War, commodity prices had risen. And as the purchasing power of the dollar had therewith declined, it had declined signally in its ability to buy gold — which is to say, the price of gold had gone up. From this and less dramatic evidence came the Warren proposal: raise the price the Treasury would pay for gold, and prices, farm prices being of particular concern, would rise.

In his proposal Warren had the support of Irving Fisher and one of his influential Yale colleagues, James Harvey Rogers, both of whom, however, were thought by their fellow economists to take a somewhat more sophisticated, if still dangerously erroneous, view of the matter. In the autumn of 1933, to the applause of the disciples of Bryan and the Committee for the Nation, the administration began to offer progressively higher prices for gold that was brought to the Treasury to be traded into dollars. This was metal that had been newly mined; privately possessed gold, as noted, had already been turned in.

Herewith the major flaw in the design. Had people been allowed to retain their gold in the first instance, they would have been able to realize a windfall gain in dollars when they turned it in. Perhaps — no one knows — the consequent spending would have boosted prices. But the gold having been sequestered, this could not occur, and now those who had neglected, however thoughtlessly, to surrender their hoard could not even confess their default by converting it and spending the proceeds. The dollar fell on the foreign exchanges as foreign currencies, which were still on the gold standard and exchangeable for gold, now bought more dollars — a depreciation of the dollar. From the cheaper American money came, presumptively, some improvement in exports. But this effect was slight in a country heavily committed to its own markets.

What was not slight was the reaction of the economics profession — as also that of the reputable financial community. Their response was not to the evident ineffectiveness of the policy; it was to its seemingly reckless impairment of the principle of a solidly grounded currency exchangeable into gold, which was above and secure from any government manipulation. Far better the deflation than such foolhardy disregard of sound classical principles.

The most famous monetary authority of the time was an exceptionally amiable Princeton professor, Edwin W. Kemmerer (1875–1945). His monetary expertise had been achieved during his leadership of missions to countries as diverse as the Central American republics and Poland to put their currencies in order. His therapy had consisted in arranging a loan for them with New York banks, the proceeds of which, in gold, would return the debauched currency of the unfortunate country to the gold standard. On occasion the currency would be given a new name for some theoretically beloved figure in the nation's past. The Kemmerer achievement would be richly hailed; it would only be well after his return to Princeton that the country in question would, in the frequent case, slip again off gold.

Now Professor Kemmerer turned his attention to the gold standard in his own country. The Economists' National Committee on Monetary Policy was established under his leadership. It united all sound classical opinion in opposition to what had come to be called the Warren Plan. There was strong support from the press and the financial community for the National Committee, and its opposition to the Warren Plan was encouraged and enhanced by the well-publicized protest and resignation of three high Treasury officials — Dean Acheson, later Secretary of State, James Warburg, a liberal figure from Wall Street who was eventually to repudiate his highly exceptional descent into orthodoxy, and O. M. W. Sprague, a Harvard professor who had a reputation as a major authority in financial matters. It was also repeatedly pointed out that Professor Warren was an *agricultural* economist. This was a greatly and, many believed, rightly denigrated part of the economics profession — a matter also for later comment — and it was not deemed fitting that any policy having to do with money should be authored by an agricultural — or, as commonly then called, a farm — economist.

In January 1934, in consequence in no small part of the reputable and professional pressure but also almost certainly reflecting the evident lack of effect of the gold-buying policy on prices, the Warren Plan was abandoned. The price of gold, up from the long-established level of $20.67 an ounce, was stabilized at $35 an ounce, where it remained for slightly more than a third of a century.

The modern student will ask, all but automatically, why this policy was centered on the price of gold. Why not, once gold payments had been suspended for domestic purposes, a strongly liberal policy emanating from the Federal Reserve System? Let the borrowing rate — the rediscount, later the discount, rate — at the Federal Reserve be low; let the Reserve banks buy government securities and expand the reserves of the commercial banks; let the commercial banks lend freely and, through the consequent deposit expansion, increase the supply of money.

All this had, in fact, been done. Interest rates were lowered during the later Hoover years to, by modern standards, nominal levels; by 1931, the New York Federal Reserve Bank's rediscount rate, which had been 6 percent before the crash, had been reduced by 0.5 percent steps to 1.5 percent. Many banks were replete with cash; one of the common tabulations of the time was of the excess reserves in the commercial banks that were available to support lending. There was no appreciable effect. The banks emerging from the great banking crisis of the early 1930s, which had closed all their doors on the day of Roosevelt's Inaugural, were in a mood of unexampled caution, more precisely fear and even panic. And borrowers struggling against low prices and, in the case of the citizenry at large, to make ends meet did not come to them to borrow.

To the stock of economic metaphors, a prodigious accumulation that is still growing, was now added one involving a string: you can, as by pulling on a string, diminish the volume of bank lending by austere central bank policy and thus arrest an increase in the supply of money or effect a reduction. You cannot, as by shoving on a string, increase bank lending and the money supply.

This asymmetry in monetary and banking policy would be important for Keynes in the coming years. It was now evident that it was within the scope of government power to expand demand by the borrowing and spending of government funds; it was not within its scope to get an ensured increase in demand from easing interest rates and expanding bank lending. So public spending to stimulate demand became the answer to the ineffectiveness of monetary policy during the depression.

Meanwhile depression and price deflation had led to two other and more spectacular efforts to raise prices, one by direct action and the other by limiting supply.

The direct action to raise prices, principally industrial prices, was through the National Recovery Act — the NRA and its richly symbolic Blue Eagle. Sellers were brought together to agree on minimum prices. As a *quid pro quo* they were required to allow labor to do likewise — to bargain collectively and in good faith. There was something distinctly plausible about this effort. A high measure of industrial concentration had been achieved, as Berle and Means had shown, and there were, in consequence, a manageable number of firms in most industries to assemble and to agree. Oligopoly, not competition, was now the industrial norm. So situated, each individual firm could strongly influence its own prices; and, in particular, by pressing down its wages, it could operate profitably or with less loss at lower prices and thus gain at least a temporary advantage over the other firms in the industry. The others would then respond. From this process would come a competitive downward spiral of wages and prices, the counterpart in all respects of the upward spiral that would someday be recognized, albeit with reluctance, as a new and powerful form of inflation. By agreement the firms joining in an NRA code acted to arrest the downward spiral.

This view of matters was not, however, accepted. No such economic justification was accorded the NRA by economists. Instead they saw it as the most formidable assault on the classical system ever designed. Market competition to reduce prices was proclaimed by the NRA to be bad — against the public interest — and monopoly, the great and conceded flaw in the classical system, was proclaimed acceptable, something the NRA codes sought to create. As a further and not negligible step, the antitrust laws, long seen as the single great support needed from government for the classical system, were set aside. What, indeed, of the classical system was left?

There was no organized attack by economists on the NRA such as the one on the gold-purchase program; as always, money and its impairment induced a greater liturgical response. A few economists — it was a time when employment was much needed — served the NRA; it was at least permissible to be in the office created to speak for the interests of the consumer. For the profession as a whole the NRA was a symbol of egregious public error, as it so remains in histories of the time.

On May 27, 1935, the Supreme Court invalidated the code-making provisions of the National Recovery Act, thus bringing the experiment to an abrupt end; it is not beyond belief that the adverse view of the economists was, in some sense, a supporting brief in the case.

In recent times the NRA and its context have had, as just noted, a mirror-image sequel. Wage and price interaction — wages pressing up prices, prices pulling up wages — has been seen as a plausible cause of inflation. Government intervention to arrest the spiral — wage and price controls, more amiably a wage and price policy — has become an issue, and the classical response that operated so strongly against the NRA has once more been in influential opposition. Again the past as a harbinger of the present.

The second major effort at price enhancement was equally an attack on the classical faith, and it occurred in agriculture, not in industry. There, competition ruled in a reasonably faithful replica of the classical model; thousands, even millions, of producers accommodated to prices that no one of them controlled or dreamed of influencing. There was no visible unemployment in agriculture; the return to labor did, plausibly, adjust down to a marginal return.[10] This return the worker — the independent farmer, sharecropper, hired farm hand — had to accept. No economist in the classical tradition could look on this model without approval. But even in the 1920s it had been a source of grave discontent to the participants; in the early 1930s it became economically, socially and politically unendurable.

The Hoover administration was forced to act. Through the encouragement of cooperatives by a special fund and body that had been set up for the purpose, the Federal Farm Board, it hoped to give farmers some of the control over their prices that was commonplace in the industrial sector. It was an idle hope; except for a limited range of products — oranges, raisins and peaches being prominent examples — the organization required was too great. By 1933, it had become inescapably necessary to do something to mitigate the distress in this idyllically acceptable sector of the system. Its prices, as Gardiner C. Means, now an adviser in Washington, was intent on showing, had been far more vulnerable to the deflation of the depression than those of industry.[11]

The rescue operation was, in overwhelming measure, led by economists, but by a theoretically and ideologically uncommitted branch of the profession. Beginning in the last century, the United

10. The agricultural work force grew during the depression as workers discarded by industry sought survival on the farms.

11. *Industrial Prices and Their Relative Inflexibility*, Senate Document 13, 74th Congress, 1st Session (Washington, D.C.: 1935).

States government and the states, through the land-grant colleges and universities, had been supporting agricultural experiment and education. A share of their support had gone to research and instruction in the general economics of agriculture and the operation of the individual farm business. In the United States Department of Agriculture in Washington there was a large and intellectually active center of such research in the highly regarded Bureau of Agricultural Economics.

Its examination of farm price behavior, agricultural credit sources and use, farm cooperatives, farm markets and marketing and farm management was highly pragmatic; funds from legislators could not be wholly assured were it otherwise. And the farm economists were in close communication with other agricultural specialists and their farm clients, who pressed them for answers as to how farm revenues and operations might be improved. So occupied, they had little commitment to the classical system of which many were only distantly aware; instead, from the 1920s on, their principal concern was with the economic problems — particularly the low prices — of the farmers. Various scholars — John D. Black, formerly of the University of Minnesota and by then a professor at Harvard; M. L. Wilson of the University of Montana; Howard R. Tolley, the head of the Giannini Foundation of Agricultural Economics at the University of California; and others — began an intense discussion of remedial action, of means for raising prices. Perhaps this should be done by controlling agricultural production, perhaps by separating domestic farm prices from low world prices — instituting a two-price system. This latter would be accomplished by export subsidies — dumping — with domestic markets suitably protected by tariffs. Whichever means was chosen, the classical competitive design would be rejected. Government, not the market, would be a determining influence on farm prices.

With the arrival of the new administration in 1933, the agricultural economists also came to Washington. Under their aegis and under the nominal direction of long-time advocates of farm legislation, the Agricultural Adjustment Administration — the Triple A — was born. And born, more remarkably, was a policy of setting minimum prices or returns for the major agricultural products and, as necessary, limiting production and providing storage so as to achieve those prices. The policy would survive and would have its counterpart in all the industrial countries. The branch of the economy that conformed most closely to the classical ideal would no longer be left to perform according to classical principles.

The reaction to the agricultural heresy by the exponents of the accepted economic ideas was markedly less severe in the New Deal years than had been their organized response to the gold-buying monetarism and their more generalized objection to the NRA. Agriculture was a special case; the good professional economist did not pretend to understand its economic and political aberrations. Agricultural economists were a cult unto themselves. Thorstein Veblen had distinguished between esoteric and exoteric knowledge, the first being of high prestige but low practical effect and the second of low prestige but high practical use. The agricultural economists in the universities and colleges had long been regarded by their economist colleagues as rather sordidly exoteric. And this was true now of the policies they initiated.

The feeling that price and production controls in agriculture are systemically wrong has not quite evaporated. As late as the early 1980s, the Reagan administration at first accorded them what would quickly be recognized as rhetorical opposition, but very soon there was renewed intervention at previously unequaled cost. Professors Samuelson and Nordhaus in their textbook dismiss the policy with brief contempt: "A common government program is to raise the incomes of farmers by lowering agricultural production. . . . Because the demand for most foods and feeds is inelastic, crop restrictions raise [their] incomes. . . . Consumers, of course, pay through the snout."[12]

12. Samuelson and Nordhaus, p. 389. Perhaps as a consequence of his farm belt location — he is a professor at the University of Nebraska — Campbell McConnell deals rather more seriously and sympathetically with the policy. McConnell, pp. 634–638.

The policy is not one to be so dismissed. That the classical system in its purest form will not be tolerated by its participants is a highly significant fact of modern economic life. That it is not so tolerated in any of the industrial countries strongly affirms the point. Not in Japan, where agricultural prices are strongly protected; not, certainly, in the European Common Market, where farm prices command a major share of attention and money; not in allegedly free-enterprise Switzerland, where cows live on the mountain grass and their owners on the subsidy that the government provides. The point must again be urged: it is a major fact in the modern history of economics that the classical market system is not now tolerated where it occurs in its purest form.

XVI

The Birth of the Welfare State

ONE OF THE MOST significant responses to the Great Depression in the United States was the creation of what, in time, would be called, partly in approval, frequently in condemnation, the welfare state. It would be this which would most endure from the Roosevelt Revolution. But there can be no parochial American claim to its development; the United States was in many respects a late starter. For the contextual and intellectual sources of this significant change in economic life, one must go over to Europe and back a full half century. The welfare state was born in the Germany of Count Otto von Bismarck (1815–1898).

In the 1880s, social action in Germany was untroubled by the Ricardian and classical constraints on the role of the state. The German economists concerned themselves with history, and their work was not generally a source of grave warnings about the intrusions of government. In the Prussian and German tradition the state was competent, beneficent and highly prestigious. What was seen as the principal danger of the time was the active intelligence of the rapidly growing industrial working class and its well-perceived openness to revolutionary ideas, in particular to those emanating from their recently deceased countryman Karl Marx. In the clearest example of fear of revolution as an inducement to reform, Bismarck pressed for amelioration of the more stark cruelties of capitalism. In 1884 and 1887, after considerable controversy, legislation was passed in the Reichstag that provided in an elementary way for accident, sickness, old-age and disability insurance. Similar action followed, though in fragmentary fashion, in Austria, Hungary and elsewhere in Europe. Those who currently condemn the welfare state are in a great historical tradition; the debate over its worth and legitimacy is now almost exactly one hundred years old.

A more comprehensive and, in some ways, more influential step in this process came in Britain twenty-five years after Bismarck's great initiative. Here it was the result far less of the fear of revolution than of the conscientious and informed agitation of socially concerned men, women and organizations — Sidney and Beatrice Webb, H. G. Wells, George Bernard Shaw, the Fabian Society and the by then influential and articulate trade unions. Under the sponsorship of Lloyd George, the chancellor of the Exchequer, legislation was passed in 1911 that provided for sickness and invalidism insurance and then unemployment insurance. A non-contributory system of old-age pensions had previously been written into law, though without the requisite taxes to support it. The British provision for unemployment compensation went well beyond the German precedent, which Lloyd George had personally investigated; Germany did not, in fact, have unemployment insurance until 1927.

In close association with the accompanying taxation — for which provision had been made in the 1910 budget — the British social-welfare legislation provoked unprecedented political conflict and turmoil. This led to elections in 1910 and to a noted constitutional crisis in which the opposition of the House of Lords was overcome only by a threat from the Liberals to create enough new peers to approve the necessary taxes. If in Britain as in Germany the welfare measures protected the fortunate from a later aggressive onslaught, the need for them was not something that the privileged could easily perceive at the time.

In a very real sense, the triumph of Lloyd George in 1910 and 1911 paved the way for the American action a quarter of a century later. Britain was the home of the classical orthodoxy, but it had now accepted, however reluctantly, this major modification of the system — more specifically, this truly substantial amelioration of its rigors. The example was one for the United States to emulate.

There was a perceptible mellowing of classical attitudes toward welfare legislation in Britain in the years following the Lloyd George initiative. In 1920, Arthur C. Pigou (1877–1959), the successor to Alfred Marshall in both prestige and professional position at the University of Cambridge, published his basic work on economics, the counterpart of Marshall's *Principles* of thirty years before. It was called, significantly, *The Economics of Welfare.*[1]

Pigou was not given to radical innovation; as late as 1933, he affirmed that "with perfectly free competition [which largely, although not completely, he assumed] there will always be a strong tendency toward full employment. Such unemployment as exists at any time is due wholly to the frictional resistances [that] prevent the appropriate wage and price adjustments being made instantaneously."[2] But he was subversive of the classical doctrine on a subtle but basic point. Rigorous theory had always held — and even after Pigou continued to hold — that the marginal utility of money for the acquiring individual, unlike the marginal utility of individual goods, did not fall. It remained constant; more did not give any lessened satisfaction per added unit. And the established theory held, even more strongly, that interpersonal utilities could not be compared. With greater quantities of a specific good, the user had diminishing satisfaction from the increments. But it was not possible to say that the one with more goods had less satisfaction from an increment than the one who had fewer. The feelings of different people were not comparable; to make such comparisons was to deny the depth and complexity of human emotions, and this was a

1. (London: Macmillan, 1920.)

2. This passage, cited by Paul A. Samuelson and William D. Nordhaus in *Economics*, 12th edition (New York: McGraw-Hill, 1985), pp. 366–367, is from Pigou's *The Theory of Unemployment* and is accompanied by their observation that unemployment in the United States at the time of Pigou's writing was at around 25 percent of the labor force.

denial of the scientific modes of thought to which all good and reputable economists aspired.

However esoteric all this may seem, it had an impressive practical result. It meant that there could be no strict economic case for transferring income (or accumulated wealth) from the rich to the poor. The appreciation and enjoyment of money by the rich did not decline with increased amount. Accordingly, it could not be said that the rich, being rich, suffered less than the less affluent from some loss of marginal wealth or income. Nor could it be said that the satisfaction from the consumption they gave up was less than the satisfaction — the utility — gained by the poor. In strict economic theory this was an illegitimate comparison. Classical economics, accordingly, did not support a redistribution of income. And now the key point: in one form or another, welfare measures would always involve such a redistribution, and so classical orthodoxy remained opposed to them. For the affluent this was again a highly convenient conclusion.

From this line of classical thought Pigou provided release. He held that so long as total production was not reduced by the action, economic welfare — the sum total of satisfaction from the system — was enhanced by the transfer of spendable resources from the rich to the poor. The marginal utility of money did, he held, decline with increasing amount; accordingly, the poor man or family did get more enjoyment than the rich from an increment of income and the goods so obtained.

This was not a completely mortal blow to orthodox attitudes; the comparison of interpersonal utilities remained suspect. To some extent it still does. But Pigou's views gave resounding support to the redistribution of income that welfare measures involve. And this sanction came from well within the current established thought.

The breach in the classical orthodoxy just noted was one factor in the movement toward the welfare state. More important in the United States was the appearance of an influential group within the profession who were directly committed to its purposes.

By the mid-1930s, a considerable number of younger economists had descended upon Washington. In addition to the major concentration in the Department of Agriculture — to which, more than incidentally, Rexford Tugwell had come as assistant secretary — there was a generous scattering through other agencies. Because of them the word *professor* had acquired for many an opprobrious political connotation, somewhat like *sexual deviant.* Just as the agricultural economists, who were academically exempt from classical restraint, had moved in to take charge of agricultural policy and administration, so the institutionalists, who were similarly exempt from classical restraint, undertook the advocacy and design of the welfare state.

While there were outriders at other places — Eveline M. Burns (1900–1985) at Columbia University, Paul H. Douglas (1892–1976)[3] at the University of Chicago — the University of Wisconsin was the source of both the ideas and the practical initiative basic to the welfare legislation. John R. Commons (1862–1945) of that university is the American companion figure to Bismarck and Lloyd George.

In his mature years Commons was the brilliant and exceedingly influential end-product of a chaotic education and a disastrous early academic career. The latter took him to a succession of midwestern and eastern colleges and universities — Ohio Wesleyan, Oberlin, the University of Indiana, Syracuse University. All, as in the case of Veblen, found it more agreeable to have him teach elsewhere. It was less remarkable, perhaps, that he was so often fired than that he was so regularly hired.

A principal rescuer of Commons was Richard T. Ely (1854–1943), himself a pioneer figure in American economic dissent and, as indicated earlier, a founder of the American Economic Association. Ely eventually brought Commons to the University of Wisconsin, where he wrote learned books that were broadly and at times somewhat incoherently concerned with the bearing of orga-

3. Who was in the process of combining a notable academic career with a distinguished political one as a United States senator.

nization, including the state, on the citizen. They detailed the legal foundations of this relationship and its history in thought and practice over the centuries.

Commons's books are now, as they were by many when they were first published, largely unread. His greater achievement was in assembling and leading a brilliant and devoted coterie of colleagues and students who, untroubled by the classically orthodox views, set out in a highly practical way to redress the evident social grievances of the time. Their primary instruments were the Wisconsin state government in Madison, which was conveniently adjacent to the university, and its governing family, Robert La Follette and his two sons.

The Wisconsin Plan, the joint accomplishment of economists and politicians, included a pioneer state civil service law, the effective regulation of public utility rates, a limit on usurious interest (although it was kept to the still prohibitive rate of 3.5 percent a month, or 42 percent a year), support to the trade union movement, a state income tax and finally, in 1932, a state unemployment compensation system. This last had a penetrating effect on economic and political attitudes; nothing else contributed so directly to the federal legislation on the subject three years later. And it was the Commons and Wisconsin economists who again led in the federal design. Edwin E. Witte (1887–1960), a professor of economics at the university and an architect of the Wisconsin Plan, was executive director of the staff of the Cabinet Committee on Economic Security that drafted the federal legislation. And associated closely with him was Arthur J. Altmeyer (1891–1972), who had also been involved in the Wisconsin reforms. Any visit to the origins of the welfare state must include a respectful sojourn in Madison, Wisconsin.

The initial federal step, legislation drafted in 1935 by Thomas H. Eliot (1907–   ), grandson of a Harvard president, a young Massachusetts lawyer, later a congressman from that state and later still the chancellor of Washington University in St. Louis, provided a series of grants to the states for the needful old and dependent children and for other welfare purposes. And it provided for a federal-state system of unemployment compensation and a compulsory national system of old-age pensions for workers in the main industrial and commercial sectors of the economy.

The pension plan, which was exceedingly modest in scale, was designed to build up reserves from a specific tax levy on pay; this would provide for the greater eventual claims when the larger generations of current workers reached retirement age. In a country still suffering from severe deflation it was openly deflationary; more was removed from the stream of purchasing power than was returned in current pensions. The alternative, which would have been to pay claims out of the general federal budget, would have added to the deficit or required a less specific tax increase, possibly an increase in the income tax. The former was ruled out by the continuing economic commitment to conservative finance, the latter by the political resistance to taxing the more affluent for the less, the young for the old. The principle that the Social Security accounts, that is, the old-age pensions, must be sustained by their own tax levies has remained nearly unchallenged ever since. In fact, only seeming political expediency at the time of their inception kept them from being a general claim on public revenues.

Unemployment compensation financed by payroll taxes involved an intricate combination of state and federal action, with a wide variation in benefits as between states. Sadly, there was considerable encouragement to states to do less rather than more and thus to improve their competitive position by imposing a lesser burden on their established industry or that which they sought to attract. But at least here was a beginning.

The response from orthodox economists to the Social Security Act, like that to the agricultural legislation and in contrast to their reactions to the NRA and especially the gold-purchase experiment, was relatively muted. Unlike the NRA or the gold purchases, the proposed new legislation involved no frontal assault on classical belief.

Unemployment and the economic disabilities of age did exist; perhaps these flaws should be remedied. Unemployment compensation was a plausible bridge over the down side of the business cycle. The old-age pensions paid their own way; they were, after all, insurance, not a radical thing. As prestigious a figure as Pigou had given a measure of sanction. And the Wisconsin scholars, however dissonant their views, were, at least in general designation, true economists, not members of some lesser part of the profession.

The business community, the views of which call for a special word here, was not so tolerant. No legislation in American history was more bitterly assailed by business spokesmen than the proposed Social Security Act. The National Industrial Conference Board warned that "unemployment insurance cannot be placed on a sound financial basis"; the National Association of Manufacturers said it would facilitate "ultimate socialistic control of life and industry"; Alfred P. Sloan, Jr., then the sovereign head of General Motors, stated firmly, "The dangers are manifest"; James L. Donnelly of the Illinois Manufacturers' Association proclaimed it a design for undermining the national life "by destroying initiative, discouraging thrift, and stifling individual responsibility"; Charles Denby, Jr., of the American Bar Association said that "sooner or later [it] will bring about the inevitable abandonment of private capitalism"; and George P. Chandler of the Ohio Chamber of Commerce advised, somewhat surprisingly, that the downfall of Rome could be traced to such action. In a comprehensive paraphrase of all their positions, Arthur M. Schlesinger, Jr., wrote, "With unemployment insurance no one would work; with old-age and survivors insurance no one would save; the result would be moral decay, financial bankruptcy and the collapse of the republic." Representative John Taber of upstate New York spoke in Congress for the business opposition: "Never in the history of the world has any measure been brought in here so insidiously designed as to prevent business recovery, to enslave workers, and to prevent any possibility of the employers providing work for the people." A colleague, Representative Daniel Reed, was more succinct: "The lash of the dictator will be felt." The Republican opposition voted all but unanimously to recommit, that is, kill, the bill, but when it came to the floor of the House, there were commanding second thoughts. It passed by a huge — 371 to 33 — majority.[4]

It was, however, just the beginning. Health insurance, fully established aid to families with dependent children, housing for lower-income families and housing subsidies, job training and other welfare supplements to the needful, were all to come. And as in the United States, so in all of the industrial countries.

To come also was a continuing flow of concern and complaint from those who, like the business leaders just mentioned, saw welfare measures as the natural enemy of free enterprise, the destroyer of the motivation that drives its wheels. In later times avowedly conservative administrations in the United States and Britain would make of this anxiety and criticism a chorus. And compliant acolytes would come forth to affirm, often with a self-gratifying sense of novelty, the earlier truths of Bentham, Spencer and William Graham Sumner.[5]

As the anger and alienation of the unpossessed subsided, calmed by the welfare state itself, so did the Bismarckian fear of revolution. And socialism, beset by deep-seated problems of performance, diminished as an alternative. The result was that the vocal attack on welfare measures was intensified. But, to a remarkable degree, the ample and effusive rhetoric did not translate into action. Not anywhere in the industrial world. Faced with reality, including the undoubted political consequences from attempts to dismantle the welfare state, legislators and administrators have retreated,[6] as did the American House of Representatives on that initial vote. The welfare state, the oratory notwithstanding, has

4. See Arthur M. Schlesinger, Jr., *The Age of Roosevelt:* Vol. 2, *The Coming of the New Deal* (Boston: Houghton Mifflin, 1958), pp. 311–312. I am here indebted to Professor Schlesinger's account of the opposition.

5. See George Gilder, *Wealth and Poverty* (New York: Basic Books, 1981), and Charles Murray, *Losing Ground: America's Social Policy, 1950–1980* (New York: Basic Books, 1984).

6. On this, see David Stockman, *The Triumph of Politics* (New York: Harper & Row, 1986).

become firmly a part of modern capitalism and modern economic life. Social Security is both reviled and loved, but love triumphs.

The business reaction to the Social Security Act marked the beginning of a change in the relations of economists and the business world; henceforth there would be a measure of tension. Economists would no longer be the source of a benign classical rationalization of economic events as in all earlier times; some were now the source of deeply antithetical ideas and action. There had been indication of this adverse role in the gold purchases; now, with the beginning of the welfare state, it became evident. And soon, with John Maynard Keynes, it would be vividly so.

A question arises as to why the business interests resisted economic measures so patently designed to protect the economic system, a question that was to come up again strongly and urgently with Keynesian action. Traditionally this resistance has been attributed to the shortsightedness — by the untactful, the social unintelligence — of businessmen, and of their more articulate spokesmen in particular. This is a limited view. Personal pecuniary interest is not transcendent in these matters; religious conviction also has a role. For active business participants the classical system was — and remains — more than an arrangement for producing goods and services and defending personal reward. It was also a totem, a manifestation of religious faith. It was thus that it was to be respected and protected. Businessmen, business executives, capitalists, rose above interest to defend faith. This, many still do.

And there was yet another reason for their attitude. Business is not only a search for money; it is also a search for distinction and resulting self-esteem. It is a hard but inescapable fact that in assessing whether these have been obtained, comparative achievement is more easily perceived in bad times than in good. In periods of general misfortune the successful and articulate businessman can see in clear detail what by his own efforts (or those of a worthy ancestor) has been accomplished and what has been escaped. If everyone is well or even modestly endowed, this exercise in self-approval is less rewarding. There ceases to be the gratifying thought and statement "Well, *I* made it" or the possibility for any reflection on the superior qualities that allowed it. To attribute to intellectual myopia or to narrow pecuniary interest the resistance of business to the ameliorative tendencies of Social Security (and later of Lord Keynes) is to misunderstand much that is important in competitive and capitalist motivation. Something, perhaps much, must also be attributed to the pleasure of winning in a game where many lose.

XVII

John Maynard Keynes

BECAUSE OF the relentless pressure of events on economic ideas and the overriding pressure of the Great Depression, the 1930s were, especially in the United States, the most innovative of decades. As already told, the drop in industrial and agricultural prices was directly addressed; relief and public works employment were provided; in 1935 came unemployment compensation and old-age insurance. There still remained the grave failure of the system as a whole. In 1936, the fourth year of the New Deal, and after some, as it was to develop, very temporary recovery, personal expenditures were low; 17 percent of the American labor force was still unemployed; and real Gross National Product was only 95 percent of the now distant 1929 level. So much for the strong annual increases all politicians promise. In 1937, there was another sharp slump; since there was already a depression, a new name had to be found, and it was called a recession. A recession was a depression within a depression.

To none of this could the classical orthodoxy respond. Therein, to repeat once more, the economy found its equilibrium at full employment, and from full employment came the flow of demand that sustained it. Say's Law. Temporary shortfalls were possible and, indeed, accepted, but certainly nothing that could last, as by 1936 this one now had, a full, endlessly grim six years. A century earlier Thomas Robert Malthus had argued the case for overall overproduction, the counterpart of a shortage of demand.[1] On this he had been deemed possibly eccentric, certainly wrong. The accepted truth had remained with Say, David Ricardo and the rejection of what was all but universally termed the undercon-sumption–shortage of demand fallacy. If a shortage of demand could not exist, there could be, rather obviously, no case for public action to enhance demand. Apart from being unnecessary, it violated the canons of sound public finance. The government, like the private household, lived within its means — or should.

Perhaps, indeed, interest rates might be lowered by central bank action, but by the mid-1930s, these were already at nearly nominal levels; one could not further encourage borrowing and investment by pushing on that string.

Out of these circumstances — and its force can be seen only in their light — came, with enormous effect, the work of John May-nard Keynes (1883–1946). The essentials of his case were simple and forthrightly designed to release antidepression policy from its classical constraints. The modern economy, he held, does not necessarily find its equilibrium at full employment; it can find it with unemployment — the underemployment equilibrium. Say's Law no longer holds; there *can be* a shortage of demand. The government *can and should* take steps to overcome it. In a de-pression the precepts of sound public finance must give way to this need.

The underemployment equilibrium, the repeal of Say's Law, the call for government spending uncovered by revenues to sustain demand — these were the essence of the Keynesian system, and to them I will return. They made up what, with some harmless hyperbole, came to be called the Keynesian Revolution.

Not the least remarkable feature of this revolution was by how many it had been anticipated. There were Keynesians well before Keynes. One was Adolf Hitler, who, exempt from any restraining

1. See Chapter VII.

economic theory, launched a major program of public works construction upon taking office in 1933, the *Autobahnen* being the most visible example. Civil works expenditure was followed only later by that for arms. The Nazis were also indifferent to the constraints of tax revenue; deficit financing was taken for granted. The German economy recovered from the devastating slump it had previously suffered. By 1936, the unemployment that had been so influential in bringing Hitler to power had been substantially eliminated.

The economic world was not impressed; Hitler and the National Socialists were not a model to be imitated. When visiting the Reich in those years, economists and the more expressive voices of financial wisdom all but unanimously predicted economic disaster. As a result of reckless, if not insane, economic policies, the German economy would, they said, collapse; National Socialism would be discredited and disappear. Heinrich Brüning, the relentlessly orthodox chancellor who had presided over the previous unemployment and distress, joined the faculty at Harvard, where he told any available audience of the grave consequences that would flow from Germany's having abandoned his rigorously austere policies, policies that he adamantly denied had had anything to do with the despair that led to the rise of fascism.

More civilized and far more closely associated with deliberate and concerned economic thought was the case of Sweden. Here for two generations an alert group of economists had engaged in critical discussion of economic ideas as they bore upon public affairs. And going beyond discussion, teaching and writing, they had carried their concepts and policies into practical politics and public administration.

The founding figure of the first generation was Knut Wicksell (1851–1926), a scholar in the classical and Utilitarian tradition but with a strongly independent and original mind and a talent for unpredictability or, on occasion, forthright heresy. He was severely criticized for his pioneer advocacy of birth control; in 1908, when he made some less than devout references to the Immaculate Conception in a public lecture, he was committed to jail for two months. It was thought that economists should be less eclectic in their heresy.

Wicksell's views were the forerunner of much later discussion; specifically, in anticipation of Chamberlin and Robinson, he thought that monopoly and competition were at the extreme ends of a spectrum with many forms of market organization in between. This and other irreverent attitudes toward the orthodox concepts brought him into lifelong conflict with Gustav Cassel (1866–1944), the pillar of Swedish and, in some measure, European economic conservatism. Cassel was an unswerving defender of the classical system, the gold standard and, if not a minimal, at least an appropriately limited role for the state. Being powerfully committed to his own views, and these being greatly applauded by conservatives throughout Europe, Cassel inspired a strong dialectical response. What was to be Sweden's break with economic orthodoxy owed much to the availability of so staunchly orthodox an opponent.

Prominent in the opposition to Cassel was a second generation of remarkably independent-minded scholars, Gunnar Myrdal (1899–   ), Bertil G. Ohlin (1899–1979), Erik Lindahl (1891–1960), Erik F. Lundberg (1907–   ) and Dag Hammarskjöld (1905–1961), later secretary-general of the United Nations, who died in its service. With a full knowledge of the relevant theory and a strong resistance to its constraints, they all addressed themselves to the practical problems of the Swedish economy, society and polity. As the depression deepened, their attention turned especially to the resulting price deflation, diminution of production, unemployment and agricultural distress. In the compact Swedish community, the economists were in close, indeed everyday, association with political leaders and public officials or acted in these roles themselves. There emerged from this association a broad design for minimizing the hardships and improving the overall functioning of the economy. This included what was by the standards of the time a well-developed social security system. Also support to agricultural prices. Also, as a supplement to, and corrective of, ordinary capitalist and competitive enterprise, a highly structured system of farmer and consumer cooperatives.

Of greatest present relevance, however, was the deliberate use of the government budget to sustain demand and employment. The depression led the Stockholm economists to abandon hope that central bank action to lower interest rates would serviceably expand investment, investment expenditure and demand. Again the futile shoving on the string. Instead, they held that in good times the public budget should be balanced, but in depression it should, by contrast, be unbalanced deliberately so that the excess of expenditure over income would sustain demand and employment.

All of this was being said and done in Stockholm in the 1930s well in advance of Keynes; in a terminologically exact world the modern reference would be not to the Keynesian but to the Swedish Revolution.

By the middle of the decade, word of developments in Swedish thought were, indeed, seeping through to Britain and the United States. To a world troubled by the idea that socialism and communism were the only alternatives to a rigorously orthodox capitalism, Sweden, with its now well-developed social welfare system, its consumer and farmer cooperatives, its general tolerance of modification and amendment of classical rigor and its demand-sustaining budget, was being pictured as the Middle Way.[2] But as Ben B. Seligman has observed,[3] the language barrier was for a long time forbidding. And great economic ideas were not expected to come from small countries.

There were antecedents to Keynes in the United States as well. In the 1920s, William Trufant Foster (1879–1950) and Waddill Catchings (1879–1967), the former an economist of eccentric reputation, the latter a *Wunderkind* of the great investment trust promotions

2. Part of the title of Marquis W. Childs's widely read book, *Sweden: The Middle Way* (New Haven: Yale University Press, 1936).

3. In *Main Currents in Modern Economics* (New York: The Free Press of Glencoe, 1962), p. 539 *et seq.* This enormous work is greatly and rightly admiring of the Swedish economists.

(and disasters) of the years before and following the 1929 crash, published a series of books strongly urging government intervention to sustain and enhance demand. Say's Law and the supporting economic beliefs were their target: "These lords of the domain of economic theory [the classical economists] merely assumed, without even an attempt at proof, that the financing of production itself provides people with the means of purchase."[4]

The ideas of Foster and Catchings were not wholly without public appeal; in the early depression years they had a considerable lay audience and discussion. But among reputable economists they served principally as an example of popular and superficial error, and they were cited in everyday instruction to show the tendency to such error.[5]

Finally in anticipation of Keynes there was a highly practical application in the United States of what would be his central prescription; namely, that there should be government expenditure financed by borrowing to sustain demand and employment. Through most of the 1930s, the federal government ran a substantial deficit. Beginning in 1933, this was increased by expenditures for direct relief, public works and other public employment, the latter through the Federal Emergency Relief Administration, Public Works Administration, Civil Works Administration and Works Progress Administration. By 1936, after three full years of the New Deal and in, as it may be described, the year of Keynes, federal receipts were only 59 percent, a little more than half, of expenditures. The deficit was 4.2 percent of the current Gross National Product.[6] Harsh circumstance, that intractable force in economic policy, had already required what Keynes was to urge. What was necessary was not, however, approved. Circumstance did not excuse fiscal error. In

4. William Trufant Foster and Waddill Catchings, *The Road to Plenty* (Boston: Houghton Mifflin, 1928), p. 128.

5. But not by all. John H. Williams (1887–1980), for long a much respected Harvard professor who specialized in money and banking — and who was also an officer of the New York Federal Reserve Bank — interested his classes and startled his colleagues by saying that Foster and Catchings had a point that could not be ignored.

6. By way of comparison, the ardently discussed deficit of 1986 was around 4.9 percent of the Gross National Product.

consequence, in the minds of many, not excluding Franklin D. Roosevelt, Keynesian economic policy would long be seen not as an act of economic wisdom but as a sophisticated rationalization of what had been shown to be politically inescapable.

Early advocacy of Keynesian policy included strong attempts at persuasion by Keynes himself. In a notable Open Letter to the President in *The New York Times* on December 31, 1933, during the first year of the New Deal, he told the new administration that he placed "overwhelming emphasis on the increase of national purchasing power resulting from government expenditure, which is financed by loans,"[7] and the following year he had a rather unsuccessful meeting with Roosevelt to press the point. However, none of this earlier effort ranked in importance with the publication of *The General Theory of Employment Interest and Money* in 1936,[8] which was an event in the history of economics comparable in significance with the publication of *Wealth of Nations* in 1776 and the first edition of *Capital* in 1867. It was, as Keynes intended it to be, a lethal blow at the classical[9] conclusions as to demand, production and employment and the resulting policy.

As will now be obvious, *The General Theory* owed much of its acceptance to the Great Depression and to the failure of classical economics to contend with that pervasively unsettling event. But it also owed much to Keynes's assurance in economic argument and analysis, the confident originality of his expression and mood. The confidence should especially be stressed. No economist is ever more highly regarded than he regards himself or followed with more

7. Quoted by R. F. Harrod, *The Life of John Maynard Keynes* (New York: Harcourt, Brace, 1951), p. 447.

8. (New York: Harcourt, Brace.) Keynes eschewed commas in the title; later commentators almost invariably supply them.

9. I here note again that, as did Keynes, I use the word *classical* for the whole sweep of orthodox thought from Smith and Ricardo on. By the time of Keynes the common reference was to neoclassical economics, this being thought a step upward from classical economics. There was, however, no sharp break with the older argument; the new term took cognizance only of the numerous refinements of which mention has been made in this history. Classical economics is a more nearly valid description of the traditional current of thought at least until Keynes.

certainty than that which he himself manifests. And Keynes's influence also owed much to his personal background, reputation and prestige. Had *The General Theory* come from someone who lacked these qualifications, it might well have sunk without trace. Of them now a word.

Keynes's family and academic credentials could hardly have served him better. His father, John Neville Keynes, was a University of Cambridge economist of excellent reputation. For fifteen years he was the registrary, that is to say the chief administrative officer, of the university. Maynard Keynes's mother, Florence Ada Keynes, was a devoted community leader and in later life mayor of Cambridge. Both outlived their famous son and were at his funeral in Westminster Abbey in April 1946.

John Maynard Keynes went to Eton and on to the University of Cambridge, where he was a student with Lytton Strachey, Leonard Woolf and Clive Bell. They, along with Virginia Woolf, Vanessa Bell and a number of others, would later make up the much celebrated — let it perhaps be said, the considerably overcelebrated — Bloomsbury group in London. For Keynes these friends would be an opening to a world and to a kind of conversation in engaging contrast with the austere concepts of economics; for his friends Keynes would be a highly improbable, even mystifying, link with economics and practical political affairs.

After he took his degree at Cambridge in 1905, he sat for Civil Service examinations and did badly in economics: "I evidently knew more about Economics than my examiners."[10] Surviving this official ignorance, he served for a time in the India Office, wrote a highly technical and well-received book on the theory of probability, began another on Indian currency and returned to Cambridge on a fellowship provided personally by Professor Arthur Pigou.

The 1914–1918 war and its aftermath accorded Keynes fame, and also the assurance that would thereafter mark his public voice and

10. Keynes, quoted in Harrod, p. 121.

make it influential and eventually irresistible. During these years he served at the Treasury, where he achieved a significant reputation for his competence and resourcefulness in handling British foreign exchange earnings, loan proceeds and receipts from foreign securities conscripted and sold abroad. Also for distributing the proceeds over needed imports and overseas expenditures and for guiding and helping the French and Russians on the same matters. So well was he known by the end of the war for his ability in economic policy and administration that he was selected to serve with the British delegation to the Paris Peace Conference in 1919, an assignment of no slight interest and distinction.

The behavior of a young specialist — Keynes was now thirty-six — brought into such awe-inspiring company as that at the Paris Conference — David Lloyd George, Georges Clemenceau, Woodrow Wilson — and to such an awe-inspiring task as ensuring the peace of the world ought to be wholly predictable. One so chosen and favored should enjoy the resulting self-gratification and the envy of others not so fortunate; he should offer advice with all appropriate deference; and he should accept and even defend the result, however unwelcome, unwise or bizarre, as the best that could be done. To behave otherwise would be to deny the wisdom that led to his selection and to impair his own self-esteem. Keynes, in no need of any enhancement of self-esteem, left Paris in June 1919 in a mood of deep contempt for the proceedings. He returned to England to write *The Economic Consequences of the Peace*[11] over the period of the next two months. It was published in England later that year, sold eighty-four thousand copies in the British edition, was widely translated and still stands as the most important *economic* document relating to World War I and its aftermath.

It is also, as has often been said, one of the most eloquent diatribes ever written. It pictured the Paris mood as vengeful, myopic and deeply unrealistic. So also the great statesmen — Wilson, this "blind and deaf Don Quixote";[12] Clemenceau, who had "one illu-

11. (New York: Harcourt, Brace and Howe, 1920.)
12. Keynes, *The Economic Consequences of the Peace*, p. 41.

sion — France; and one disillusion — mankind";[13] Lloyd George, in a passage that was deleted at the last moment, "this goat-footed bard, this half-human visitor to our age from the hag-ridden magic and enchanted woods of Celtic antiquity."[14]

However, it was the reparation clauses that invited Keynes's professional condemnation. Germany could not, he held, meet the amounts contemplated out of any conceivable export earnings; the effort and the resulting trade and financial dislocation would penalize not only the defeated enemy but all of Europe as well. From this conclusion, more than from any other source, came the view in the 1920s and 1930s that the peace terms had been, in fact, Carthaginian. In consequence, Germany ceased to be seen as a punished aggressor and came, instead, to be thought of as a victim. Such was the legacy of Keynes.

And there was a longer reach. After World War II, the idea of reparations from Germany and Japan in the form of monetary transfers was uniformly rejected; the error celebrated by Keynes must not be repeated. Instead this time there would, more sensibly, be reparations in kind, notably in the form of physical plant and equipment. Sadly, except in being somewhat impractical, reparations in this form turned out to be, if anything, considerably more dislocating and cruel. Workers and whole communities had to view the factories and machines on which their livelihoods depended being dismantled, loaded up and carted away. For the moment, at least, all hope for the future was gone. A truly Carthaginian exercise, limited only by the practical problems in moving and using the plants.

In the 1920s and early 1930s, Keynes wrote prodigiously, interested himself in the arts, was chairman of the *New Statesman and Nation*, served on the major Government Committee of Enquiry into Finance and Industry, was chairman of the board of an insurance company, was a Fellow and the bursar of King's College,

13. Keynes, *The Economic Consequences of the Peace*, p. 32.
14. Keynes, quoted in Harrod, p. 256.

Cambridge, and speculated, at first disastrously — he had to be rescued by his father and City friends — and later with success, on his own behalf and, more remarkably in light of the sensible restraints customary on such action, on behalf of King's College.

In 1925, the issue of the gold standard, and the threat soon realized of what he called a tempestuous season, brought him into brilliant polemical conflict with the then chancellor of the Exchequer, Winston Churchill. It was over the return of the pound, after wartime deterioration, to its old gold value of 123.27 grains of fine gold, its old parity with the dollar at $4.87 to the pound. This, all solemn financial wisdom and tradition required, but the expensive pound also priced British export products, including in particular coal, some 10 percent above the world market. In its effect on exports and imports, it was the precise reverse of the Roosevelt gold-buying, gold-price-depreciating policy of eight years later and the counterpart of the high American dollar in the mid-1980s.

To remain competitive, British export prices and, with them, costs, notably wages, had to come down. Gradually, painfully, after a long and bitter strike in the coal fields and the great General Strike of May 1926, wage reductions were achieved. Britain's return to gold in 1925 still stands as one of the most transparently wrong decisions in the long and impressive history of economic error.

Keynes was ruthless in opposition and especially in his criticism of Churchill, who, it was later revealed, had also had serious doubts as to the wisdom of the action. Keynes asked, "Why did he [Churchill] do such a silly thing?" and then answered his own question by saying he had "no instinctive judgment to prevent him from making [such] mistakes. . . . [He] was deafened by the clamorous voices of conventional finance; and . . . gravely misled by his experts."[15] Having earlier found a good title, Keynes did not hesitate to use it a second time. The essay conveying this attack was called "The Economic Consequences of Mr. Churchill."

Finally, in 1930, Keynes published the two-volume *A Treatise*

15. John Maynard Keynes, *Essays in Persuasion*, cited in Robert Lekachman, *The Age of Keynes* (New York: Random House, 1966), p. 47.

on Money. It was hailed as a polar work of its time. Included was a fascinating history of money, the remarkable thought that gold owed its distinction to a Freudian appeal and the calculation that the world's total accumulation of the metal from the beginning of time until the present could then (as doubtless still) be carried across the Atlantic on a single ship.

There were also ideas that anticipated *The General Theory:* "It might be supposed — and has frequently been supposed — that the amount of investment is necessarily equal to the amount of saving. But reflection will show that this is not the case."[16] Here in moderate language was a major later point: all income cannot be depended on to flow back in the form of demand for goods and services, as had been prescribed by Say's Law. Some of it may be lost by way of unused or uninvested savings.

On other matters, however, Keynes reached conclusions in this book that he was presently to assail in *The General Theory*. He failed to deal with factors causing changes in output and associated employment in the economy as a whole, and this he acknowledged: This "dynamic development [that is, the changes just mentioned], as distinct from the instantaneous picture, was left incomplete and extremely confused."[17]

Keynes was a lucid and resourceful master of English prose, as were Smith, Bentham, Malthus, the two Mills, Marshall and Veblen. Ricardo possibly excepted, no one of great importance in the history of English-speaking economic thought was otherwise. *The General Theory of Employment Interest and Money*, however, is a complex, ill-organized and sometimes obscure work, as Keynes himself recognized, noting that the general public, "though welcome at the debate, are only eavesdroppers" at this necessarily technical effort to persuade his fellow economists. Very few people outside the field of professional economics have ever accepted Keynes's invitation to listen.

16. John Maynard Keynes, *A Treatise on Money* (New York: Harcourt, Brace, 1930), Vol. 1, p. 172.

17. Keynes, *The General Theory of Employment Interest and Money*, p. vii.

Yet the central ideas are, as I have already indicated, relatively untroublesome. The decisive problem of economics is not how the price of goods is established. Nor is it how the resulting income is distributed. The important question is how the level of output and employment is determined.[18] As output, employment and income increase, consumption from the additional increments of income decreases — in Keynes's historic formulation, the marginal propensity to consume declines. This is to say that savings increase. There is no assurance, as the classical economists held, that, because of lowered interest rates, these savings will be invested, which is to say spent. They may be held unspent for a variety of precautionary reasons that reflect the individual's or firm's need or wish for liquid assets — again, in Keynes's term, his, her or its liquidity preference. If revenue is saved and unspent, the effect is to reduce the total of the demand for goods and services — effective aggregate demand — and therewith output and employment. And the reduction will continue until savings are reduced. This happens as an increasing marginal propensity to consume is pressed, even forced, by lessening income. The reduced savings are then absorbed by the less rapidly falling level of investment expenditure.

As in the classical view, savings and investment must be equal; savings must be offset by investment. The difference is that they are no longer necessarily or even normally equal at full employment. To make savings equal to investment and so ensure that savings are spent may require diminishing incomes and deprivation. The equilibrium situation in the economy, it follows, is not at obligatory full employment; it can be at different and even severe levels of unemployment. This became known, as we have seen, as the underemployment equilibrium. It was something that could be observed with the naked and untrained eye in 1936.

There was another jarring Keynesian note. When unemployment occurred in the classical context, apart from those workers in the process of changing jobs or out of work because skills and require-

18. Leading on to the later and common concern for the rate of expansion called growth.

ments were in bad fit, the accepted cause was wages that were too high or too rigid. Unions and their demands were an obvious cause. The return from adding workers, the marginal revenue from increasing the work force, simply did not pay the required wages. Lower the wages over whatever resistance, and the idle workers would be back on the job. With Keynes, this, most significantly, was no longer so; what was true for the individual employer was not true for all. This, to remind, is what economists speaking of the tendency to proceed from the simple to the complex, as from family finances to those of the state, call the fallacy of composition. Were employers generally to lower wages in a time of unemployment, the flow of purchasing power — the aggregate of effective demand — would diminish, *pari passu*, with the diminished wages. The reduced effective demand would then increase unemployment. Unemployment could not be blamed on high wages — or on trade unions. Herbert Hoover and Franklin D. Roosevelt, the latter through the NRA, had agreed on at least this one policy: both had opposed wage reductions. Economists, in keeping with their classical faith, had strongly criticized both Presidents, but Keynes made them both right.

With the diagnosis came the cure. No longer could governments wait for self-correcting forces to provide a remedy; the underemployment equilibrium could be stable and persistent. No longer could they wait for unemployment to bring down wages; that could lead to equilibrium at a lower level of output and employment. Low interest rates could not be counted on to increase investment and investment spending; perhaps they only reinforced liquidity preference. Why give up the various advantages of holding cash for a nominal return? Even more plausibly, there was the all too evident fact of the current economic scene; even the admirably low interest rates then obtaining did not stimulate investment in the presence of great excess capacity and the absence of a plausible return.

There remained one — just one — course. That was government intervention to raise the level of investment spending — government

234

borrowing and spending for public purposes. A deliberate deficit. This alone would break the underemployment equilibrium by, in effect, spending — willfully spending — the unspent savings of the private sector. It was a powerful affirmation of the wisdom of what was already being done under the force of circumstance.

Such are the hard essentials of the Keynesian Revolution. They were not so put by Keynes. The economic discussion that followed the publication of *The General Theory* wrestled endlessly and pleasurably with the complexities and obscurities of the book. There was a certain professional satisfaction in surrounding them with a veil of mystery; what learned scholars struggled to master, the layman could hardly be expected to understand.

One feature of the Keynesian Revolution went largely unmentioned: impressed with how much had changed, economists did not pause to reflect on how much remained unchanged. Henceforth the state would be responsible for the overall performance of the economy. There would be disagreement as to the measures to be employed; there would be no disagreement as to the responsibility of the government or, at a minimum, of the central bank. The belief in autonomous full employment at stable prices, eccentricity apart, was gone. However, instruction and debate as to how full employment and price stability could be achieved would now be separated off into a special branch of economics, which would be called macroeconomics.[19] In an especially tasteless contraction, some economists would refer to their specialty as "macro." Left untouched and untroubled by Keynes was what would be called microeconomics or, in equally repellent professional slang, just "micro." In microeconomics the market was as before, also the business firm and the entrepreneur. And monopoly, competition,

19. With no slight damage to economic understanding. As will later be noted, economic life is of a piece, and the separation between macroeconomics and microeconomics prevented a proper appreciation of the strong macroeconomic influence on microeconomic developments, that of the modern corporation and trade union and the interaction of wages and prices in particular.

imperfect competition and the theory of distribution. Here, in short, was the classical system largely intact. This system functioned within a managed flow of demand; within that managed flow economic life was mostly unchanged. The distribution of power as between corporation, trade union, individual worker and consumer was as classically perceived. On these matters the state had no need to intervene any more than it had in the past.

Keynes lifted the incubus of depression and unemployment off capitalism, or such was his design. He thus removed the feature that it could not explain and that, as Marx had held, it could not survive. But that was all or mostly all. The Keynesian Revolution, so viewed, was not only a limited but an intensely conservative thing.

In 1935, on New Year's Day, in response to a letter from George Bernard Shaw urging attention for a point made by Marx, Keynes replied: "To understand *my* state of mind, however, you have to know that I believe myself to be writing a book on economic theory which will largely revolutionise — not, I suppose, at once but in the course of the next ten years — the way the world thinks about economic problems."[20] The expectation was not entirely unjustified. Change there was. But in contrast with the change that Marx both urged and foresaw, the achievement of Keynes was in how much he allowed to remain the same.

In the next two decades, especially in the United States, Keynes's name would acquire a marked overtone of radicalism. In the business and banking community Keynesians would be considered as inimical to the established order as Marxists and rather more of a clear and present danger. Here another great constant in economic life: as between grave ultimate disaster and the conserving reforms that might avoid it, the former is frequently much preferred.

20. Keynes, quoted in Harrod, p. 462.

XVIII

Affirmation by Mars

IN THE AUTUMN of 1936, a few weeks before the presidential elections of that year, Harvard University celebrated its 300th anniversary.[1] Each of the several departments was invited to recommend candidates for the honorary degrees to be bestowed on that occasion. In an admirably liberal gesture the views of the younger scholars — instructors and assistant professors — were solicited. Junior members of the government department, wishing to be as disconcerting as possible, proposed the name of Leon Trotsky. Younger economists, not wishing to be more amenable, offered the name of John Maynard Keynes. Both suggestions were thoughtfully rejected.

In place of the degree for Keynes one was conferred on Dennis (later Sir Dennis) Robertson (1890–1963) of Trinity College, Cambridge, an economist of exceedingly pleasant manner and reputation. Robertson was not a stern classical ideologue; he had early joined Keynes in the rejection of Say's Law, holding that since savings and investment were by different people and institutions, there was no good reason to expect them to be equal. But he also associ-

1. I should confess that I am here citing an incident earlier told in *Money: Whence It Came, Where It Went* (Boston: Houghton Mifflin, 1975), pp. 227–228. I also draw in this chapter on another earlier exercise. In 1965, *The New York Times Book Review* discovered with sorrow that the original edition of Keynes's *General Theory* had never been reviewed — in retrospect, an impressive oversight. At their request I used much of an issue for a review-article called "How Keynes Came to America," which was published on May 16 of that year.

ated unemployment with unduly high wages and was otherwise committed to the established view. He traveled from the one Cambridge to be honored at the other, taking recess from a continuing dispute with Keynes over the latter's heresy.

The division thus demonstrated between the younger and the older generations at Harvard was both symbolic and substantive. It was to younger economists everywhere that Keynes appealed; his views were a welcome alternative to the unemployment and misery that could no longer be defended and also to a commitment to Marx and revolution that, though gaining ground, was undeniably inconvenient for comfortably situated young scholars. But the response of the younger Harvard economists was specific; it was through their agency that the Keynesian system was to come to the United States. As Wisconsin would be the source of Social Security and Yale of monetarist innovation, Harvard, previously a citadel of the high orthodoxy, would be the germinal point for Keynesian economics in the United States.

There were, of course, older converts. But most of the economists of established reputation stood firm, and quite a few saved themselves from temptation by not reading *The General Theory.* One who did read it was Joseph Schumpeter, by now for several years at Harvard. He condemned the book in firm tones: among Keynes's more grievous flaws and faults, in Schumpeter's view, was his insistence on uniting economic theory with practical policy.[2] On another occasion Schumpeter said Keynes was afflicted by "the curse of usefulness," but for those who were ardently in search of a policy against the depression that did not seem a compelling objection.

Far more influential was Alvin Harvey Hansen (1887–1975), who came to Harvard in 1937. He was then a fully qualified advocate of the market, liberal international trade and the generally self-correcting mechanisms of the classical system. A kindly, open-hearted

2. Joseph A. Schumpeter, review of *The General Theory of Employment Interest and Money,* in the *Journal of the American Statistical Association,* Vol. 31, No. 196 (December 1936), pp. 791–795.

and open-minded scholar and teacher, popular with colleagues and students alike, he had previously rather sternly corrected some of Keynes's early and more technical writing. He now read *The General Theory* with quiet disapproval: "Not a landmark in the sense that it lays a foundation for a 'new economics' . . . more a symptom of economic trends than a foundation stone upon which a science can be built."[3] Then in the months ahead, as Hansen defended his criticism and participated in discussion, he changed his mind, a relatively rare professional happening, which is much remarked when it occurs. Eventually he became the single most effective spokesman in the United States for the Keynesian diagnosis and more especially for the Keynesian remedy, the one close rival being his associate, assistant and devoted younger friend Paul A. Samuelson (1915–), whose textbook carried Keynes to millions of students around the world from 1948 on.

In the late 1930s and continuing after the war, Alvin Hansen's seminar on fiscal policy drew participants from as far away as Washington and frequently overflowed from the crowded seminar room into the adjacent hall. His articles and books were read and avidly discussed, most especially his *Fiscal Policy and Business Cycles*,[4] published five years after *The General Theory* and a decidedly more lucid and empirically more substantial statement of the basic Keynesian view. In an important sense Hansen went beyond Keynes to argue that the underemployment equilibrium — in his language, a tendency to secular stagnation — was normal and predictable in the modern economy; it could be offset only by determined government action.[5]

Hansen not only led the discussion of the Keynesian system as

3. Alvin H. Hansen, review of *The General Theory of Employment Interest and Money*, in *The Journal of Political Economy*, cited in Robert Lekachman, *The Age of Keynes* (New York: Random House, 1966), p. 127.

4. (New York: W. W. Norton, 1941.)

5. For a complete discussion of Hansen's views as well as for a highly readable, professionally competent account of Keynes, Keynesian theory and its influence, the reader is referred to the above-cited *The Age of Keynes* by Robert Lekachman. To both the author and the volume I happily acknowledge my obligation.

it applied to the United States, but he also served as a bulwark of defense for the younger scholars who were similarly engaged. In later years, as knowledge of the Keynesian heresy penetrated otherwise resistant minds, there was a minor witch hunt, an effort to extrude from academic and public positions the sources of this sorcery. Again the already noticed righteous anger at seemingly unlicensed efforts to save the economic system. Thus, in the years after World War II, the governing boards of Harvard University expressed grave concern over this Albigensian deviation. Their committee to visit the department of economics was aroused from normal acquiescence and somnambulance to resist such error. A group of Harvard graduates formed the Veritas Foundation, with the task of extirpating Keynes from Harvard instruction, for Keynes could not be reconciled with truth. A much larger national constituency addressed the graver problem of Samuelson's textbook, seeking if not its suppression, at least the prevention of its adoption and use. Against these currents, Hansen stood as a rock. So long as he was there, they swirled around ineffectively; no one could persuasively assail a midwesterner of mature years and solid Scandinavian antecedents, the epitome of academic calm and respectability. Hansen himself did not escape criticism, but he dealt with it according to an explicit rule: never, under any circumstances, respond.

Much of the American reaction to Keynes, political and academic, did not come until after the war; not until then did he achieve the distinction of being a recognized threat. Marx, it was often said, had been protected on this side of the Atlantic by the general confusion of his name with the Marx Brothers and the great clothing firm of Hart, Schaffner and Marx. After World War II, the name of John Maynard Keynes lacked even that kind of security. This, however, runs ahead of the story. We must go back to the influence of Keynes in the late depression period and during the war.

In the years following the publication of *The General Theory* its message was carried from Cambridge, Massachusetts, to Washington by younger American economists, as also by young Canadian economists to Ottawa, especially in the latter case by Robert Bryce, who had been in Keynes's seminar at King's College before going to Harvard. Canada, in consequence, was the first country, the special case of Sweden apart, to accept and implement Keynesian management of its economy.

The principal Keynesian voice in the American government was Lauchlin Currie (1902–), also earlier at Harvard, whose book *The Supply and Control of Money in the United States*[6] had anticipated Keynes in some important respects, a circumstance that, at the time, could well have cost him a Harvard promotion. In Washington he went initially to the Federal Reserve Board, and he was later and more influentially the first, if still unofficial, White House economic adviser. He used both positions with marked effect to urge Keynesian policies on the government and to encourage the employment of those who held similar views to his own.

At the Federal Reserve, Currie had the support and active advocacy of its chairman, Marriner Eccles (1890–1977), a Utah banker from a prominent Mormon family, who, before joining the government, had watched with sorrow the farmers he served surrender in bankruptcy to the deflationary forces of the depression. He had been led to wonder if the rigid monetary and fiscal orthodoxy and the hands-off policy of the government were justifiable, given the result. Not previously had a central bank shown itself so vulnerable to such heresy, and certainly none has so shown itself since.

In the years after *The General Theory*, the Keynesians in Washington met regularly for mutual support and approval and to consider means, opportunities and avenues of persuasion. It would have been celebrated as a conspiracy had the frequency of their meetings been known. They were reinforced in their views and helped in the persuasion by the sharp recession of 1937–1938, which, in turn, followed a well-publicized drive toward a more conservative fiscal policy — tax increases, expenditure curtailment and renewed promises of a balanced budget.

6. (Cambridge: Harvard University Press, 1934.)

There was also at the time a muted debate between the Keynesians and, as they may be called, the adhering classical liberals. The latter, searching for a reason for the continuing stagnation, believed themselves to have found it within the framework of classical orthodoxy. The cause was the decline of competition, the inroads on the market of monopoly and corporate concentration. This had restricted production and therewith employment. There was seeming proof in the high incidence of unemployment in highly concentrated heavy industry, the low or nonexistent incidence in classically competitive agriculture. So if monopoly were extirpated and the tendency to corporate concentration reversed, the economy would function in accordance with the classical model. Employment would extend out to embrace all or nearly all workers.

The practical consequence of this view was a considerably revived commitment to antitrust enforcement. This was led by Thurman Arnold (1891–1969), a former Yale law professor of strong economic interests who was currently the assistant attorney general in charge of the Antitrust Division.[7] And in 1937–1938, the classical liberals in the executive branch of the government united with legislators of like view or inclination in the Congress to set up the Temporary National Economic Committee, the TNEC. This was a combined legislative and executive body formed to look into the whole competitive structure of the American economy and recommend as to reform. It was here — in microeconomics, as it would soon be called — that one could find the causes of macroeconomic failure. Not alone unfair competition, not alone consumer exploitation, not alone monopoly profits, but the unemployment and idle plant capacity of the depression had their source in monopoly or imperfect competition.

Emerging thus from the very heart of classical theory was a cause of the present despair. It took the accepted, even revered, rationale

7. He was also the author, before coming to Washington, of *The Folklore of Capitalism* (New Haven: Yale University Press, 1937), a widely read volume that rather strenuously attacked and discounted the role of the antitrust laws. Consistency is, as ever, the hobgoblin of little minds.

of capitalism itself and turned it against its own progenitors. Salvation required only that the high priests of capitalism adhere to the approved doctrine. The classically competitive system does indeed work. The reformer asserts only its basic principles against those who, in yielding to monopoly and industrial concentration, have deserted them in practice. This reformer was not a radical of the left; rather he was simply affirming more strongly the principles to which conservatives, the defenders of the system, were presumed to adhere.

The war brought this final upsurge of classicism largely to an end. The last report of the TNEC in 1941, unlike the earlier committee hearings, attracted no notice and was lost in the urgent concerns of wartime. Enforcement of antitrust legislation was suspended for the war, along with the free markets it was assumed to protect. There would be a modest revival of interest in antitrust enforcement after peace came, when it would be recommended to and, in degree, enforced upon Japan and Germany. There it was seen as an answer to the great corporations, combines and cartels that ardent classical economists and antitrust lawyers, in their tolerant company with Marxists, would hold to be at least partly responsible for the Japanese militarists and for National Socialism and Adolf Hitler. Antimonopoly policy would remain in the United States as an answer to ostentatious monopoly, flagrant price fixing and consumer price abuse and would have a deeply respectful treatment in textbook instruction. It would not again emerge as a serious explanation of overall nonperformance and unemployment.

For the Keynesian system the war had major consequences. As already indicated, it brought economists into positions of power in Washington; all of the war agencies were in greater or lesser measure either administered or guided by economists, and these were, extensively, the younger Keynesian protagonists. The older classical generation was not similarly attracted — or recruited. Business executives did come to Washington in force, but, with notable exceptions, they were the public relations spokesmen for their firms or, on occasion, those who could best be spared. And, again with exceptions, they lacked a usable conception of the larger economic task involved in war mobilization or, in all but the rarest cases, a vision of what the economic system could be made to accomplish. Into this vacuum the younger economists moved with no noticeable reluctance. They had the support also of high authority: Alvin Hansen came to the Federal Reserve Board. And John Maynard Keynes arrived from England to conduct negotiations for His Majesty's Government. In Washington he met with his younger disciples and did not conceal his approval and support:

> There is too wide a gap here in Washington between the intellectual outlook of the older people and that of the younger. But I have been greatly struck during my visit by the quality of the younger economists and civil servants in the Administration. . . . The war will be a great sifter and will bring the right people to the top. We have a few good people in London, but nothing like the *numbers* whom you can produce here.[8]

As Keynes predicted, so it developed. The war extensively ensconced the Keynesians in positions of influence.

The further service of the war was to bring vividly into view a statistical model of the economy that gave strong quantitative support to the Keynesian ideas. This was the work of Simon Kuznets (1901–1985). Kuznets, a quiet, retiring man never involved in anything even approaching public advocacy, was, nonetheless, with Alvin Hansen, one of the two most influential proponents of the Keynesian system. His instrument was the National Accounts. On the basis of important prior work — that of Colin Grant Clark (1905–   ) in England, Wilfred I. King (1880–1962) in the United States and others — and with the aid of a group of committed younger scholars, Kuznets gave the present form and statistical

8. Letter of July 27, 1941, from John Maynard Keynes to Walter S. Salant, one of the aforesaid disciples and for long after the war a much respected figure in the Brookings Institution. Reprinted in *The Collected Writings of John Maynard Keynes:* Vol. 23, *Activities 1940–1943*, edited by Donald Moggridge (Cambridge, England: Cambridge University Press, 1979), p. 193.

values to what are now the commonplace concepts of Gross National Product, National Income and their components.

For many decades statistics had been the poor and largely passive relation of economics. Index numbers of prices, the earlier work of Irving Fisher, had been invented and calculated; these showed that prices behaved as almost everyone had known they did. Production figures in agriculture and industry had become available. Sampling techniques had been developed, surveys conducted and correlation analysis derived to associate cause and effect. None of this had had a major influence on the development of economic thought. In university departments of economics the professor of statistics, certainly a necessity, was thought to be well outside the mainstream of economic interest. Thus at Harvard University W. Leonard Crum had gone on from unsuccessfully disproving the conclusions of Berle and Means on the concentration in American industry[9] to correcting the findings of *The Literary Digest* on its projections of the election results in 1936. These had shown Alfred Landon winning by a substantial margin; correcting for sampling errors, Crum showed Landon winning by even more. It was, in a general way, what was expected of statisticians when they moved beyond the simple tabulation of population, production and prices. Even on urgent matters there were serious statistical gaps. Until well into the depression years the United States had no useful figures on the level or distribution of unemployment. There was a certain classical logic in this; one did not spend money collecting information on what, in high economic principle, could not exist.

From this pedestrian tradition now came the statistics that, in their powerful practical effect, made Keynes inescapable. They showed the value of the total production of goods and services of all kinds, public and private. The Gross National Product. And in companion tables they showed the income derived therefrom by kind and source. National Income. That the latter needed to be sufficient to buy the former was a thought that no one could

9. See Chapter XV.

henceforth escape. Nor, more specifically, the thought that savings from the income now shown might not all be used — that they might not be absorbed by the spending for investment goods also shown in the tables. And it was evident how serviceably an increment of income, as from government expenditure, would make up any shortfall in investment spending or consumer borrowing and add to the purchase and production of goods.

It was one thing to resist Keynes's theory; it was something else and much harder to resist the Kuznets statistics.

And there was an even more powerful effect. The Kuznets figures in the early 1940s showed how far below capacity, by the standards of past performance and with the normal increase in the labor force, the economic system was operating. They showed how much the economy could produce for both civilian consumption and military requirements from currently unused capital and manpower.

In one of those coincidences by which even undeserving officialdom is redeemed, one of Kuznets's most talented and persuasive students, Robert Roy Nathan (1908–   ), was actively associated with war planning in 1940 and 1941 and in charge of planning at the War Production Board after its creation in 1942. In 1941, in the last months before the attack on Pearl Harbor, Nathan and his staff outlined a schedule of weapons production — aircraft, tanks, ordnance, ships — called the Victory Program. It far exceeded anything that others in Washington, including their later colleagues on the War Production Board, thought possible, even sane. But there were the tables; they showed how great were the unused and available resources.

The Victory Program was adopted and with no undue difficulty achieved. After its implementation Nathan became a powerful force, along with Kuznets, in the scheduling of its components and then in restraining the more irresponsible military demands and proposals. He came also to be greatly resented by men who found themselves unable to contend with his statistics. When he was drafted into the army in 1943, it was an occasion for much quiet, and some expressed, relief.[10]

In Britain counterpart calculations of Gross National Product and its components were also a guiding framework for mobilization, a thing there of great completeness and competence. Germany, in contrast, had no useful National Accounts; the concept of Gross National Product — perhaps incidentally, extensively Jewish in origin — had not effectively penetrated the Third Reich. In the absence of knowledge of how resources were being used, civilian consumption and man- and womanpower use in the civilian sector remained uncontrollably high throughout nearly the whole of the war.[11]

Simon Kuznets stands as one of the least recognized of the pillars of Allied power in World War II. Here again the Kuznets contributions: he and his associates put Keynes into statistically influential form, showed the wartime rewards from breaking the underemployment equilibrium and producing at capacity and made the Gross National Product a household expression. All this is still highly relevant. Without "this great invention of the twentieth century [the National Accounts] . . . macroeconomics would be adrift in a sea of unorganized data."[12]

The final contribution of the war to the propagation of Keynes's beliefs was that it showed what his economics could accomplish through the agency of the state. From 1939 to 1944, the wartime peak, Gross National Product in constant (1972) dollars increased from $320 billion to $569 billion, not a great deal short of doubling.

10. I am grateful to Robert Nathan himself for help on this account.

11. See the *U.S. Strategic Bombing Survey: The Effects of Strategic Bombing on the German War Economy* (Washington, D.C.: U.S. Government Printing Office, 1945) and Burton H. Klein, *Germany's Economic Preparations for War* (Cambridge: Harvard University Press, 1959). The first competent measures of German aggregate product and its components were made by American statisticians as they assessed the effects of the air attacks after the war.

12. Paul A. Samuelson and William D. Nordhaus, *Economics*, 12th edition (New York: McGraw-Hill, 1985), p. 102.

Amid much talk of wartime deprivation, personal consumption expenditures in similarly constant dollars did not diminish; they increased — from $220 to $255 billion.[13] Unemployment was an estimated 17.2 percent of the civilian labor force in 1939; in 1944, it was a nominal 1.2 percent.[14] Metal-using durables, such as new automobiles, had disappeared from the living standard, but, over-all, in the last full year of the war Americans were living better than ever before. That this was the result of the upward pressure of public demand on the economy — federal government pur-chases of goods and services in these years increased from $22.8 billion in 1939 to $269.7 billion in 1944[15] — no one could seri-ously doubt. Mars, the god of war, had, in his ineluctable and unpredictable course, fashioned for Keynes a demonstration beyond anything that could — or indeed should — be asked.

The state had not been passive in this period, as classical and *laissez-faire* doctrine required; instead it had been active and inter-ventionist on an unprecedented and previously unimagined scale. The result was an achievement on which all Americans reflected with pride.

Some forms of the wartime government intervention did not survive. Comprehensive price controls supported as necessary by rationing held prices nearly stable from the time they were fully deployed in 1943 until they were lifted in the autumn of 1946. The black market was small — perhaps, considering the extent of the controls, insignificant. World War II, unlike World War I or the late 1970s, does not stay in the social memory as a time of inflation.[16] But control of prices or wages was not part of the Keynesian sys-tem. Though revived for the Korean War and by Richard Nixon in

13. Both sets of figures are from the *Economic Report of the President* (Washing-ton, D.C.: U.S. Government Printing Office, 1985), p. 234. The base of constant 1972 dollars is one that is commonly used.

14. Cited in Lekachman, pp. 142, 150.

15. *Economic Report of the President*, 1985, p. 235.

16. I have dealt generally with these matters in *A Life in Our Times* (Boston: Houghton Mifflin, 1981), p. 124 *et seq.* See also the recent study *Drastic Measures: A History of Wage and Price Controls in the United States* by Hugh Rockoff (Cam-bridge, England: Cambridge University Press, 1984).

1971–1973, it was later to have only a fugitive existence in economic thought and policy in the English-speaking countries. The very word *control* would be excised; if restraints were needed on wages and prices, it would be not wage and price control but an incomes and prices policy.

Of greater eventual importance was the effect of the war on taxation. Taxes, by modern standards, had been insignificant before 1941. In 1939, federal revenues were just under $5 billion; by 1945, they were in excess of $44 billion in current dollars.[17] In ensuing years they remained at around ten times or more the prewar level. In 1929, the highest marginal rate on the personal income tax had been 24 percent; it rose during the New Deal years, and by 1945 it was 94 percent.[18]

With the war, and in justification of these taxes, had come the notion of an approach to equality of sacrifice: the poor would pay with their lives or anyhow with their military service or their toil; the affluent, especially the nonserving rich, would pay with their taxes. A proposal by President Roosevelt in 1942 that for the duration of the war personal incomes be subject to an upper limit of $25,000 after taxes was received adversely by those who made more and was not adopted; the principle of a strongly progressive, effectively an income-redistributive, tax survived until recent times.

As noted, the wartime achievements of the United States and Britain were regarded with wide approval. They were the achievements of government — of the state. This did not escape professional or public mention. And the conclusion was evident: what had served so well in war could surely serve as well in peace. As the war had affirmed Keynes, so it had dealt a heavy blow to classical *laissez faire*.

The voices of the great tradition were, however, by no means stilled. In 1944, at the peak of the wartime effort and intervention, Professor Friedrich von Hayek, by now at the University of Chi-

17. *Economic Report of the President* (Washington, D.C.: U.S. Government Printing Office, 1964), p. 274.
18. These data are from Joseph Pechman of the Brookings Institution.

cago, returned to the charge, rigorously and sternly asserting the rules of the classical economy: "The price system will fulfill [its] . . . function only if competition prevails, *that is, if the individual producer has to adapt himself to price changes and cannot control them.*"[19] But even he stressed not the inefficacy of government intervention but its threat to liberty. To this threat, its impairment of the freedom to choose, he and his coadjutor, Professor Milton Friedman, would increasingly return.[20] The war, nonetheless, dealt the classical disapproval of government intervention a heavy blow. It was not, during the war years, a persuasive theme. Millions had then enjoyed the more immediately relevant freedom of employment and money to spend, a freedom that those who speak with the greatest solemnity of freedom are most disposed to ignore. And in the economics profession a new view of government and a new reliance on its intervention would be one of the major economic consequences of the war.

Here once again it was events, not economists, that took charge — events silent, without voice and, since unrecognized, unresisted.

19. Friedrich A. von Hayek, *The Road to Serfdom* (Chicago: University of Chicago Press, 1944), p. 49. Italics added.

20. Friedman most specifically in the widely read *Free to Choose* (New York: Harcourt Brace Jovanovich, 1980), which he wrote with his wife, Rose Friedman.

XIX

High Noon

A FTER A WAR the wise victor consolidates his gains. So after
World War II did the Keynesians. The war had eliminated
unemployment. Let there now be steps to ensure that what
had been a passive consequence of wartime mobilization would
become an active purpose of public policy. The Keynesians were
still, and influentially, in Washington and had found allies in the
business world, soon to be mentioned. They moved, accordingly,
to have the Keynesian precepts written into law. Full employment
would no longer be considered the autonomous consequence of the
competitive economy. The underemployment equilibrium would
now be assumed, and henceforth it would be a deliberate purpose
of government to break that equilibrium and ensure full employment in its place.

Movement in this direction began even before the end of hostilities. In the United States, as also in Britain, the predictable oratory
of the time held that those who were risking their lives against
Hitler and the Japanese militarists should expect something better
on their return than the unemployment and economic despair of
the depression years. To this end, the Beveridge Report in Britain,
extensively influenced by Nicholas Kaldor,[1] promised a greatly
improved social insurance system; in the United States there was
much seriously unfocused talk about postwar planning — plan-

1. See Chapter XIV.

ning to ensure that reconversion would be accomplished effi-
ciently and that economic life would otherwise flourish without
too much impairing change. And there was talk with a sharper
focus that extended into the business community. In the war years
a group of liberal businessmen — Ralph E. Flanders, a machine-
tool manufacturer in Vermont, later a senator from that state;
Beardsley Ruml, a former economics professor and then a high officer of R. H. Macy's, the great retail store in New York; and others — formed the Committee for Economic Development. Its purpose was to consider how unemployment could be lessened and
economic performance improved when peace came. The committee did not publicly embrace Keynes; that would have repelled too
many sober-minded executives and entrepreneurs. Nor did it approve
deficit financing by the federal government; that was still a manifestation of grave irresponsibility. In a formula devised by Ruml, it
held that the federal budget should, indeed, be balanced but balanced specifically at full employment.[2] A shrewd counselor always
accentuates the positive.

In January of 1945, with the end of the war in sight, there was a
stronger and economically far more influential step. The Keynesians in the executive branch drafted, and four senators — Robert F.
Wagner of New York and three from the liberal West, James E.
Murray of Montana, Elbert Thomas of Utah and Joseph O'Maho-
ney of Wyoming — took the lead in sponsoring, a bill (S380) to put
the economics of John Maynard Keynes firmly and fully into law.[3]
In its early versions this legislation committed the government to
a policy of ensuring *full* employment, declaring plainly that "to
the extent that continuing full employment cannot otherwise be

2. See The Committee for Economic Development, *Jobs and Markets* (New York:
McGraw-Hill, 1946). When I reviewed this book for *Fortune*, I was asked by Theodore Yntema, the chief economist of the committee, if I would be careful not to
identify the ideas therein with Keynes.

3. The history of this legislation is dealt with at length by Stephen Kemp Bailey in
Congress Makes a Law: The Story Behind the Employment Act of 1946 (New York:
Columbia University Press, 1950).

achieved, it is the further responsibility of the Federal Government to provide such volume of Federal investment and expenditure as may be needed to assure continuing full employment." The bill called for the annual submission of a national budget detailing, among other things, the size of the labor force, the prospects for its employment and the additional federal expenditure and investment required to yield "a full employment volume of production."[4] Provision was made for a strong executive authority to prepare and submit this full-employment budget and for a companion congressional committee to receive and act on it. The legislation as first proposed stands as the high-water mark, not alone in the United States but in all the industrial lands, of the Keynesian system.

The tide, to continue the metaphor, soon receded. The now familiar battle between those who believe themselves to be saving capitalism and those concerned to save it from its saviors was promptly rejoined. The National Association of Manufacturers, then the most influential of all business organizations, led the fight against the bill — and against the trade unions and the National Farmers Union, the most liberal of the farm organizations, both of which had rallied to its support. The principal NAM document in opposition held in successive section headings that the bill would mean added government controls, would destroy private enterprise, would increase the powers of the Executive, would legalize federal spending and pump priming, would lead to socialism, would promise too much and would otherwise be ridiculous.[5] A comprehensive indictment.

Against such consequences, the bill as originally written could not be passed. But neither, given the specter of renewed unemployment, could the need for such legislation be denied. "Full employment" was therefore reduced to "employment"; no one could

4. Both quotations from the bill are in Bailey, p. 244.
5. See Robert Lekachman, *The Age of Keynes* (New York: Random House, 1966), p. 168.

seriously object to a policy in favor of that. The bill sternly warned in its final form that it was designed for those "able, willing, and seeking to work"; this also was reassuring. It advised that the energies of industry, agriculture and labor would be coordinated and utilized in "a manner calculated *to foster and promote free competitive enterprise* and the general welfare."[6] The classical system was clearly not being relegated to the past.

The retreat went further. The full-employment budget was abandoned and likewise the executive and congressional machinery to implement it. Instead, three men or women of economic competence, a Council of Economic Advisers, would henceforth advise the President on measures to enhance employment and economic policy in general. Each January the Council would report on the economic prospect to a joint committee of the House of Representatives and the Senate, although the latter was, thoughtfully, denied any legislative power. Admirers of the art of legislative emasculation have, on occasion, taken the action on the Employment Act of 1946 as a model.

President Harry S. Truman reacted to the bill with marked calm and did not for some months get around to appointing his new advisers. When he did, he designated as chairman Edwin G. Nourse (1883–1974), an economist of exceptionally pleasant manner, orthodox credentials and mature years, who had been long at the Brookings Institution. Nourse was free from any evident Keynesian taint; it is unlikely that he had ever read *The General Theory* or thought it a worthwhile use of his time.[7]

Nevertheless, and the emasculation notwithstanding, the passage of the Employment Act of 1946, with its provision for a Council of Economic Advisers, was a step of marked importance in the

6. This quotation from the Employment Act of 1946 is in Bailey, p. 228. Italics added.

7. He was soon succeeded by Leon Keyserling (1908–   ), a former aide of Senator Robert Wagner's and an ardent and articulate advocate of the purposes of the legislation and the Council it established. It was not in Keyserling's favor in dealing with the more sensitively self-conscious of academic economists that, although thoroughly schooled in economic issues, he was, like Adolf Berle, trained originally as a lawyer.

history of economics. It established economists and economic counsel firmly in the center of modern American public administration. There would be similar if less formal steps in the other industrial countries.

The quarter century following the passage of the bill was very good in economic performance and, without question, the best professionally for economists in the history of the discipline. Unemployment in the United States and elsewhere in the industrial world was relatively — relative, that is, to earlier or later experience — trivial. So were price movements; there was only a minor upward drift. In only three of these twenty-five years did the American Gross National Product, a term now fully in common usage, fail to increase, and two of the three slippages were slight. For this, economists, including those in positions of prominence, were given full credit. And this credit, not reluctantly, was accepted. In January 1969, as the Employment Act was rounding out its twenty-second year, the Council of Economic Advisers was led to reflect on its achievements. Its self-gratifying cerebration is worth repeating at some length:

> The Nation is now in its 95th month of continuous economic advance. Both in strength and length, this prosperity is without parallel in our history. We have steered clear of the business-cycle recessions which for generations derailed us repeatedly from the path of growth and progress. . . .
>
> No longer do we view our economic life as a relentless tide of ups and downs. No longer do we fear that automation and technical progress will rob workers of jobs rather than help us to achieve greater abundance. No longer do we consider poverty and unemployment permanent landmarks on our economic scene. . . .
>
> Ever since the historic passage of the Employment Act in 1946, economic policies have responded to the fire alarm of recession and boom. In the 1960s, we have adopted a new strategy aimed at fire prevention — sustaining prosperity and heading off recession or serious inflation before they could take hold. . . .

Meanwhile, a solid foundation has been built for continued growth in the years ahead.[8]

Economists of these years were surely wise in one respect: they chose the right time to be operative in their craft. Not since Adam Smith and not again after this postwar period could or would economists look with more approval on their own achievements or, perhaps a more important matter, be generally so approved. All are reminded, however, that "Jove strikes the Titans down / Not when they set about their mountain-piling / But when another rock would crown the work." In the late 1960s, Jove was in wait for economists as they moved to crown their Keynesian edifice.

The adverse blow would come partly in consequence of a misapprehension of the economic conditions in the twenty-five good years. In these years a series of expansive forces, completely apart from any economic guidance, had stimulated the American and world economies. These forces included the release into consumer expenditure of the lush wartime accumulation of savings — approximately $250 billion in the United States by the end of the war.[9] The money so available turned the all but universally predicted postwar slump into an unprecedented boom, one that sustained itself as consumers found that the depression and unemployment against the threat of which many had been saving had not materialized.

Reinforcing domestic expenditure in the United States was an inflow of purchasing power from abroad. In these years, because the country had been exempt from wartime devastation, it had a strongly favorable trade balance, which is to say that foreigners were spending more on American products and employment than Americans were spending abroad, with resulting stimulative effect. This is still a poorly appreciated point. It is in sharp contrast with circumstances in the 1980s, when a strongly adverse trade balance meant that Americans were spending much more on foreign prod-

8. *Economic Report of the President* (Washington, D.C.: U.S. Government Printing Office, 1969), pp. 4–5.
9. Lekachman, p. 164.

ucts and travel abroad than foreigners were spending in the United States. Money so spent abroad is a marked subtraction from effective demand at home.

Further, as time passed, there were the expenditures for the Korean War, for the weapons responsive to the cold war and later for the increasing involvement in Vietnam. In earlier times Keynes had proposed that pound notes should be buried in abandoned coal mines, because their digging up would add beneficially to employment and purchasing power. Weaponry of vast cost that was unusable because of its nearly infinite destructive power was now, and increasingly, serving the same economic purpose as the buried money.

Finally, there was the modest stabilizing effect of the welfare state. Unemployment compensation was discovered in these years to have the convenient tendency to increase when economic activity and employment slackened, acting thus as a compensatory force against economic contraction and unemployment. Other welfare expenditure cushioned and secured the flow of purchasing power.

In 1948, federal expenditures and outlays of all kinds reached their postwar low of just under $30 billion; twenty years later, in 1968, the year that gave rise to the above-cited reflection on economic success, they were in excess of $183 billion, approximately six times as much.[10] The federal government had thus contributed to a reliable and increasing flow of expenditure. A substantially progressive tax system, one transferring income from the affluent to the needful and spending poor, also modestly supported the marginal propensity to consume of both those taxed and those receiving income from the government.

None of this — not the more effectively expended savings, not the favorable trade balance, not the arms expenditure in the two wars, not the unexpected stabilizing effect of welfare expenditures — could be attributed to a deliberate economic design. Economics, often the victim of adverse events and soon to become so

10. *Economic Report of the President* (Washington, D.C.: U.S. Government Printing Office, 1985), p. 318.

again, was for once the beneficiary of highly favorable circumstance.

There was in 1964, however, one step that *was* attributable to studied economic activity. It was the tax-reduction measure of that year, led in its advocacy by Walter W. Heller (1915–   ), who, with Leon Keyserling in an earlier administration, was one of the two most influential members of the Council of Economic Advisers in the history of that institution. The marginal rate on the personal income tax, then at a theoretical 77 percent, was reduced to 70 percent; there was companion reduction in other brackets; the basic rate on the corporate income tax was also reduced. None of this reflected a diminished need for revenues; it was deliberately designed to expand purchasing power and employment and avoid a depressive budget surplus at full employment.

This was perhaps the most discussed tax measure in American history to this time, that leading to the permanent adoption of a personal income tax in 1913 possibly excepted. Certainly no action was more influential in the example it set. It would, seventeen years later, be the often-cited precedent for large tax reductions by the administration of Ronald Reagan.

Nonetheless, throughout the twenty-five good years the range and power of economic advice was again, as so often before, generally subordinate to the commanding power of events.

Economic ideas, it has been sufficiently seen, are also extensively the product of adversity. During war and depression, in rationalizing or, more rarely, contending with poverty and deprivation, economists are forced or encouraged to thought. In good times there is an agreeable tendency to relax in self-approving contentment. If there are no great and pressing problems, none is addressed.

So economics lost its sense of urgency in the twenty-five good years. There was active concern for the problem of postwar reconstruction in Europe and Japan, the reconstruction in no slight measure preceding the evolution of a guiding theory. There was also for the first time a lively interest in the nature of the development process in the countries newly released from colonial rule. Economic development became a separate field of research and study, one that suffered significantly from an inclination to urge on countries in earlier agrarian modes the policies and associated administrative apparatus appropriate to advanced stages of industrial development. And, as in Central America, there was a tendency to ignore feudal political structures that were wholly inimical to development of any kind because they were intractable. But the history of these concerns must await another book — and author.

Mathematical formulation of economic relationships — of cost in relation to prices, consumer income in relation to the shape of the demand function and much else — also flourished in these years. And there was a continuing debate as to the usefulness of mathematical economics, often called mathematical theory, with those proficient in the science of numbers taking a favorable view and those not so equipped taking a cautiously unfavorable view of what they did not understand. Mathematical accomplishment in economic theory did attain a certain objective value as a ticket of admission to the economics profession, a device for keeping out those with a purely verbal talent. And while such theory did not, it was agreed, contribute greatly to practical policy guidance, it did serve another function. The increasingly technical formulations and the debate over their validity and precision provided employment for many of the many thousands of economists now needed for economics instruction in universities and colleges around the world. Had these voices all sought a hearing on practical matters, the resulting clamor would have been distracting, perhaps unendurable.

Mathematical economics also gave to economics a professionally rewarding aspect of scientific certainty and precision, adding usefully to the prestige of academic economists in their university association with the other social sciences and the so-called hard sciences. One of the costs of these several services was, however, the removal of the subject several steps further from reality. Not all but a very large number of the mathematical exercises began (as they still do) with the words "We assume perfect competition." In the real world perfect competition was by now leading an increasingly esoteric existence, if, indeed, any existence at all, and mathematical theory was, in no slight measure, the highly sophisticated cover under which it managed to survive.

Two other developments in this period had substantially greater practical utility and effect. One, tracing back to the 1930s and distantly, as also earlier told, to François Quesnay, was the Input-Output Analysis of Wassily W. Leontief. A superbly simple concept, the Leontief tables, to remind, showed the value of what each industry and, with increasing work and refinement, what subsections of each industry sold to each other and received from each other. The resulting great complex showed how any given change is distributed through the economic system — what an increase in automobile production, for example, would require of the several elements of the steel industry and from the steel industry on to coal and ferro-alloys. Or, an important point for Leontief, what the military power absorbed in resources and returned in sales.[11]

In the years following the war this most informative, as well as somewhat costly, statistical enterprise was taken on by the government. Discontinued by the Eisenhower administration, it was resumed in 1961 in the Kennedy years. Nearly all of the industrial countries — Britain, Japan, Canada, Italy, Holland and others — sought similar insight into their interindustry relations. And so did the Soviet Union and its satellites.

Born in 1906 in St. Petersburg of a textile-manufacturing family of social revolutionary, which is to say anti-Bolshevist, political commitment, Leontief had come to the United States by way of Berlin and China in self-imposed political exile some years after the Russian Revolution. The interindustry tables that he later devised and developed, if interesting and informative for capitalism, proved to be highly functional for socialist planning as well, since it is an elementary and inescapable need of such planning

11. See Wassily W. Leontief, *Input-Output Economics* (New York: Oxford University Press, 1966), and my earlier discussion of Professor Leontief in Chapter V.

that there be knowledge of what each industry requires in any considerable amount of each other industry. In consequence, it was Leontief's remarkable fate, after having lived and worked in the United States, to be celebrated in the Soviet Union and welcomed back to the land of his birth as one of the most useful contributors to socialist economic success.

The second, somewhat later and related development of these years, a product of the great engineering advances in data storage and processing techniques, was the econometric or computer models of the economy. Though a matter of considerable mystery to the layman, the econometric models are not, in their essentials, difficult to grasp. Going beyond Keynes, Kuznets and Leontief, they seek to reproduce with the help of computers the widely distributed effects of all great changes in the economic system — changes in public expenditures, taxes, interest rates, wages, profits, industrial production by industries, housing construction, a great deal else — as these, in varying association with other changes, affect or are assumed to affect all other economic magnitudes. Human judgment, needless to say, enters into the equations that denote the effect of any given change.

Pioneering work on these models of the economy was accomplished by Jan Tinbergen (1903–   ), an economist from the Netherlands of international reputation and respect, who extended his innovative concerns to numerous other matters, including guidance of Dutch economic policy and problems of development in the poor countries. Following Tinbergen's early work was that of John Richard Stone (1913–   ) of the University of Cambridge, Lawrence R. Klein (1920–   ) of the University of Pennsylvania and Otto Eckstein (1926–1984) of Harvard, along with literally hundreds of anonymous but informed and diligent assistants. For this (and associated) accomplishments Tinbergen, Klein and Stone each received the Nobel Prize. No other economic effort, it may be added, was ever commercially so lucrative. From the models came forecasts and more specific information relevant to corporate decisions

of a highly saleable character. In 1979, Data Resources, an econometric consulting firm established by Otto Eckstein, was sold to
McGraw-Hill, the publishing company, for $103 million. Not many
economics professors have created so much capital value in one
lifetime.

A major service of the models, as indicated, was forecasting — of
output, income, employment and prices in the economy as a whole
and of how these might affect individual industries. This calls for
a special word. Organized, as distinct from casual or off-the-cuff,
forecasting was not a new function for economists. In the 1920s,
as a product of the great economic hubris of that era, the Harvard
Economic Society had been formed by a group of Harvard economists with the purpose of foretelling major economic developments. Elementary econometrics was brought to the task. The
Society did not have a happy history. In the summer and early
autumn of 1929, it forecast a modest setback in business conditions, and when the setback came in October, its percipience was
admirably confirmed. Unfortunately, it continued to emphasize the
modest character of the downturn, and as that downturn became
more serious, it proclaimed the certainty of a prompt recovery, for
such was the basic tendency of the business cycle in the classical
mode. Its encouraging forecasts continued as the economic conditions continued to worsen. Eventually the forecasting effort suc-
cumbed to the depression, along with so much else, and was
liquidated.

Forecasting did not become a wholly reputable economic phenomenon until the building of the full-court econometric models.
With this development the factors bearing on business conditions
and the results — the flow of business, consumer and government
expenditures, their sources and components and the expected
responding production, employment and prices in aggregate and
detail — were envisaged as to effect and were measured. Having
been so measured, the larger economic consequences could, it was
felt, be anticipated. There was further encouragement from the

feeling that some of the determining factors in the forecasts, notably government expenditures and taxation and central bank interest rates, were under public control, which meant that the economy so managed or at least guided had a predictability not known in the pre-Keynesian world.

However, the new faith in forecasting spread far beyond the econometric models.[12] Few economists in the post-Keynesian years passed a week, some not a day, without being asked for their professional view as to the prospect for economic growth, that is, for prospective increases in the Gross National Product, or as to what prices, employment levels and the outlook for particular industries could be expected. In those good years economists were thought worthy of trust. Many responded not out of knowledge but more or less automatically out of professional habit. These were things economists were expected to know. Rarely in history has so much questionable information been so confidently offered.

Forecasts are, in fact, inherently unreliable. Were they otherwise, those responsible for them would never give them to the public; that would be an act of unimaginable generosity, for were they kept for the private pecuniary use of the men, women or organizations making them, the resulting accretions of wealth would be nearly infinite. Returns from investment in accordance with such forecasts would be completely certain; purchasable assets would flow relentlessly into the hands, or more precisely the portfolios, of people or organizations that could not lose. Such perfect certainty having been achieved, capitalism, the free enterprise system in any form now known, would cease to exist. It would, in truth, be gravely vulnerable to any forecast with an ensured accuracy of more than 50 percent.

There are two reasons that forecasts fail. The equations linking change to result — interest rates to investment, net government expenditure to consumer demand, the latter to prices — are, as earlier noted, based on human judgments supported by statistical

12. A matter I touched on in Chapter I of this history.

knowledge of such relationships in the past. Judgments can err; relationships can change. Further, many of the forces that initiate change cannot be predicted; they are outside the knowledge of economists. War and international tension, the monetary manipulations of central bankers, the rise and fall of international cartels, decisions by debtor countries to pay or forgo payments on their debts, the outcome of wage negotiations and much, much else are all, by their nature, unknown. The best equations relating interest rates to real estate values will tell nothing of the latter in the absence of knowledge of the operative interest rate.

Nonetheless, a supporting reason for this great economic preoccupation remains. Every day in thousands of different contexts business executives and government officials must make decisions requiring an assumption as to the future — a future that by its nature is unknown. The modern large business enterprise, in contrast with its flexible, quickly accommodating, small entrepreneurial predecessor, must also plan. Planning always involves the future. The forecasts — what the econometric models tell an industry as to prices or costs or probable demand for products — help establish probable magnitudes and keep decisions within the range of plausibility. But far more important in the modern practice, the forecasts lift from the person who must make decisions as to the future a heavy, even perilous, responsibility. Since he cannot know the demand for the fertilizer, urban office space, recreation vehicles or rail, air or road transport for which provision must be made, the forecast allows him to yield his judgment to the forecaster. If the judgment is then wrong, it is not his; instead it is the best professionally available — a significant protection in a world of tense bureaucratic conflict.

The rise of the forecasting industry and syndrome as a major episode in the history of economics in the years after Keynes was not the result of enhanced certainty in the economic prospect. It owed much, as earlier observed, to the increased self-confidence of, and confidence in, economists. But, far more important, the forecasters saved business executives — vulnerable bureaucrats charged with knowing the future — from the consequences of an inescapably flawed knowledge of what was to come.

The twenty-five good years came to an end. The exuberant confidence of this period had, as I have indicated, prevented introspection. The separation of macroeconomics from microeconomics preserved in the latter an approach to the classically competitive structure, but, as we shall see, it also, alas, diverted attention from developments deeply adverse to macroeconomic or Keynesian management. And a strongly inhibiting circumstance, one not yet fully appreciated, emerged as regards Keynesian economics. That was its grave political asymmetry. What was politically possible against deflation and depression was not politically possible or feasible against inflation. To this saddening history we now turn.

XX

Twilight and Evening Bell

ALTHOUGH increasingly evident, the decline of the Keynesian system went unremarked for a long time, and it is still not fully recognized. As the last chapter indicated, what seemed economically symmetrical in the operation of the system proved to be politically asymmetrical. Deflation and unemployment called for higher public expenditure and lower taxes, which were politically very agreeable actions. Price inflation, on the other hand, called for lower government expenditure and higher taxes, which were far from politically agreeable. Moreover, a matter soon to be seen, they were not easily effective against the modern form of inflation — against wage-price inflation, as it came to be called. Keynesian policy was a one-way street or, more precisely, an avenue that presented a pleasant and easy downhill passage but a very difficult and uncertain effort in ascent.

There were two reasons that this was not recognized in most economic discussion. Keynes's *General Theory* was, eminently, a tract of the Great Depression. The problem then was of unemployment and falling prices; the early Keynesians gave little or no attention to inflation and none to the political aspects of its restraint. This neglect continued and was made greater by the growing divorce of economics from politics. What in the last century had been called political economy was, after Alfred Marshall, called economics, and in pursuit of an earnestly sought reputation as a science, economic

266

instruction and policy advice were ever more severely separated from political constraints.

In the United States over most of the twenty-five good years inflation was not, in fact, an issue. The brief price pressures of the Korean War apart, there was only a small upward drift in prices — until 1966, only a percentage point or two a year in the Consumer Price Index. Economists, as ever, did not concern themselves with what was not visibly troublesome.

The rate of inflation began to accelerate, however, after 1966; it went up more than 6 percentage points between 1969 and 1970, nearly 8 between 1972 and 1973 and nearly 14 percentage points from 1974 to 1975,[1] the final increase lodging the phrase "double-digit inflation" disastrously in American economic terminology.

In these new circumstances, the political asymmetry became entirely evident. Where the economic advisers to the President had once come to his office to urge the relative merits of lower taxes or higher public expenditure, they now came to speak of tax increases and expenditure reduction. Where once their appearance on a White House calendar was welcomed, it was now a sordid and depressing prospect, one to be postponed by any, however implausible, excuse.

A further and yet more serious problem in all the industrial countries was the new form of inflation. This was price and wage increases coming from the interaction in the modern economy of great organizations. With industrial concentration, corporations had achieved a very substantial measure of control over their prices, the control that orthodox economics conceded to monopoly and oligopoly without quite conceding its full existence in real life. And trade unions had achieved substantial authority over the wages and associated benefits accorded their members. From the interaction of these entities had come a new and powerful inflationary force: the upward pressure of wage settlements on prices, the upward pull of prices and living costs on wages. This was the interacting dynamic that came to be called the wage-price spiral.

1. *Economic Report of the President* (Washington, D.C.: U.S. Government Printing Office, 1985), p. 291. In the Consumer Price Index, 1967 = 100.

For contending with this dynamic the Keynesian Revolution had left a strongly negative legacy. Wage and price determination was a microeconomic phenomenon, and microeconomics had been separated off by Keynes and left to the classical market orthodoxy. In orthodox microeconomics the wage-price spiral could not occur; producers of goods and the wages they paid their workers were still subject to market forces that the producers did not control. And if, as with monopoly or oligopoly, they did control them, it was in order to maximize profits, not to retrieve increases in wage costs forced by the unions.

The separation of microeconomics from the purview of Keynesian economics and policy thus preserved a microeconomic model that could not be accorded an inflationary role. This separation was important; it was at the very heart of the great compromise of Keynes with the classical tradition, the compromise that preserved the market nexus. To admit of the inflationary role of the wage-price spiral was to destroy that compromise. Worse still, it was to invite policies — wage and price restraints or controls — that surrendered the market, in greater or lesser measure, to the authority of the state.

And there was a further objection. Quite evidently, in their ability to influence prices and wages, not to mention their ability to influence consumers through advertising and salesmanship, corporations (in conjunction with trade unions) now had an important effect on the allocation of capital, labor and materials — of economic resources. This also could not be conceded, so with no slight solemnity it was said that any restraint on wages and prices would interfere with resource allocation.

In Europe — in Germany, Austria, Switzerland, Holland, Scandinavia — and in Japan the Keynesian compromise, the separation off of microeconomics as the privileged preserve of the market, was less influential than it was in Britain and the United States. Accordingly, as inflation became increasingly a threat in the 1970s, those countries more readily accepted the inflationary effect of wage-price interaction. In further consequence, steps to limit wage increases to what could be afforded from the existing price structure became normal, accepted policy. In Austria, the most advanced and successful case, controls on wages and a counterpart system of restraint on corporate prices were put into effect with considerable formality through what was called the Social Market Policy. In other countries the procedure was less formal; wages were negotiated within the framework of existing prices and with a general view to keeping those prices stable.

In the United States and Britain, as also in Canada, there were in these years hortatory, voluntary and some legal efforts to arrest the wage-price spiral, and in 1971–1973 the administration of Richard Nixon introduced formal wage and price controls, which, in combination with a relaxed fiscal and monetary policy, helped him enormously in the 1972 election. But none of these efforts was thought serious or legitimate. They were temporary steps, wise or not so wise, meant to serve until the Keynesian macroeconomic policy came somehow to perform its established function in combining reasonably full employment with stable prices. Since neither unions nor business firms in the English-speaking countries were inclined to accept government interference with wages and prices, the traditional defenders of the integrity of the microeconomic market had decisively powerful allies.

Finally, beginning at the end of 1973, there came the large increase in oil prices, the result of the cartel action of the oil-producing states, OPEC. Between 1972 and 1981, the index of the prices of household fuels in the United States climbed from 118.5 (1967 = 100) to 675.9, a nearly sixfold increase.[2] This, too, was a microeconomic change beyond the reach of Keynesian macroeconomic policy.

The role of the oil price increases as an inflationary force was recognized. Their exceptional character was made evident in the terminology of the time: the oil shocks, they were called. The increase in the price of oil accounted for perhaps 10 percent of the inflationary effect in these years, but its proclaimed effect was much

2. *Economic Report of the President*, p. 292.

greater. Domestic prices and wages being inconsistent as causal factors with the prevailing orthodoxy, it was extremely convenient to pass blame for inflation over to distant Arabs and their co-monopolists.

As wage-price inflation was beyond the reach of the Keynesian orthodoxy, so too were OPEC prices. The Keynesian system, in consequence, was visibly impotent. In 1975, President Gerald Ford called into conference some of the country's better-known economists to prescribe for inflation — 13.5 percent in the Consumer Price Index in that year. There was full professional agreement on only one remedy: that government regulations should be reviewed to remove any obvious impediments to market competition. For practical effect, this was no better than the President's own prescription, which was the wearing of buttons inscribed with the insignia WIN, for Whip Inflation Now.

There remained, however, one highly available political course of action: there could be a resort to monetary policy — monetarism. This had articulate and influential advocates; by the mid-1970s, it was also and more impressively the residual legatee as to policy, nothing else being politically possible.

Since the end of the gold-purchase episode in the Roosevelt years, monetary policy in the United States, as in the other industrial countries, had had a passive, even exiguous, existence. During World War II, it had had no role at all; interest rates were kept low and constant; movements in the money supply, however measured, attracted no attention. Matters did not change much in the twenty-five good years. Little thought needed to be given to managing the money supply in order to control prices if prices were stable anyhow. The legacy of Irving Fisher had not been lost, but any economic scholar who dwelled too persistently on the role of money in the guidance of the economy risked being called a monetary crank. Information on the current money supply — M or hand-to-hand coinage and currency, M' or bank deposits subject to check — could still be had by the economist of more arcane tendency in these years, but no newspaper featured these aggregates, and if printed, they attracted no attention or comment.

Waiting his time in the 1960s and early 1970s was, however, perhaps the most influential economic figure of the second half of the twentieth century. This was Milton Friedman (1912–) of the University of Chicago, later of the Hoover Institution on War, Revolution and Peace, a diligent, even indefatigable, advocate of the policy that was to fill the post-Keynesian void, especially in the English-speaking countries.

A small, vigorously spoken man, uniquely determined in debate and discussion, entirely free of the doubt that on occasion assails intellectually more vulnerable scholars, Friedman was, as he remains, the leading American exponent of the classical competitive market, which he held still to exist in substantially unimpaired form except as it had suffered from ill-advised government intrusion. Monopoly, oligopoly and imperfect competition played no important part in his thinking. Friedman was a powerful opponent of government regulation and government activity in general. Freedom, he held, was maximized when the individual was left free to deploy his own income as he wished.

On the other hand, Friedman, unlike less sophisticated practitioners of his faith, was not wholly indifferent to the freedom that accrues from having income to spend. To this end, he was the author of the most radical welfare proposal in the years following World War II. The income tax, he proposed, should, as always, diminish to zero as the lower income brackets are approached. And then in the lowest brackets it should return income, the amount increasing with increasing impoverishment. This was the negative income tax, a secure minimum income for all. Not many economists of the left could lay claim to such an impressive innovation.[3]

Friedman's central contribution to the history of economics was,

3. The negative income tax, in modified form, was taken up by the Nixon administration at the behest of Daniel Patrick Moynihan, one of its leading advocates and later senator from New York, and by then Senator George McGovern, who made a

however, his insistence on the controlling influence of monetary action on the economy and specifically on prices. After a lag of a few months, prices, he held, would always reflect movements in the money supply. So if one controlled the money supply — limited its increase to the slowly expanding requirements of trade, the T in Fisher's historic equation — prices would remain stable. In a statistically impressive demonstration, Friedman, in company with Anna Jacobson Schwartz, sought to show that this relationship had held, or appeared to have held, long in the past.[4] So, presumably, it must in the future.

Friedman did not understate his case. As with most statistical relationships, there were questions as to what was cause, what was effect and also what was coincidence. Perhaps it was movements in prices or in the volume of trade that caused changes in the money supply. Nor was the economic nexus between the supply of money and prices ever fully explained. Various relationships in the field of nature and natural science, Friedman said, also held true even though they eluded explanation.

There was a further, more grievous difficulty with the Friedman prescription, one we have already observed, and that was that no one knew with certainty what, in the modern economy, is money. Hand-to-hand currency and checking deposits certainly. But what of savings deposits subject to check and savings deposits readily convertible to checking accounts? Also what of the purchasing power lying back of credit cards or unused lines of credit? Further, could these monetary aggregates, designated however arbitrarily as money, be, in fact, controlled?

As it turned out, they could not. Friedman was eventually to accuse both the Federal Reserve System and the Bank of England of gross incompetence in their efforts to do so. An economic policy, it might be pointed out in response, needs to be within the

variant a major plank in his 1972 presidential campaign. Unlike old-age pensions, unemployment compensation and health insurance, it generated no effective and enduring political support.

4. See Milton Friedman and Anna Jacobson Schwartz, *A Monetary History of the United States, 1867–1960* (Princeton: Princeton University Press, 1963).

competence, however limited, of those available to administer it.

Acting against these objections and supporting Friedman's relentless and effective advocacy was, again, the context, the post-Keynesian world in which microeconomic concerns were separated off from macroeconomic management. Monetarism would protect the microeconomic orthodoxy. In that orthodoxy there was no original inflationary effect; competition and the market still ruled; there could be no direct intervention to control or influence wages or prices. Monetarism would also circumvent the uncomfortable political asymmetry of Keynesian policy. No tax increases would be necessary nor any curtailment of public expenditure. Nor would there be any enlargement of government function; all monetarist policy could be accomplished by the central bank, in the United States the Federal Reserve System, with only a negligible staff.

For some, monetary policy had (and has) another, even greater, appeal, which was curiously, even unforgivably, overlooked among economists: it is not socially neutral. It operates against inflation by raising interest rates, which, in turn, inhibit bank lending and resulting deposit — that is, money — creation. High interest rates are wholly agreeable to people and institutions that have money to lend, and these normally have more money than those who have no money to lend or, with many exceptions, those who borrow money. An unduly evident truth, as sufficiently emphasized already. In so favoring the individually and institutionally affluent, a restrictive monetary policy is in sharp contrast with a restrictive fiscal policy, which, relying as it does on increased personal and corporate income taxes, adversely affects the rich.

Conservatives in the industrial countries, especially in Britain and the United States, have given strong support to monetary policy. Their instinct in this matter has been far better than that of the economists, who, along with the public at large, have assumed its social neutrality. The applause for Professor Friedman from the conservative affluent, which has been great, has been far from unearned.

As the 1970s passed, inflation persisted. Higher taxes, lower public expenditures, direct intervention on wages and prices, were all ruled out as remedies. As sufficiently observed, only monetary policy remained. So in the latter part of the decade, by the ostensibly liberal administration of President Jimmy Carter in the United States and the avowedly conservative government of Prime Minister Margaret Thatcher in Britain, strong monetarist action was initiated. The Keynesian Revolution was folded in. In the history of economics the age of John Maynard Keynes gave way to the age of Milton Friedman.

By now, however, the Keynesian system had captured both the economic mind and the textbooks. Accordingly, the resort to monetary policy was not, on the whole, well received by economists. And its initial results in the late 1970s and early 1980s were far from reassuring.[5] Economic expansion was arrested, but wage-price interaction continued. So did the effects of the OPEC cartel. And so did inflation. Another singularly offensive word was added to the economists' lexicon, *stagflation*, which describes a stagnant economy in association with continuing inflation.

In the end, inflation was crushed. Money is not related to prices through the unrevealed magic of Fisher's equation and Friedman's faith but through the high interest rates by which bank (and other) lending and deposit creation are controlled. In the early 1980s, interest rates were brought to unprecedented levels in the United States: now against double-digit inflation stood double-digit interest rates. The latter curtailed demand for new housing construction and for automobiles and other credit-supported purchases. And in 1982 and 1983, they brought a sharp restriction in business

5. As the policy came into full effect in the United States and Britain in the early 1980s, large random movements in the money supply, as it was variously and arbitrarily defined, also continued to occur. It was then that Friedman was led to his stern condemnation of the competence of the central bank effort at control. Toward the close of his life Marx had rebuked working-class deviants from his system in a famous passage: "If this be Marxism, I am no longer a Marxist." In 1983, Professor Friedman was led to say "If the policy the Federal Reserve has followed is monetarism, I am not a monetarist." His conservative friends were thought to be distressed about the possible nature of his reading matter.

investment expenditure. With this came a large increase in unemployment — to 10.7 percent of the civilian labor force in late 1982. Also the highest rate of small-business failures since the 1930s[6] and severe pressure on farm prices. Further, the high interest rates brought in a strong flow of foreign funds, which bid up the value of the dollar, curtailed American exports and strongly encouraged imports, especially from Japan. The overall result was the deepest economic depression since the Great Depression.[7] But in 1981 and 1982, there came a marked decline in the rate of inflation in the United States, a further drop in 1983, and, toward the end of 1984, the Consumer Price Index was nearly stable. There was a similar, although considerably less dramatic, decrease in the inflation rate under similar monetarist policies in Britain.

Monetarism, or more precisely the restrictive consumer-spending and business-investment effect of high interest rates, had worked, it was evident, by producing a severe economic slump, a cure not less painful than the condition remedied. The success of the policy in the United States was also the result of a related and, by economists, little foreseen circumstance. This was the exceptional vulnerability of the modern industrial corporation to a combination of restrictive monetary policy, the high interest rates through which it operates and the resulting adverse exchange rates. These effects were enhanced by a developing corporate senility, with further advantages to foreign competition.

That unemployment — the unemployment induced by monetarist policy and high interest rates — would lessen trade union

---

6. *Economic Report of the President*, 1985, p. 337. In 1940, the business failure rate had been 63.0 firms per 10,000 enterprises. In 1982, it was 89 per 10,000 and in 1983, 109.7.

7. The terms *recession* and *depression* have no precise meaning; each reflects an instinct in economics for semantic disguise. In the last century men spoke of *panics* and *crises*. These terms then came to seem too harsh, even violent, and thus alarming, so with the economic setback after World War I, there came the reassuring reference to a mere *depression*. Then in the 1930s, the word *depression* took on the ominous coloration of the contemporary disaster, and in 1937, when the temporary recovery abated, there was talk, as we have seen, of a mere *recession*. Now as the word *recession* has acquired discomforting overtones, we hear of *rolling readjustments*, *growth adjustments* or periods of *economic pause and waiting*.

bargaining power was not surprising. Orthodox economics accepted that unemployment would lower wages; it was in such fashion that classical full employment was achieved. The trade union was merely a resistant force in this adjustment; were the unemployment serious enough, it would have to yield.

Not foreseen, however, was the effect on the employing corporation. In the steel, automobile, machinery, mining, airline and other industries the aggregate effect of the policy, including the foreign competition, curtailed sales, led to extensive plant idleness and threatened bankruptcy and the cessation of operations. In this situation unions were forced not only to forgo wage increases but to negotiate wage and benefit reductions. While they could in some degree ignore the misfortunes of unemployed workers — the majority that was still employed was the decisive voice — they could not ignore the unemployment of all workers, which might result if plant or industry faced a general shutdown. And that became the prospect in the early 1980s in a number of the American heavy industries. It had not previously been realized that strong trade union action required a strong employer position. The weakening of the latter deeply impaired the former. So, impressively, did the microeconomic developments affecting the competence of the aging corporation.

The Keynesian compromise, as noted once more, left the microeconomic economy to the classical market. The wage-price dynamic, with its macroeconomic effects, was a serious assault on this compromise. And there was a further assault arising from the changed and changing internal character of the participating business units. This, in recent times, has produced a substantial economic literature and an even more general discussion. It has also shown again the resistant powers of classical orthodoxy.

Central to this new development is the rather obvious fact that the modern economic enterprise, the characteristic large firm, requires a very large organization in order to conduct its business. This means an intricate division of labor as to task — production, marketing, advertising, finance, labor relations, public relations, government relations, new product development, acquisition strategy and much more. There must also be a division of labor as to intelligence. Different people bring to the firm diverse qualifications in science, engineering, design, law, finance, marketing and economics. It is the organization comprising all these specialists that possesses the power of decision; power no longer rests in any perceptible measure with the owners of the enterprise. The pioneer conclusions of Berle and Means[8] are now conceded by all but the most motivated traditionalists. The resulting characteristics of organization, in turn, have prime microeconomic importance.

There is, first, the relationship to profit maximization of the authority within the organization. Obviously no economist in the great classical tradition can either regret or deny profit maximization. And none can suppose that it is other than a deeply personal motivation, something one does for oneself and not gratuitously for others. Yet the modern corporation is assumed to require of its management that profit maximization be for others, for stockholders who are both powerless and unknown. In fact, and often spectacularly in recent times, profit maximization has come to be for those with the power of decision. Management pay, bonuses and perquisites, golden parachutes in case of loss in a takeover struggle, are set by management for itself. These costs are not subject to any minimizing calculation; they are enhanced by the most orthodox of classical motivation to serve the interests of organization.[9]

8. See Chapter XV.

9. See "Why Executives' Pay Keeps Rising," *Fortune*, April 1, 1985, pp. 66–68. The point has penetrated the textbooks, although with an evident reluctance on the part of their authors. Professors Samuelson and Nordhaus, after first assuring that "generally speaking there will be no clash of goals between the management and stockholders," go on to warn that "insiders, i.e., the management, may vote themselves and friends or relatives large salaries, expense accounts, bonuses, and fat retirement pensions at the stockholders' expense." Paul A. Samuelson and William D. Nordhaus, *Economics*, 12th edition (New York: McGraw-Hill, 1985), p. 444. Professor Campbell McConnell, after similar comment on personal profit maximization by management, observes that "the separation of ownership and control raises important and intriguing questions about the distribution of power and authority . . . and the possibility of intramural conflicts between managers and stockholders." *Economics*, 9th edition (New York: McGraw-Hill, 1984), pp. 102–103.

With the passage of plenary authority to management, the latter rewards itself not only with income but also with prestige. That, as well as the justification for managerial pecuniary return, is notably enhanced by corporate size. Size, accordingly, becomes for those in authority an important goal, along with return. From these new needs and motivations have come the modern conglomerates and the supporting takeover movement. These are not thought by any but exceptionally disciplined believers to improve efficiency, as traditional theory would hold. Rather, such mergers and combinations, in contrast with old-fashioned growth, are a much abbreviated route to the power, prestige — and also compensation — that go with greater size.

From the foregoing motivations, in turn, come the strategic planning and "paper entrepreneurship"[10] that are central to modern corporate concern. Although these developments have produced a wide-ranging discussion, they have, like managerial income maximization, had only a marginal effect on established economic theory and instruction. Professors Samuelson and Nordhaus, in a competent detachment from the issue, conclude that "economists have reached no consensus on [such questions] . . . so perhaps the best policy is to keep a watchful eye."[11]

A further and powerful tendency operates within the modern corporate enterprise. Personal prestige and position in any organization turns in substantial measure on the number of one's subordinates. And one's comfort and contentment are notably improved by the availability of subordinates to whom tedious

10. The phrase "paper entrepreneurship" comes from Robert Reich's *The Next American Frontier* (New York: Times Books, 1983).

A useful survey of this development is in *Megamergers: Corporate America's Billion-Dollar Takeovers* by Kenneth M. Davidson (Cambridge: Ballinger, 1985). Mark Green and John F. Berry, in *The Challenge of Hidden Profits: Reducing Corporate Bureaucracy and Waste* (New York: Morrow, 1985), have dealt energetically, if perhaps a trifle too vividly, with this issue, as well as with others raised in this chapter.

11. Samuelson and Nordhaus, p. 549.

thought and duty can be passed. Therefore the first instinct of any-one appointed to a corporate post at any level above the lowest is to acquire the assistants who are so serviceable to both prestige and ease of effort. From this, in turn, comes the powerful dynamic of bureaucratic expansion. In the recession of 1981–1983, many of the large American corporations — automobile, heavy machinery, steel, banks — announced the shedding of corporate staff, in several cases the departures numbering in the thousands. In all instances this was hailed as a contribution to efficiency. The question was not asked as to why these people were there in the first place and why under financial duress they were so advantageously expenda-ble. The answer lies in the organizational or bureaucratic expansion just described, and with this, also, modern microeconomics has not come to terms in any way.

Nor has there been a reaction to the well-recognized tendency toward organizational stasis and senility in the modern great enter-prise. The entrepreneur of traditional economic theory ages and is replaced as to both capital and its direction by newcomers riding new waves of innovation. This is the process — "the gales of cre-ative destruction" — that was made famous by Joseph Schumpe-ter.[12] Not so the modern corporation. It suffers from the grave operational handicap of immortality; there is no therapeutic death.

These characteristics of the modern bureaucratic firm have been frequently discussed.[13] The superior performance of the younger, hence mentally and thus organizationally more flexible and adapt-able firms of the newer industrial countries — Japan, South Korea, Taiwan, Singapore — has been recognized. As have the problem of bureaucratic stasis in the socialist world — the USSR, China, Poland,

12. See Joseph A. Schumpeter, *The Theory of Economic Development*, translated by Redvers Opie (Cambridge: Harvard University Press, 1934).

13. Notably of late in *Iacocca, An Autobiography* by Lee A. Iacocca with William Novak (New York: Bantam, 1984) and *The Reckoning* by David Halberstam (New York: Morrow, 1986), both of which deal convincingly with these tendencies in the automobile industry.

Romania and others — and the diverse efforts to deal with it. Again, however, they have not penetrated the conventional economic theory of the firm and its motivation.

Finally, and as yet somewhat on the fringe of current discussion, is the possibility that the command relationship, a deeply established and accepted feature of the industrial firm since the Industrial Revolution and the birth of classical economics, is obsolescent.

Within the management of the modern corporation there are principals and subordinates, bosses and bossed. But also, as a recognized requirement and virtue throughout the organization, negotiation tempers command. As a wholly normal circumstance, the technician, designer or salesman may be more important to the enterprise than the person to whom he or she reports. When this is true, the one in higher authority does not direct; he or she must ask, encourage, persuade and learn. A cooperative relationship replaces a hierarchial one. Increasingly this relationship extends to the shop floor; there the worker is an original force for quality control, productivity and the guidance of more and more technically automated operations. An emerging literature, some of it looking especially at the Japanese experience, argues that tradition and the self-gratification of the boss are protecting a relationship that is, in fact, outworn.[14]

There is a final blow here to the microeconomic orthodoxy. As the organizational ethic and practice come to embrace ever more of those employed, the classical equivalence of marginal wage cost and marginal revenue becomes an improbable caricature. Such equivalence had an intelligible relevance only for a generally homogeneous labor force, a labor force that could be hired and fired at will and without grave organizational cost. The employment of highly specialized workers and staff in the context of complex

14. See specifically Samuel Bowles, David M. Gordon and Thomas E. Weisskopf, *Beyond the Waste Land: A Democratic Alternative to Economic Decline* (Garden City, New York: Anchor Press, Doubleday, 1983).

organization and its hierarchy allow of no easy calculation of marginal labor cost and return.

Thus the fate of the Keynesian Revolution. Like so much in economics, it was right for its time, and its nemesis was the passage of time. The years have brought the political asymmetry and the microeconomic dynamic and change of a highly organized world with which Keynesianism cannot effectively contend. Explained here in part is the low estate to which modern economics has descended or is widely thought to have descended. To this and the prospect we now turn.

XXI

The Present as the Future, 1

H ISTORY DOES NOT END with the present; it extends on, changing without limit, into eternity. The difference is only that the historian does not accompany it there; his journey, however tempting the prospect, must end with the present. But not entirely. For as there is much of the past that is in the present, so also there is much of the present that will be in the future, including not a little that is yet to be evident. This will enter fully into the general consciousness only with the aid of time. Of this — what in the past and the present in economics will be part of future history — the economic historian can say a word.

The most famous forecast of the future of economics was written half a century and slightly more ago by John Maynard Keynes, who observed: "From the earliest times of which we have record — back, say, to two thousand years before Christ — down to the beginning of the eighteenth century, there was no very great change in the standard of life of the average man living in the civilised centres of the earth. Ups and downs certainly. Visitations of plague, famine, and war. Golden intervals. But no progressive, violent change."[1] Going on to the vast increases in industrial productivity and production since the Industrial Revolution and guessing, presciently, that technical progress "may soon be attacking agricul-

1. John Maynard Keynes, *Essays in Persuasion* (New York: Harcourt, Brace, 1932), p. 360.

ture,"[2] Keynes concluded that "the economic problem is not — if we look into the future — *the permanent problem of the human race.*"[3] The study of economics, he thought, would become an occupation for useful but unspectacular specialists, "like dentistry." And he added, "If economists could manage to get themselves thought of as humble, competent people, on a level with dentists, that would be splendid!"[4]

After fifty years Keynes's prediction has shown itself to be less than perfect. It is true that some of the formerly powerful economic influences are diminishing in the industrial countries. As will presently be held, the production of goods is a far less urgent matter than it was. As is the question of how those goods are priced. And, if in lesser measure, how the income from safe and secure production is distributed. But economics as a discipline has a survival value that is not related to the urgency of the economic problem. Scholarly and larger economic self-interest has intervened to sustain its traditional or classical form and seeming relevance. And new problems have emerged, notably, as we have seen, that of the certainty or uncertainty with which employment and the resulting income are provided.

Also, along with the achievements of great organization — of bureaucracy — have come its socially and economically regressive tendencies. These Keynes did not foresee. Nor did he see or anyhow stress the appalling and increasing differences in well-being of the rich countries and the poor. Nor, reasonably enough, the differences in productive efficiency as between the older industrial lands and those that are newly industrialized — South Korea, Taiwan, Hong Kong and, of course, Japan — and how, a point for later mention, the latter would ravage the bureaucratic and sometimes senile industries of their older competitors.

More generally, Keynes, in contemplating the future of econom-

2. Keynes, p. 364. On this, Keynes, to use his famous phrase concerning a decision of President Roosevelt's, was magnificently right.

3. Keynes, p. 366. The italics are his.

4. Keynes, p. 373.

ics, did not foresee the depth of the commitment of traditional economists to the classical values and concepts and the way their validity and importance would be asserted in the face of intruding change. Their strength comes, as noted, from service to professional and larger economic interests, to the vested interests whose power Keynes thought inferior to that of ideas. When we contemplate the future of economics, the continuing power of classical theory must first be emphasized.

Holding economics in the classical or neoclassical tradition, there is, first of all, the vested intellectual commitment to established belief. This is a powerful constraint. Few economists wish to reject what was accepted in their earlier education and subsequently defended and elaborated in their own teaching, writing and scholarly discourse. To abandon what they have learned and taught is to admit to earlier error; this we all resist. As we do, it may be added, the demanding thought required in accommodating to change. The latter, economists, far from uniquely, find inconvenient, even painful.

Accommodation to changing reality is also resisted, as in the past, because of the desire to view economics as a science. In the academic world, where economics is taught, the standard of intellectual precision is set by the hard sciences. To the intellectual reputation of chemists, physicists, biologists and microbiologists, economists and other social scientists, perhaps inevitably, aspire. This requires that the ultimately valid propositions of economics be essentially given, like the structure of neutrons, protons, atoms and molecules. Once fully discovered, they are known forever. Unchanging also, it is held, is human motivation in a competitive market economy. Such fixed and permanent truths allow economists to view their subject as a science. It is the paradox of the discipline that it is the wish so to see itself that commits economics to an obsolescence in a changing world that, by any scientific standard, is to be deplored.

Also holding the subject to the past and to the classical model is, as it may be called, the technical escape from reality. The central assumption of classical economics — pure competition in the market extending on from the prices of products to the pricing of the factors of production — lends itself admirably to technical and mathematical refinement. This, in turn, is tested not by its representation of the real world but by its internal logic and the theoretical and mathematical competence that is brought to bear in analysis and exposition. From this closed intellectual exercise, which is fascinating to its participants, intruders and critics are excluded, often by their own choice, as being technically unqualified. And, a more significant matter, so is the reality of economic life, which, alas, is not, in its varied disorder, suitable for mathematical replication.

A further force that holds economics to the classical orthodoxy and that will continue to do so is the previously stressed power of economic interest. The great dialectic in our time is not, as anciently and by some still supposed, between capital and labor; it is between economic enterprise and the state. Labor and labor unions are no longer the primary enemies of the business enterprise and of those who direct its operations. The enemy, the wonderfully and dangerously rewarding role of military production apart, is government.

It is government that reflects the concerns of a constituency that goes far beyond the workers — a constituency of the old, the urban and rural poor, minorities, consumers, farmers, those who seek the protection of the environment, advocates of public action in such areas of private default as housing, mass transportation and health care, those pressing the case for education and public services in general. Some of the activities thus urged impair the authority or autonomy of the private enterprise; others replace private with public operation; all, in greater or lesser measure, are at cost either to the private enterprise or to its participants. Thus the modern conflict between business and government.

For the defense of private enterprise against the state the commitment to the classical market is of vital importance. If the market is broadly optimal in performance, the burden of proof lies heavily on those who urge public intervention or public regulation.

As this book goes to press, avowedly conservative governments are in office in a number of the larger industrial countries, and there has been an especially strong revival of market rhetoric in the United States with President Ronald Reagan and in Britain with Prime Minister Margaret Thatcher. This is both plausible and predictable. The market rhetoric of present-day conservatism is firmly and very effectively grounded in economic interest; the economic commitment to the classical market, its instruction and its broadly pervasive role in the public consciousness, is strongly in the service of that interest, and it has a theological quality that rises well above any need for empirical proof.[5]

Finally, classical economics will endure because it solves the problem of power in the economy and polity. That the modern great business is an instrument for the exercise of power — power, greater or lesser, over its workers and their wages, its prices to suppliers and consumers and, through advertising, over consumer market response — is not in doubt. But the classical tradition serves to cast this exercise of power into a greatly subdued light. Power is effectively subordinated to the market. The market, it is said, sets wages, salaries, interest and prices for suppliers and the sovereign consumer. The market having this authority, neither the individual nor the enterprise can be possessed of it. To the charge of misuse of power there is the simple, all-embracing answer: your quarrel is with the market. The paradox of power in the classical tradition is, once again, that while all agree that power exists in fact, it does not exist in principle.

In assessing the future of economics, no one will wisely discount the service and therewith the durability of the classical-neoclassi-

5. As sufficiently seen, economic interest traditionally produces a sanctifying economic response, and this has been the case here. What is called supply-side economics came forward in the United States specifically to license the tax reductions and welfare curtailment sought by the Reagan administration. It has not, it should, however, be said, achieved a significant foothold in established economic instruction and thought. It was too obvious in its intent, an unduly unsophisticated accommodation to pecuniary interest.

cal tradition. Its influence is not, however, plenary nor will it be in the future. Reality also has its claims on thought, a persisting, obtrusive presence that commends itself by its practical relevance and, to some, by its very inconvenience. To the reality as it will intrude on neoclassical conformity we now turn.

There is, first, a matter of little novelty: the dominant, highly visible role in the modern economy of the great enterprise and its preemption in all the advanced industrial states of a large share of all production. As frequently observed, some two thirds of industrial production in the United States comes from the one thousand largest industrial firms.

Competition between these firms and their overseas counterparts continues. But in their pricing they have a sensitive concern for the action that the prices they set will precipitate from their rivals. The result and likewise the prices negotiated with suppliers and trade unions have no theoretical relation to what occurs in the competitive market. This is not denied by neoclassical theory but rather is accepted as a basic characteristic of oligopoly. What is stressed is that the dominant large firm and its cohorts — General Motors, General Electric, General Dynamics, General Mills — are somehow a special case and thus outside the main current of classical theoretical discussion.[6]

As reality intrudes on neoclassical orthodoxy, economics will deal increasingly with the external and also the internal dynamics of the large firm — externally as it influences or controls its price and market relationships and goes on to guide and shape the reactions of its consumers, not excluding the attitudes and actions of government; internally as it organizes the experience and intelligence of its workers.

Organization is one of the great facts of contemporary life. It

6. "Despite the doubts which both Schumpeter and Galbraith have tried to implant in the minds of their colleagues, economists — whatever their other differences — are still inclined to view the megacorp and its accompanying oligopolistic market structure as a departure from the ideal of multitudinous enterprises competing in atomistic markets." Alfred S. Eichner, *Toward a New Economics* (Armonk, New York: M. E. Sharpe, 1985), p. 23.

accounts for the most significant achievements of modern industry and government in tasks that go far beyond both the physical
and intellectual reach of the individual. This it does by combining
diversely specialized intellectual qualifications for results superior
to those otherwise available. And since many varied scientific,
engineering and experiential qualifications bear upon each decision, the organization encompasses the crucial power of decision.
The future theory of the firm, if it is to have relevance, will of
necessity be a theory primarily of bureaucratic structure and organization. The classical theory of the firm will stay alive only as it
has relation to the smaller, small-business sector of the economy.
The individual entrepreneur, the economists' hero, will still be celebrated, but only as he operates in a secondary sector of an economy that is dominated by great corporate enterprise.

As the role of great organization is more fully appreciated in economic life, the nature of another curious modern accommodation
to reality will be understood. In universities and colleges throughout the United States and in other countries as well, economics in
its various fields of specialization is a popular subject of study. But
it is no longer thought to be relevant to a career in economic life.
For that the student studies business administration.[7] In business
schools, among students and faculty alike, the business enterprise
is seen as it really exists. There the assumption is of organization — bureaucracy; it is for survival, advancement and problem-
solving in bureaucracy that education in business administration
is designed. It is within such an organizational structure the student sees his or her future.

It is not to be assumed that these matters are being ignored, for
there is now a younger generation of economists[8] that is question-

7. Or, increasingly, the law, from which comes the knowledge needed to understand the mergers, acquisitions and paper entrepreneurship mentioned in Chapter
XX.

8. Among others, Samuel Bowles, Herbert Gintis and Barry Bluestone at the University of Massachusetts, Bennett Harrison at the Massachusetts Institute of Tech-

ing the tenets of the neoclassical system and urging a notable array of amendments and modifications: reform of bureaucratic and static management of the business enterprise; participation by labor in management and ownership; an active investment role by the state, especially as regards technological innovation; a strengthened welfare program; stronger support for education and human capital development; and much else.

None of this has yet crystallized into a system, but it is a current of thought that will, as certainly one hopes, be much a part of the future.

The classical concerns of the textbooks will suffer a more commonplace blow in the years ahead, one that is also evident now but that is ignored. That blow will be aimed at the traditional preoccupation of economics with value and distribution, with how the prices of goods and services are determined and the resulting income is shared. The determinants of prices of individual products, as distinct from price movements in general — inflation or, more improbably, deflation — have already diminished enormously in interest and importance. In the future the economist who is too exclusively concerned with what anciently has been called price theory will, indeed, shrink to a public stature not above that of Keynes's dentist.

The controlling fact here is, simply, that in a rich country individual prices are not socially very important. In the earlier world of poverty, how much food, clothing, fuel and shelter cost was profoundly a gauge of the suffering or enjoyment of life. A high price for any necessary good, there being few goods that were not, meant deprivation as regards either that or some competing requirement. The consequence was the detailed attention that economics accorded the setting of prices; it was addressing an issue of great individual and social significance. Of obvious and pressing concern was any

---

nology, and Stephen Marglin at Harvard. Mention should also be made of the marginally more orthodox but able, diligent and prolific Lester Thurow, also at MIT.

correctible inefficiency or incompetence in the production of goods or any monopoly power in the setting of price.

Now no longer. The modern living standard in the industrial countries at all but the lowest levels of income extends to a wide range of products and services and out to items of considerable, even extreme, frivolity and unimportance. Only the price of housing — shelter — continues to be a source of substantial consumer concern and anxiety, and especially so in the United States. The inadequate provision of housing at modest cost in contrast with that of, say, automobiles or cosmetics, can be considered the single greatest default of modern capitalism.

In great measure, wants are now shaped by the advertising done by the producing firms that supply the products or services. That this is possible is itself an indication that the individual product or service has little consequence. When the price for a particular product is noticeably high, the result may be complaint or indignation, but there is no suffering or hardship as in the past. Accordingly, while the mechanics of price formation is still the central textbook topic, not even the most talented future defender of classical orthodoxy will be able to accord it the urgency it once had.

A further consequence will be that monopoly in its various forms and its correction will decline in importance as a public issue. In the United States the antitrust laws will sink into neglect; indeed, under the regime of Mr. Reagan this is already occurring.

So much for prices. Time and increasing well-being will also overtake the concern about how their proceeds are distributed. That again can be assumed, for it is already happening. In the industrial countries most people, *when employed,* are not primarily preoccupied with the size of their income. They seek to increase it, often with commanding diligence, but inadequacy of income is not their first concern in the broad generality of industrial life. Their principal worry is the danger of losing all or most of their income — of losing employment and the consequent loss of all or most of the means of their livelihood. This fear afflicts men and women at nearly all levels — on the shop floor and throughout the middle structure of administration and management. In consequence, the factors affecting the security of employment are now socially far more important than those determining the level of reward. This being so in the present, so it will be in the future.

During the severe recession of the early 1980s in the United States and elsewhere in the industrial world, the production of goods and services declined over a broad range. No one was thought, however, to suffer because of what was not produced, housing again apart. Deprivation of this kind received no mention at all. All suffering was identified with the interruption in the flow of income — with unemployment or loss of employment. That, not prices or the unequal distribution of income, is demonstrably the prime social anxiety of our time. In the modern industrial economy production is of first importance not for the goods it produces but for the employment and income it provides.

XXII

The Present as the Future, 2

THE OLDER industrial countries, it has been evident, taught the later countries their economics, not omitting, it is also clear, what was to their own advantage in trade matters. Thus the lessons of Britain to Germany and the United States on the classical market and free trade, the later less specific German instruction on historical method to a generation of American scholars at the end of the last century and the widely generalized American instruction in modern times. In the next stage Japan, hitherto a prime consumer of American economic ideas, will become the source of economic thought for yet newer countries on the industrial scene and, in reverse flow, for the United States and Europe.

Again the future can be seen in the present. The industrial world, and not least the United States, has already become deeply concerned with the economic ideas and more especially their practice in Japan, making that country and its economic life an important field of study.

The ideas central to Japanese economic thought derive extensively from the American and British tradition but with a stronger Marxian component than is thought reputable in the English-speaking countries. It has often been observed that those Japanese who become business executives and high civil servants frequently begin their lives as Marxists. There is no serious expectation of revolution, but the Marxian influence does have a significant consequence: it relieves Japanese economic and political thought of the notion of a social dichotomy, even conflict, between the private market economy and the state, a theoretical conflict that has a strong hold on all conventional American and British economic thinking. In Japan the state is indeed, as Marx held, the executive committee of the capitalist class; this is normal and natural. The result is an accepted cooperation between industry and government — public investment, planning and support to technological innovation — that is unthinkable, to the extent that it is not thought subversive, in the American and British tradition.

There are further lessons to come and that are coming from Japan. A clear-headed view of investment in human capital — in education in the largest sense — is implicit in Japanese economic attitudes. From this come the highly competent Japanese labor force and the ample engineering and managerial talent.

Central also to Japanese success is the avoidance of relatively sterile, unproductive investment in military operations and artifacts. The use of a generous flow of savings for civilian capital formation as opposed to military purposes and the availability of engineering, scientific and business talent for civilian industry go far to explain the industrial success and eminence of Japan, as also of Germany, since World War II. American economic thought, policy and development were, as we have seen, decisively influenced by the war, and the case was the same for the Japanese. Between 1941 and 1945 they discovered that military aggression is not the path to national greatness, and they now pursue industrial achievement instead.

A further influence from Japan is and will be a better understanding of dynamics and motivation in the modern great corporation. These function, it is now evident, with greater effectiveness there than in the Western industrial countries. A more flexible accommodation to change, possibly a more acute recognition of talent and certainly a more comprehensive sense of belonging that extends down to the workers on the shop floor are all important in the Japanese achievement, but the last is perhaps especially important.

We have seen that in the classical view a worker was added when his contribution at the margin exceeded his cost. The Japanese worker is added as an integral part of the enterprise, and for life. Not surprisingly, this induces a loyalty not likely or even plausible in the Western tradition.

The Japanese economists of the present generation — Hirofumi Uzawa of Tokyo University, who is thought of as Japan's leading economist; Shigeto Tsuru, Harvard-trained, widely known and admired in the United States (and in his youth a leading Marxist scholar); Ryutaro Komiya, also American-trained and also at Tokyo University; and Kazushi Ohkawa, the designer of Japanese national income and product accounts — will, along with others and successors in the years ahead, be increasingly recognized around the world. And unlike their American or British colleagues, they will have the support of a smoothly functioning economy. As the experience of the United States revealed in the good decades following World War II, nothing so well serves the reputation, and the self-esteem, of economists.

The rise and success of Japanese capitalism and that of the other newly industrialized countries will bring closer attention to the circumstances of international competition. The older, more rigid, more ensconced business organizations, such as those of the United States and Britain, are and will be threatened by the younger, more flexible, less sclerotic enterprises of Japan, as also those of Korea, Singapore, Brazil and, potentially, India.

There are several designs for escaping market discipline, including that imposed by younger, more adaptable, more aggressive competitors. The first is a return to tariff protection. Faced with foreign competition, the great industrial corporation seeks tariffs and also quotas that will release it from the pressure of market constraints. After ceremonial praise of the free market, the need for a worthy exception is urged. A revival of protectionist sentiment and legislation in the older industrial countries having already occurred in the present, it will do so to even greater degree in the future. Once protective tariffs were for infant industries; now they are for the old and putatively senile.

A second well-established design for dealing with competition is simply to take it over. This is the purpose of the international or multinational corporation. It has long been thought that the latter is an instrument of aggression, even imperialism, on the world stage. Far more important is its protective purpose, its profoundly important service as an escape from the constraints of the market.

Evading market discipline is increasingly apparent in a third design; this is for the older, bureaucratically and intellectually more rigid enterprise to assign to firms in the newer industrial lands work that can no longer be performed competitively in the older countries. Thus the now numerous arrangements between American automobile, computer and other electronic firms and their Japanese counterparts by which costly and demanding production is undertaken in Japan and what is produced is imported into the United States at lower cost than would be possible if the manufacturing were done at home.

Another and final recourse available to aging and inefficient private enterprises is to seek forthright intervention by the government. This, in practice, goes far beyond protection from foreign competition. In the United States, as this is written, the Reagan administration has repeatedly set aside its free market rhetoric to come to the rescue of failing banks and needful exporters and, at unprecedented costs, to protect farmers from the free market. Again there is first the speech on the eternal verities of free enterprise and then the case for the particular exception. Socialism in our time is not the achievement of socialists; modern socialism is the failed children of capitalism. So it will be in the years to come.

Three further developments in economics are part of the present and will contend against the neoclassical tradition for recognition in the future. The distinction between microeconomics and macroeconomics will blur and disappear. This distinction, which, to remind, was the legacy of Keynes, gave responsibility for overall economic performance to the state and the central bank, leaving the traditional role of the classical market to the individual sectors of the economy. Inflation and unemployment were for macroeconomic attention; if they were thereby controlled, the microeconomic performance of the market could be left in firm descent from classical orthodoxy.

In recent times the distinction between microeconomics and macroeconomics has been attacked by members of an economic convocation who are impeccably in the classical tradition; they have held that when macroeconomic measures are known — changes in taxes, public expenditure, central bank policy — they will be anticipated, with the result that their effect will be nullified. Rational microeconomic expectation of macroeconomic change will thus defeat macroeconomic policy. There is a mystical quality about this particular position — the rational expectations school — that limits its acceptance even among those otherwise subject to classical orthodoxy. It is, nonetheless, an interesting impairment of the microeconomic-macroeconomic dichotomy.

The dynamic of prices and wages as a determining factor in both inflation and unemployment will help to blur further the distinction between microeconomics and macroeconomics. Prices and wages, as they are established by the interacting power of unions and corporations, have in the past been a clear source of inflation. This, however, was never fully accepted by classical microeconomic market theory, which holds that prices and wages are determined independently of the power of individual sellers and buyers of labor. What is evident in fact is once again at least partly denied in principle. In recent times, as earlier told, the English-speaking countries, which are tied far more strongly to classical microeconomics than are Austria, Switzerland, Germany and Japan, have dealt far less effectively with wage-price inflation. They have been constrained not to intervene through wage and price restraints — an incomes and prices policy — against a source of inflation that in accepted microeconomic theory does not exist. The European countries and Japan, on the other hand, have accepted that wage negotiations must be conducted within the framework of existing prices, and such directly negotiated restraint, not unemployment and idle plant capacity, has been their socially better answer to the wage-price dynamic and the resulting inflation. Sooner or later, the English-speaking countries will be led to recognize this, and with such recognition the distinction between microeconomics and macroeconomics — as will now be evident, one of the intellectually suffocating errors of modern economics — will disappear.

Unemployment in the past has been seen, overwhelmingly, as a macroeconomic problem, something caused or remedied by the overall design and management of fiscal and monetary policy. This also will cease to be so; increasingly it will be seen that unemployment arises from the nonoptimal performance and the changing competitive position of particular industries — in the United States of such older industrial enterprises as those in coal mining, steelmaking and fabrication, automobile manufacture, textile and apparel manufacture. While macroeconomic policies can ameliorate or deepen general unemployment, they cannot remedy it, given the specifics of these industries.

As inflation requires a comprehensive view of its sources, so does unemployment. The compartmentalization of economics between microeconomics and macroeconomics hides the most stubborn cause of present-day unemployment in the mature industrial countries: the decline of the older industries. And it also hides the relevant solutions. Unemployment as it microeconomically exists can be corrected in some measure by job retraining, provision of public-service jobs, protective tariffs and by action to address suboptimal labor relations and managerial competence. It cannot be remedied in any complete way by a general tax, expenditure or monetary policy.

Another major concern in the future will be the interrelationship between domestic monetary and fiscal policy and a nation's international position. This, too, is already evident in the United States. The Reagan administration, reflecting the liberalized attitudes of the Keynesian Revolution on budgetary matters and the not surprising drive to return benefit to its own affluent constituency through tax reduction, initiated and continued a series of unprecedented peacetime budget deficits. These should have had a strongly expansive and stimulative effect. However, relatively high real interest rates — a residual from the monetarist experiment — along with a safe-haven reputation attributed to the United States, attracted a large flow of funds from abroad. For a time these bid up the dollar strongly on the foreign exchanges. In combination with the industrial desuetude just mentioned, this made the United States an easy market in which to sell goods, an expensive one from which to buy. The result was a large trade deficit relevant in magnitude to the budget deficit.[1]

Money spent abroad for goods and services and for travel by American residents in excess of what foreigners were spending in the United States had an economic effect precisely opposite from that of an expansive public deficit. The Keynesian effect of the budget deficit was thus offset in the mid-1980s by the negative effect of the trade deficit. The result was a very modest stimulative effect from the large budget deficit. Obviously it is also an effect that will change as these magnitudes in their several relationships change in the future. This, along with the income transfers to other countries that are required to service the increased public (and also private) debt, will be much a part of future economic discussion.

As these pages have surely made sufficiently clear, economics does not usefully exist apart from politics, and so it will not, one hopes, in the future. The political asymmetry of the Keynesian Revolution — the asymmetry of the political actions required to remedy general underemployment as compared with those to arrest a general excess of demand — has been adequately observed. Failure to recognize the practical consequences of this was, as it remains, one of the major misjudgments in modern economics. Another serious

1. In the calendar year 1986, the budget deficit was $205 billion. The extensively offsetting trade deficit was $140 billion.

mistake has been the belief that monetary policy is politically and socially neutral — that the revenue that high interest rates return to those who lend money has been other than a rational manifestation of the self-interest of those with money to lend. Wrong, as well, has been the failure to recognize the political role of economics itself in the dialectic between the business enterprise and the state. The continuing survival of classical theory can be understood only when it is seen that classical beliefs protect business autonomy and its income and serve to obscure the economic power exercised as a matter of course by the modern enterprise by declaring that all power rests, in fact, with the market.

The separation of economics from politics and political motivation is a sterile thing. It is also a cover for the reality of economic power and motivation. And it is a prime source of misjudgment and error in economic policy. No volume on the history of economics can conclude without the hope that the subject will be reunited with politics to form again the larger discipline of political economy.

So we come to the end of this journey. Some things, one hopes, are clear. The past, we have seen, is not a matter of passive interest; it actively and powerfully shapes not alone the present but the future. Where economics is involved, history is highly functional. The present is not to be understood in neglect of the past.

It will also, one trusts, be sufficiently clear that economics does not exist apart from context — apart from the contemporary economic and political life that gives it form or the interests, implicit or explicit, that shape it to their need. Economic ideas, as Keynes averred, do guide policy. But the ideas are also the offspring of policy and of the interests which it serves.

The long reach of history establishes another truth. That is the way change in economic life and institutions bears on all economic thought. Economics is not, as often believed, concerned with perfecting a final and unchanging system. It is in a constant and often reluctant accommodation to change. Failure to recognize this is a formula for obsolescence and for accumulating error. Of this, too, the history tells.

Finally, one yearns to believe that economics and its history need not be a grim or even a relentlessly solemn pursuit. We have here observed a far from dreary procession of events, a far from pedestrian parade of personalities and talent. Writing of this has had its greatly agreeable moments; the pleasure, one trusts, will be shared in some small measure by the reader.

INDEX